God's Federal Republic

ISAAC HECKER STUDIES
IN RELIGION AND AMERICAN CULTURE

JOHN A. COLEMAN
General Editor

God's Federal Republic

Reconstructing Our Governing Symbol

William Johnson Everett

Paulist Press
New York/Mahwah

Text design by Ellen Whitney

Library of Congress Cataloging-in-Publication Data

Everett, William Johnson.
   God's federal republic: reconstructing our governing symbol /
William Johnson Everett.
     p. cm.
   Bibliography: p.
   ISBN 0-8091-2938-8 (pbk.)
   1. Sociology, Christian. 2. Christianity and politics.
 I. Title
BT738.E94 1988   87-30709
261.7—dc19   CIP

Published by Paulist Press
997 Macarthur Boulevard
Mahwah, NJ 07430

Printed and bound in the
United States of America

Contents

Cum Sylvia

Ad Lucem Publicam

■

Preface

This book is addressed to people who wish to think afresh about the religious depths of public life. Among them are ministers, politicians, theologians, teachers and students concerned about public affairs as well as many others in the professions and politics.

While the vision developed here is clearly indebted to the historical experiences of the Mediterranean and North Atlantic peoples, I hope it will not be reduced to them, for many of the symbols, perspectives and concepts nourished there have found root in many other societies, there to take on their own configurations. I hope that readers from other regions will find in these efforts a stimulus and a challenge to their own religious and political reflection.

Every book has its generative contexts. This one has many. While my experiences in Church efforts to transform neighborhoods, workplaces, and public institutions have been formative, three arenas have been especially important for this volume. The first is the OIKOS Project on Work, Family and Faith, which I conduct with my wife, Sylvia Johnson Everett. Through it we seek to help people and institutions work out more effective patterns for integrating these three dimensions of their life. The second is the Society of Christian Ethics, whose members have enriched and shaped not only this book but my life as well. The third is the Candler School of Theology at Emory University, whose collegial support and criticism coached the final labors of this book. In particular I am indebted to Carol Newsom, James Fowler and Steven Tipton for their critical assistance. From all these springs I taste most deeply what I have come to anticipate through the symbol of God's Federal Republic.

William Johnson Everett
Atlanta, March 1987

1

Introduction

Robert Bellah and his associates have recently urged us to reclaim and reconstruct our biblical and republican heritage in order to overcome a private individualism that is killing American public life.[1] This is not an easy task. Many people want to reconstruct public life without appeal to any religious roots or transcendent loyalties. Others flee directly to traditional faith without dealing seriously with the visions as well as limits of our historical publics. Some want a public without confusing pluralism. Others want pluralism without a genuine public order.

Public life cannot be sustained without visions grounded in people's deepest faith commitments. However, fervent faith often destroys politics in order to save it. Thus, faith itself needs some politically relevant visions that enable us to entertain God's future within the actual world we inhabit. To hold these two dimensions apart is disastrous. To bind them too closely is dangerous. Our task demands a complex yet compelling interplay of both. Both liberal and socialist partners have now shown their many deficiencies. Many and various religious movements compete as chief matchmaker in the public sphere. In this struggle we face at least three contenders to preside over faith and public life: neoconservative liberalism, political-religious fundamentalism, and Marxism.

In some ways Marxism is the oldest of the three, for it arose as a critique of the political economy of nineteenth century industrialism. While popular Marxism has often degenerated into sectarian terrorism or ossified into academic and bureaucratic clichés, there is still a body of insights and claims which can exercise powerful influence. The power of Marxism in this sense is its critique of domination, especially as this is rooted in economic structures. Its greatest weakness is its inability to develop an approach to public life which can undergird the rights of dissenting minorities, voluntary association, public persuasion, and pluralism. Without these provisions, religious faith cannot exist as a partner in public argument but only as a tool of administrative policy. Religious faith must exist privately, its catacomb existence an object of deep suspicion.

Gathered at the opposite end of the field we find those loosely assembled under the banner of neo-conservatism, which is in fact a reworking of nineteenth century liberalism. Its appeal, as enunciated by people like Michael Novak or Milton Friedman, lies in its affirmation of individual creativity and responsibility.[2] Its limitation appears in its refusal to grant to public processes the right to represent the common good, which, they feel, has to arise simply out of the mutual accommodation of private interests. Like Marxism, it has an inadequate understanding of public life and is too easily reduced to an ideology for the accumulation of wealth. Their chief difference revolves around who should control economic life. Like Marxism it also tends to reduce religion to being a private interest, though in the hands of some apologists, like Richard Neuhaus, it seeks to become an active participant in the public square.

Fundamentalism, which tends to fuse religious and political life, stands apart from these because of its ostensible rejection of modern economy and mores.[3] Its power arises from its attack on the aimlessness and casual violence of modern life. In replacing these with an absolutist concept of public truth and manners, however, it represses the freedom of conscience and pluralism intrinsic to public life. It robs both faith and politics of their capacity for transcendence by rooting us in a set of revealed propositions that eliminate the freedom of the present.

Within this swirl of arguments this book responds to Bellah's invitation with a challenge to think about public life and faith in the light of a particular symbol with ancient roots and a long but tortured history—the symbol of God's Federal Republic. It is this symbol which should play in religious life the role long exercised by "Kingdom of God."

Federal and republican symbolism has come to the forefront of people's political experience in our time, whether in India, Germany, South Africa, or the Soviet Union. Federalism is rooted in the covenantal heritage of biblical faith. Republicanism and the Church are rooted in the Greek and Hebrew assembly. These are symbols with religious depth as well as political relevance. They constitute a complex symbol that can help us bridge the enormous gaps between our faith convictions and our public action, between our private lives and our public performances. It is a symbol that can grasp our aspirations as well as stand in judgment on our arrogance.

All three of the protagonists to my own effort settle for solutions that neglect the dynamic complexity of the relation between faith and public life. The first two options tend to relegate religious symbols to the private sphere for the sake of a "secular" state. The third seeks to impose religious symbols and values on the public from some absolute perch outside it. The symbol of God's Federal Republic identifies elements within both the religious and political sphere which need to be combined in a complex way. The richness of this composite symbol reflects the critical engagement which is necessary to the life of faith and public action. This kind of symbol stands at the motivational as well as intellectual heart of an adequate public theology.

The point of this project is not so much to deny the validity of these other claims but to reconstitute the public argument about how we should see the interconnection of our faith and our public life. The major way I will do this is by lifting up a rich symbol to focus and guide our loyalties, our intellects, and our actions. Key symbols do this by bringing together rich emotional associations as well as models for action and understanding.

This book is therefore not so much an exercise in argument as it is an exercise in symbolization. Rather than rehearse all the rational arguments which might constitute the public discourse it attempts to cultivate a rich symbol which undergirds the very possibility of that discourse. Decisions about such symbols are not the result of argument but its beginning. They define the options for action and discourse. Our loyalty to key symbols arises from the discernment of an organizing image for what fits our experience, hopes, and fundamental convictions.

The symbol God's Federal Republic has ancient roots in our human experience. In the course of its long development it has cultivated hard won values we want to preserve even as we reshape our fundamental orientations—values of sexual equality, participatory governance and ecological responsibility. The growth of these values is due in no small part to the traditions behind this symbol. The effort to preserve them as well as to reconstruct them demands a deep awareness of this history.

Before embarking on this journey I need to explain briefly what this approach to a new vision involves. Let us recall two major efforts to reshape our public life in recent decades—black liberation and women's liberation. Both of these have been enormous struggles to introduce the majority of the American population into a public sphere long dominated by white males. While this demanded economic changes, legal reforms, rearrangement of household life and the reconstruction of many conventions of social interaction, it finally demanded that we re-symbolize the nature of our existence. Without changing these symbolic foundations of our culture, all the other changes would be unenforceable and unrealizable.

Black liberation forced us to resymbolize the meaning of black and white, of Jesus' ethnicity, and the nature of God's action in judgment and liberation. Without this powerful resymbolization Afro-Americans could never really share power, change the public discourse, and lay claim to equal public recognition. Similar observations can be made about the movements for liberation in other parts of the world—movements which demand that we as well as they change the basic symbols by which we approach life.

Similarly, the entry of women into fuller public life demanded not only medical advances like contraception, economic changes in employment, the disruptions of World War II, and new legislation. It also demanded that we resymbolize our ultimate loyalties, whether that be to introduce gender-inclusive language or to lift up new symbols of God, and new, feminine models of courage and public service.

Like many Christians I have spent some years trying to eliminate gender exclusive language from Christian worship. In many cases this has only required substituting a word like "people" for "men." In other cases, however, we stumble into greater complexities. People begin substituting "sovereign" for the word "lord," because lord connotes feudal patriarchy. At this point I begin to feel uneasy. The project of sexual equality breaks through into the language of political theory and organization.

Do we believe in a "sovereign"? What form does and should sovereignty take in our own time? What then are the proper forms of political order? What symbols should members of religious associations use to express their longing for God's perfect order? Behind the struggle to eliminate sexism lies the need for a critical appropriation of political symbols in theology and worship.

This is a problem for all groups seeking liberation from oppressive structures, whether they be due to gender, racism, age, or class. Both black and women's liberation movements lead us to the common need for symbols that guide us in our search for a new public order. What shall guide us beyond the act of liberation? What models of life shall shape our relationships beyond the revolution? What emotional symbols should be sown in our hearts so that they flower in a garden of greater justice? Behind the struggles for liberation lie our loyalties to the ultimate symbols of God's intentions for our common life.

The essential and religiously significant conflict of our time is between those who struggle for a public world and those who would restrict or extinguish a life lived in openness, argument, and mutual promises. This, baldly stated, is the central issue behind our search for a liberation from the bondage to race, gender, nationality and age. Unless we reconstruct the core symbols of our faith our efforts to engage the publics of our world will be but a nostalgic lullaby in the storm of revolution. Unless we change our basic symbols for organizing our emotions, thought and action such social changes remain on the surface only to be washed away in the next torrent of change.

It is at this symbolic level that we must work in reconstituting the relation of faith and politics. That is the burden of this book's approach to the question raised by Robert Bellah and his associates as well as by many others. My own contribution to this discussion is the presentation of a key symbol deeply rooted in our religious and political history. It contains a theology which places the symbols and concepts of public action at the center of our faith vision. It implies a political theory which focuses on the processes of covenant and public action.

This book is an effort to engage in fundamental theological and political reconstruction. It presents a "public theology"—that is, a vision of life which is both religious and political. It is a statement which seeks to speak to religious audiences as well as the general public. It recognizes the marginalization of the pivotal patriarchal and hierarchical symbol in Christian life—the kingdom of God—and unearths an alternative governing symbol from our tradition's covenantal and conciliar heritage. As a composite symbol in our own time it emerges as God's Federal Republic. The following chapters are an apologetic for refurbishing our religious speech, worship and action with that symbol.

This presentation begins in Chapter One with an examination of the role of symbols in religion and its interaction with society. A key symbol is a two-way street. Symbols are highly charged metaphors which take familiar objects, experiences, or images and bind them to more transcendent intimations beyond our normal grasp. Symbols transmit models from life experience to the visionary longings of faith. Our faith life is infused with symbols from the common world. Family images have shaped our relationship with God and Jesus. Even our usual formulation of the Trinity is an image of family inheritance, in which the Father bequeaths his domain to the Son who is bound to him in the Holy Spirit of perfect devotion. Similarly, political images of elections and parliamentary process shape the way we order our Church life.

Religious symbols also reframe our ordinary way of approaching life. The dramas of Christian worship, for instance, yield new themes, roles, and scripts for the wider world as well. Notions of mutual service raised by a Communion service can inform our approach to professional obligations. Belief in our equality before God and the sacredness of each soul informs and conditions our commitments to democratic liberties. This process of reciprocal transformation deeply shapes the selection of a key symbol ordering our lives.

The symbol of God's Federal Republic supplants another symbol intoned in prayer, evoked in sermons, sung in anthems, choruses and hymns—that of the kingdom of God. One of the arguments of this book is that this symbol utilizing kingship metaphors is no longer appropriate for bridging faith and public life. In the revolutions of our time kingdom metaphors have lost their savor. They no longer can nourish us in a post-monarchical life, whether politically or religiously. In the decline of kingship images we gain new appreciation of the covenantal and conciliar themes embedded in the symbol of a Federal Republic. The clarification of the meaning of this symbol can have enormous impact not only on Christian faith and worship but on public life as well.

In order to grasp the significance of God's Federal Republic as our central symbol we must understand why kingship symbols endured so long, even beyond their rejection in public life. In the second chapter, therefore, we will survey the history of kingship in order to assess its enduring contributions as well as its shortcomings. We will have to see the functions it served in order to ascertain how federal republican symbolism can take them up in a new way.

Then, in order to begin our reconstruction of a central governing symbol we will do the same with "Republic" in the third chapter, tracing its early formulation in Greco-Roman life, its suppression in the feudal era and its revolutionary resurgence in modern times. We will seek to identify the enduring distinctives that commend it for our adoption as a key symbol for ordering our lives. In exploring its own limitations and ambiguities we will open up the need for a complementary symbol—that of covenant, the root of federalism.

The fourth chapter will rehearse the career of covenant and its descendant, federalism, in order to lift out key characteristics that correct the deficiencies in republican thought. Both of these historical chapters do not pretend to completeness as histories. My purpose here is to illuminate the critical components necessary for an adequate reconstruction of a central religious symbol for today. Rehearsal of these histories also enables us to feel our way into their power and meaning. In reclaiming the symbol of covenant, we discover implications for our understanding of federalism. This renewal of federal theory then becomes the major contribution which biblical faith makes to the composite symbol, God's Federal Republic.

This critical reconstruction begins in Chapter Five, where I develop a contemporary theory of public action underlying a Federal Republic. This effort requires not only a structural, sociological theory, but also a psychological theory of people as performers in that public. Moreover, it demands a cogent theory of covenant to complete the republican vision.

To develop the explicitly religious dimension of our symbol, I then engage in some reconstruction of key theological ideas under the impact of this contemporary theory of public and performer. Our new understanding of persons and publics requires changes in our understandings of sin, salvation, God, Jesus and the Church. These transformed perspectives and practices then provide the basis for supporting and criticising our efforts to become full members of God's Federal Republic.

We do not face a simple task. We all have a strong emotional investment in the faith symbols which nurtured us. They are objects of loyalty and orientation as well as reasoned argument. We respond emotionally as well as intellectually to proposals for changes like this. Nothing less, however, can respond to the challenges we face. We stand before the choice between the dark forest of nostalgia and the rugged mountain of hope. We can clutch the familiar breast of survival or reach out for the beckoning hands of risky anticipation. Standing before alternatives is nothing new to us. Occasionally, however, we are asked not merely to take another route, but to choose another map, another light, another means of transportation. It is this kind of choice that we face when we are asked to embrace a new symbol for our deepest commitments. That is the kind of struggle this book seeks to foster. It is an invitation to place a new symbol of God's governance at the center of our faith, thought, and action. For these moments I invite you to think through with me what it would be like to live in the light of God's Federal Republic.

1 In Search of a Governing Symbol

The struggle for a vital engagement of faith and public life has many dimensions. Some people concentrate on clarifying the nature of the public discourse itself. Others focus on the cultivation of personal attributes, or virtues, that are necessary for public actors. Still others attend to particular institutional arrangements that are likely to enhance religious integrity and public responsibility.

This book has its own point of entree and contribution to these efforts. It seeks to lift up a transformation in fundamental symbolism that has been going on for the past two centuries—the shift from kingship to republican images for ordering the life of faith and public action. It seeks not only to identify a transformation in the foundations of our culture but to reshape it and commend it to people of faith and public concern.

Certain kinds of discourse should flow from an immersion in this symbolism. Certain ethical dispositions and habitual ways of approaching action should emerge from this way of grasping our ultimate loyalties. Certain kinds of models for public and religious life can arise from this vision. A renewal of the public philosophy, like the renewal of faith, must emerge from some key symbols guiding our emotions, thoughts and actions. That is why we turn to this task of symbolic transformation.

In this first chapter I want to clarify the meaning of a governing symbol and orient us to our task. With construction of our vehicle we can then begin our journey with the decision to explore a particular symbol—that of God's Federal Republic.

11

I.   Symbols as Motivators and Models

Symbols preside over the marriage of thought and action. They are the bridge between emotion and behavior. They provide a focus for our deep loyalties as persons and as groups. Symbols like "kingdom of God," "body of Christ," "democracy" and "socialism" have shaped our religious and political life. Symbols like these define the nature of people's hopes and fears and therefore the shape of their argument about the future and the past. They define who can participate in the public debate and the boundaries of their discourse. Symbols do not answer particular questions of policy, strategy, and institutional arrangements. They shape the struggle to decide them.

To understand and discuss this peculiar power of symbols we need to define them more precisely. A symbol is a vivid perception (usually an image), rich with associations, which is strongly tied to basic human purposes.[1] A symbol may be a word, like democracy, a thing, like a flag, a sound, like a song, or an action, like bowing one's head in prayer.

It is rich with associations because it always has metaphorical qualities. It points to something beyond itself—the flag to the nation, the bowed head to the relation of believer and God, "democracy" to a whole set of images about governance. A symbol is usually a complex metaphor. Moreover, it is highly charged, so that it evokes action in witness to what is symbolized. As we grasp a symbol our consciousness of its metaphorical character begins to yield to devotion to its acquired meaning.

A symbol elicits deep and pre-rational responses. It is therefore a primary basis for human motivation. Symbols are highly charged because they trigger in some way an earlier pleasure, pain, fear or hope. They are locked into our own most fundamental strivings for survival, comfort, expression and acceptance. The white sheet of the Ku Klux Klan costume is a symbol of racist violence. The dove is a symbol of peace. Symbols awaken in us a sense of either advancement or repression. Our responses to them are usually positive or negative.

A symbol is thus an outward manifestation of an emotional bond. This bond may be peculiar to a single person, as in the rose that reminds a widow of her deceased husband, or, more likely, be common to a multitude and become a force uniting many people into an enduring body, as with a flag, a war memorial, or an anthem.

These commonly held symbols take our emotional bonds to familiar things and extend them to more abstract and distant objects. The symbol "fatherland" takes our bond with our father and extends it to strangers and land we may have never seen. Symbols are key ways of transferring our allegiances and shaping our loyalties beyond the narrow circle we usually move in.

Once established, symbols can then convey wider loyalties back into this parochial frame. The Puritans, for instance, often spoke of the family as a "little commonwealth," because they wanted to cultivate certain behaviors there which would be consonant with a wider citizenship. Symbols thus reshape our perceptions about what is near as well as what is far away.

In doing so they also transform our way of thinking about things. Ways we may think about government become ways we think about family. Ways we think about family shape the way we think about church. Symbols mediate among the many patterns of thought and action that arise in our homes, workplaces, churches and governments.

Symbols are not only emotional lures and reflective images, however. Enduring symbols usually take on certain models for social life. They present vivid patterns for our common action. They become *symbolic models*. For instance, "king" not only draws on deep loyalties, it also carries with it some notion of right order. If one is English, it may invoke feelings of deference and awe within a social hierarchy. If one is an American, on the other hand, it may awaken the hope for racial equality and justice that inspired Martin Luther King, Jr.

Likewise, a symbol such as "family of God" not only evokes our loyalty to the group using the symbol. It also directs us to a pattern of authority drawn from family life, in which one or both "parents" make all the important decisions and control the "children," that is, the members of the group, in a way that they think is good for them. Such a symbol reinforces and legitimates a social pattern of paternalism or patriarchy (and sometimes maternalism and matriarchy).

As the examples indicate, a model is a somewhat abstract pattern of relationships bringing together a set of functions or elements in a coherent way. A model extracts from a complex situation, say a family altercation, and makes visible the main relationships sustaining the action. In the case of the family, the model may consist of a series of triangular and unstable relationships among parents, children, friends, and the family pet.

Thus we speak of a model of the atom, in which some tinker-toy structure seeks to visualize the sub-microscopic "whatever" that seems to be the building block of the universe. Likewise, we have models for defining what is or ought to go on in business organizations, skyscraper construction, and small group interactions. Models enable us to grasp what is going on in a situation and participate in it. They are crucial to our activity in a complex world of many unfamiliar and different situations. Models, like symbols, help us to bridge the gaps between the familiar and the strange.

Symbols already imply in some inchoate fashion a model of action. "The human family" as a symbol invites us to apply to global relationships some of the patterns of family life. Symbols, however, always have a somewhat diffuse impact because of their many metaphorical meanings. Without a model we are unable to discern which patterns to advance. What is our model of family life and how can that model be activated among four billion people? A model explicates a recognizable pattern of action implied in the symbol.

Sometimes the same symbol may become associated with two or more social models. We may not have conflict between two symbols, but between two different models of action bound to the same symbol. "Body of Christ," for instance, has been used to justify a pattern of Church government in which the "head" tells the members, who are otherwise inert, what to do. It is a military model of the body. Conversely, others have used the body symbol to reinforce a political pattern of mutual communication and democratic feedback, as in Karl Deutsch's book, *The Nerves of Government.*[2] They have used a cybernetic model for the body symbol.

Symbols incorporate both the emotional and the rational dimensions of our lives. They not only evoke loyalty, they also guide action. They are a means of gaining group identity as well as group coordination. We often think of symbols only in terms of religion, where they receive heightened attention and clarification. But they are also essential to any enduring organization or culture. Symbols reach into the depths of commitment we associate with religion, but they also extend into the reason, common sense and strategies of everyday life. They are fundamental to action as well as to faith and thought. The choice of dominant symbol is crucial to an effective ethics that has cultural bite.

II.   Governing Symbols

Sometimes a symbol may come to embrace many areas of life. It performs not only as a religious or political symbol, but also as a domestic, economic, and social one as well. Not only does it coordinate action within a group or institution, it helps people bridge the gaps among them. It can anchor the same model of action in many domains. Symbols that enable people to move easily from one arena to another are what I call *governing symbols*. Some people use the terms "master metaphor," "root metaphor," or "key symbol" to identify this phenomenon.

I use the term "governing symbol" to keep before our eyes the way it governs our action, especially with respect to the public world.

Governing symbols coordinate our lives by providing familiar names, dispositions, affections, and behaviors for otherwise distinctly different activities. Governing symbols evoke our loyalties, order our thinking, and shape our patterns of action. Moreover, they help us move among many diverse arenas in life in a coherent way. They provide us with familiar and dependable patterns for living. "Family" has been such a symbol, carrying domestic models into government, economics and religion. The machine has greatly influenced the way we view organization (as interchangeable parts), the human body, thinking, and the nature of the universe. In similar fashion the army ("Onward, Christian Soldiers!") and now the computer ("Give me some feedback") serve as powerful governing symbols.

Governing symbols shape our emotional disposition, our thought, and our action. They do this in three ways. First, they offer us a vision of the way things might be. This vision may even be more compelling to us if we can imagine that somewhere and sometime things were indeed that way. Symbols like family and community have that appeal. Whether as nostalgia or as hope symbols give us a vision that evokes our action. They are, as Norman Perrin and Sallie McFague emphasize, in tension with our present world.[3]

Second, as a vision of what might be, they give rise to norms, principles and standards for judging our present action. They have a normative function. We not only live by their light, we live under it. The symbol stands in judgment as well as in promise. Our governing symbol judges as well as evokes our action. In the Christian service of Communion, or Eucharist, we are not only drawn into meal-like action, we are also judged in our failure to engage in sacrificial action to share God's bounty with others. So it is in remembering the lives of national leaders who have called us to a higher level of justice and personal sacrifice.

Finally, a governing symbol not only points to what might be, but to what already is. It opens our eyes to its manifestations around us. It focuses our consciousness and orders our awareness. When we are fixed on God as King we are more aware of the elements of lordship, subjection, and paternal care around us. We see various ways this kingship is already exercised around us. When the body of Christ fills our eyes, we gain increased sensitivity to all the organic ligaments binding our lives together.

A governing symbol throws into relief those elements of our life which reflect it. It provides a filter through which we see our world in a special way. With its appropriated model it shapes the way we see life as it is. In this way the symbol, like a mighty wave, casts up evidence for our hopes on the shores of our anticipation. It provides a bridge between what is now and what is to come.

As we explore the ramifications of God's Federal Republic as our governing symbol we will see each of these functions at work. Along with them we will also have to take account of the negative effects produced when we do not distinguish between these descriptive and normative functions. The main problem occurs when our vision of the possible future merges so completely with our view of present reality that we cannot hear the dissonance and contradiction offered up by actual human affairs. The critical distance between the symbol and our present action disappears. The symbol masks over what is really going on. In the technical sociological sense, it becomes "ideological." It becomes a screen for cloaking the way things actually fall short of our ideal. It becomes a sentimental cloak over the interests, forces, and institutional patterns serving other loyalties.

In seeking to overcome ideological blindness we must not lose the tension between the world as we know it and the symbolic visions that give our life meaning. We have to see the difference between the loyalties people profess and the way they actually think and act. Otherwise we fall back under the spell of ideology.

Along with an awareness of the problem of ideology, however, must go an awareness of our need for symbols to guide our action and hopes. We must not let go of relevant governing symbols or we will wander in aimlessness and despair. Both ideology and loss of vision are destructive of human life. The struggle for a governing symbol must preserve its capacity for critical distance as well as its engagement of our whole lives.

Change in a governing symbol marks an important cultural transition. It is a deeply emotional transformation of the way we feel, think, and act. It is an act of cultural conversion. While this conversion marks a critical change in a religion or culture, a religious or cultural tradition is not destroyed by such a change, as some might think.[4] Symbols do change and even die. Others emerge from a subordinate to a dominant status. The sustenance of a tradition depends on the coherence and relevance of its governing symbols rather than their simple preservation. This book lifts up the movement from the traditional governing symbol of "kingdom of God" to that of "God's Federal Republic." It is a step requiring an analysis of the retirement of an existing symbol and the grounds for laying hold of its successor.

III. The Collapse of Kingdom

Jews and Christians still speak frequently of the kingdom of God, the kingdom of heaven, of Lord, King, and Queen. They do this solely within "religious discourse." But rarely do they live in a monarchy. When these words are used in public discourse, they are as likely to be terms of disparagement as of approbation. They are used to identify patterns of action deviating from our underlying ethical values.

Indeed, it is principally this critical role of kingship symbolism which seems to maintain its attraction for theologians. For them it functions primarily to undermine or destabilize the present order. This is the main way kingdom language has been used all through the revival of our awareness of biblical apocalyptic, that is, the way the New Testament in particular is speaking with a profound awareness of the passing away of this world. Kingdom symbolism points to a better beyond our best.

To function simply as a distancing symbol, however, is not to function as a governing symbol. Better is not enough. Kingdom, regardless of the nostalgia or hope it may evoke in hymns, Scripture, or liturgy, is a collapsing governing symbol. It may serve to distance us from our culture but not to order our affections and actions in or beyond it. A vital governing symbol can and does serve this critical function, but it does so by ordering us toward a relevant ethical ideal that upholds rather than denies our fundamental values.

The problem with kingship in this regard, as we shall explore later, is that it does not empower our public action but withdraws us from it in search of an ideal appropriate to another cultural and, for us, historical context. Indeed, the primary distancing that the kingdom symbol may accomplish is to distance the Church from the public order and focus its attention primarily on personal and family life, the natural home of kingship. Kingship symbolism is a symptom of religion's deprivation of an appropriate public role in our world.

Kingdom has collapsed as a governing symbol for a number of reasons. Other important institutions have grown up based on other models of action. They have supplanted inheritance and birthright with markets and elections as the primary legitimate means for distributing power. They have replaced patriarchal prerogative with civil equality and constitutional due process. They have curtailed parental control with rational negotiation.

This change extends to our basic models for approaching life. Where life and legitimate governance were once seen to come as a "great chain of being" from a single cause, whether God, King, or prime mover, now they are seen as the product of many interacting powers around a coordinating center. The emotions which were once attuned to hierarchies of status have been reshaped around patterns of mutuality and cooperation, whether in marriage or government.

Both as a model and increasingly as a symbol, kingdom language is dead. The hierarchy, monarchy, and patriarchy associated with it are being overturned by currents of democratic participation, pluralism, and equality. It has lost its cultural niche. It is no longer a fitting symbol for a position of governance.

This negative judgment does not rest merely on whether kingdom symbolism is culturally fitting or not. Other ethical commitments come into play to foster this symbolic change. These are values such as sexual equality, democratic participation, and mutuality which also lie deep in our religious and political traditions. Now we bring them into prominence and let kingship fade into a subordinate position. The choice of governing symbol, then, rests on an ethical as well as sociological analysis. Both of these dimensions will appear in our ensuing examination.

This is not to say that there are no values worth retrieving from the kingdom tradition. Indeed, in Chapter Two I will identify its important historic functions and contributions. Nor is it to say that there are no cultures today for whom kingship is an appropriate, though probably transitional, form. If we are to grasp the currents of hopeful change and the struggle for justice, even in these lands, we must find an alternative governing symbol.

Our first step forward is to identify some of the possible alternatives before us. Our purpose here is not to give a reasoned argument for choosing or excluding one, but to show some of what is at stake in exploring what would happen if we chose to confirm God's Federal Republic as our governing symbol. The "choice" of a symbol may be largely pre-rational and pre-argumentative, but at least we can understand better what we are and are not choosing.

IV. Alternative Governing Symbols

The realization that other symbols, values and models have lain subordinate within our traditions awakens us to the presence of alternative symbols of organization that now vie for governing position. Indeed, the collapse of kingdom has opened up a clearing in which many plants now seek the sun.

Among the competitors for prominence we find the symbols of community, body, people, and democracy. While there are others, such as assembly, organism, or machine, they lack the historic attachments, universality, and emotional depth of the others. Why, then, not choose one of them to replace kingdom symbols?

"Body" is certainly a powerful symbol, drawn from biology.[5] It has usually been the bearer of an organic model of functional interdependence. St. Paul used it of the Church in order to stress that all the different, seemingly competing gifts were actually aspects of a single purpose—the building up of the body of Christ. It evoked in people the same care for the group that they naturally give to their own bodies. The body symbol is motivationally powerful as well as being susceptible to very complex interpretations. Moreover, the advance of the natural sciences has strengthened rather than diminished its power.

Thus, we speak of the body politic, the body of knowledge, the economic organism, the student body or, using the Latin form, the army corps. Moreover, as I mentioned before, this symbol is capable of adopting a number of social models. It has been interpreted mechanistically, hierarchically, cooperatively, charismatically, and cybernetically. It is a flexible and powerful symbol. Why then reject its claim to pre-eminence?

The problem with this kind of "body thinking" is that it conceives of a society as essentially a single actor. All others are really aspects of this single being. Body thinking accents this being's need for survival and adaptation over against its environment, but cannot recognize the plurality and equality of the actors within its boundaries. It always stresses unity and common purpose before plurality, personal freedom, or action. It reduces the drama of life to metabolism and the history of a people to the growth of an organism. Body symbolism helps us grasp the nature of what binds us together but occludes the plurality of our independent action. It denies the centrality of human freedom. It is finally not a genuinely political symbol.

"Community" arises from a more social experience, but is not devoid of wider associations.[6] We speak of plant communities, human communities, the "business community" and "community of nations" as easily as we speak of family. This symbol has the advantage of going beyond familial and ethnic bonds. It connotes interdependence, mutual aid, and common memory. These are values appropriate to our social circumstances. Why not place this image at the center?

For all its virtues community falls short in crucial respects. Like the body symbol it focuses too much on what we have in common. It masks over our differences, our plurality, and the means for living with this variety. Its reaction to the stranger is to absorb her rather than to respect her. It pretends unity where none exists. When it recognizes plurality and the need to resolve conflict, it invokes face-to-face suasion based on immediate experience. Community does not know what to do with the inevitable "impersonality" of social life and the reliance on reason and countervailing power rather than affection and solidaristic appeals to resolve differences.

Moreover, it has as much difficulty with privacy as it does with strangeness. Just as it tends to obliterate differences, it also is deeply suspicious of private life. Communities, in assuming pervasive commonality of interests, are suspicious of those who refuse to share everything with them. They expect the same sharing among five hundred or one million people that we do within a family.

Community as a symbol represents as much a reaction against social complexity and rationality as it does an advance beyond a restrictive familism and ethnicity. Though it embraces more than the household, it grasps less than the globe. It represents an unrealistic yearning for unity that can easily mask over the realities we have to deal with in actual life. "Community" points to a form of organization in between family and republic. Though important, like "body," it must be subordinate to a more expansive governing symbol.

What about "people"?[7] Here is a fully social and historical symbol with a long history. It embraces the immense variety of persons and groups. Moreover, by lumping everyone together it has a highly democratic and participatory bias. It does not subordinate one sex to the other. Nor does it distinguish among races, ethnies, and traditions. Phrases like "We the people" and "the people have spoken," as well as ideas of populism, popular vote, and people's republic, have powerful appeal and practical application. We speak of the people of God in our religious life as well as the people of El Salvador in our political affairs. Here indeed is a powerful contender for our affections and directions.

However, "people" errs on the other side from body. It is too diffuse in its connotations. While it bears many of the values we seek to advance with Federal Republic, it offers little in the way of models for action. It is more like an ocean than a building. We might swim in it but we can't live in it. Appeal to the people can be a powerful solvent of rigid authoritarianism, hierarchy, and arbitrary privilege, but it offers little in the way of practical, structural alternatives.

So, for instance, at the Second Vatican Council of the Roman Catholic Church critics of the hierarchical model sustained by the symbol body of Christ tried to counter it with appeals to the Church as the people of God. This symbol was indeed admitted to the pantheon, but because its proponents had no alternative model for Church structure, it failed to sustain the reforms its advocates vaguely hoped for.

"Democracy" has similar limitations. It is the closest star to the constellation of republican symbolism. While it has widespread appeal, however, it points simply to the value of individual equality and widespread participation in decision-making. Moreover, its usual theory of personality tends toward an atomism which views the public order as a conglomeration of individuals.

The social gospel theologians Walter Rauschenbusch and Shailer Mathews used democracy as a way of talking about the kingdom of God.[8] This usage could highlight Jesus as our friend and underline our baptismal equality before God, but did not and I believe could not adopt or adapt other central elements in both religious and political traditions. While we treasure democracy's light we must find our primary orbit elsewhere.

We need a symbol that is human enough to arise from our own actions and history, inclusive enough to embrace our plurality, and complex enough to provide us with adequate models for social life. It must remind us of the historical character of God's action that is evidenced by the symbol kingdom of God, but must be more transparent to the ethical visions nurtured and constrained under its ancient care. It is not enough simply to exclude sexist language from our Bibles and lectionaries, for the old language clothed an entire model of governance. It will not do simply to criticize the old symbol of "lordship" if we only replace it with "sovereign," because the issue at stake is the whole pattern of governance. Similarly, it is not enough to pit "solidarity" over against oppressors, or black against white. We must go deeper and uncover the root symbol of governance seeking to be born amidst the pains of liberation in our time.

I have set forth a definition of a governing symbol to guide our inquiry into God's Federal Republic as the governing symbol for a biblical and republican faith in our time. It is a change that may well find resonance among Jews as well as Christians, public spirited citizens as well as traditional believers. The functions of governing symbols, with their capacity for transcendence as well as relevance, have been clarified in preparation for examining the history of our traditional as well as proposed governing symbol. Finally, we have seen some of the ethical and sociological considerations for pursuing this symbol over others.

2 | Kingship and Kingdom: The Heritage and the Harvest

We are engaged in the transition from one governing symbol to another. The symbols are significantly different but they also display important continuities. Some of the old soldiers gather under new banners. Crucial values have been nurtured under the old symbol which need to be preserved, even though with new bearers. Not only do we need to know the nature of the battle. We also need to recognize the tender shoots that were nurtured under kingship's erstwhile care. Even a cursory examination reveals that republican and federal symbolism have evolved in conflict as well as companionship with monarchy.

Therefore, we turn to the history of kingship to begin our task of reconstruction. We need to see its complexity. We need to see how it was woven into religious symbolism and advanced enduring religious and political concerns. We have to identify the functions this symbolism played in religious and political life. Only then can we approach the ways that the symbol God's Federal Republic might supplant its role in mediating the interaction of faith and politics. Only then can we be attuned to the complexity of our enterprise.

My purpose here is to survey the history of kingdom symbolism in order to lift up the dominant themes, motivations, and functions bound up in this complex image. We cannot present a detailed history of this symbol, with its many interpretations and peculiar historical uses. Our purpose is selective. We want to find out what basic forms of social life it legitimated. What kind of social context nurtured it? What were its typical psychological underpinnings? What were its typical functions? What in general has kingship meant in our civil and religious history?

Then we can turn to the ethical and theological task of winnowing out the elements to be preserved in a more appropriate symbol for our own situation.

I. The Heritage

A. Ancient Near Eastern Origins

Biblical symbols of kingship arose in the confluence of Egyptian, Babylonian, and early Hebraic cultures. Some characteristics appear in all three: the king is the keystone of right order; the order of kingship is rooted in supra-human forces, whether these be "natural" or "divine"; the welfare of the king and the land are inextricably bound to one another; and the king mediates in a priestly manner between the people and God (or the gods) in some representative way.

These features are manifested in differing ways. In ancient Egypt the king was the incarnate manifestation of the divine power underlying the essence of things (*maat*). Just as the cosmic order is grounded in God (Amon-Re), so the social-economic order is grounded in the king.[1] Everything participates in the one *maat* according to which the seasons revolve in their pattern of life and death. The king is the personal presence of the divine power behind life, both nature and society.

In Babylonia we also find this belief in an underlying order of things, but this order is construed as a law-like pattern established by the council of the gods. The king, like all other beings, must live in accord with this law. The king is the mediator and executor of this divine order, but is not the personal presence of the gods themselves. The king is merely a "great man." Here we find a more genuinely political sense of ultimate order, contained in the image of a council of the gods and a more legalistic approach to social order. Here the king is more a servant of law and order than the incarnation of the Creator. However, we still have the profound sense that all social order revolves around the right action of the king.

Because the Egyptian pharaoh was divinity incarnate, he was a sacred character. He absorbed all priestly potentialities, even though there were lesser priestly officials to administer the cult. There was a high degree of congruence between the priestly concern to observe the regularities of the universe and the regal concern to respond to challenges with fresh initiatives. This epitomizes the traditional society's desire to absorb the unpredictable future into the certain past.

The king is not only the keystone of right social order, his very designation arises from supra-human agency. Kingship was a way of removing social affairs from the unpredictability of human action. The primary way stability was achieved was through hereditary succession. This was the pattern in Egypt. The transfer of power would have the same irresistible force as the transfer of life. A second, though less stable way was through belief in divine election, revealed through success in battle or some charismatic quality. This was more the Babylonian pattern. Though there was hereditary kingship, it usually had to be confirmed in terms of some kind of election.

In both societies governmental stability was closely linked to an agricultural social order. The king exists to ensure the welfare of the land, whose condition is due more to the mysterious workings of uncontrollable natural forces than to distinct human actions. This accentuates the king's position as some kind of magician or priestly mediator. The more clearly circumscribed Egyptian world evinces a stronger sense of self-contained natural order dependent on the seasons of the Nile. Hence, the Egyptians tended to merge the roles of priest and king.

Babylonian culture accomplished this to a much lesser degree because its empire was less clearly defined by geography and its people were more aware of conflict and the uncertain fate of kings. Thus, the Babylonians portrayed more warfare at the heart of things. They saw creation as the result of a cataclysmic struggle with a monster and the ongoing order of the world as a consensus among a plurality of powers in a heavenly council. The king was more a servant than a divine mediator. He exercised great initiative in battle but exposed himself more surely to disaster.

The Hebrew development of kingship took this element of struggle and human limitation further.[2] Hebrew kingship was based on the charismatic warrior. Saul epitomizes this conception. Kings were not originally governors of a settled land but leaders in battle. They were not law-givers but saviors from invaders. They were not priests but generals.

Early priests like Samuel did exercise military authority, but this sacral function of legitimation was soon distinguished from the pragmatics of military action. After Samuel priests only legitimated kings. They did not lead them in battle. However, the union of priest and king persisted in Hebrew memory, arising again in the saga of Judas Maccabeus and of course with Jesus of Nazareth.

The union of priest and king in the mysterious figure of Melchizedek ("king of righteousness"—Gen 14:18), though evidently legendary in himself, became the plumbline of this precipitate. Since Melchizedek was king of (Jeru)Salem, we can assume that this figure was intended to legitimate David's throne by associating his office with that of the figure who even blessed Abraham.

Warrior imagery is also closely connected with Israel's earliest image of God. The king and YHWH draw on the same role, so crucial to Israel's early survival. As a savior from pharaoh's army and Canaanite defenders, YHWH was indeed a warrior god. It was YHWH, in Israel's belief, who fought for them. In this sense it was easy, in later times, to draw close parallels between the earthly and heavenly kings.

Even though these kings exercised striking charismatic leadership in war, it was really YHWH who was doing the fighting. Kings could only make limited claims for themselves. When the tribal leaders came to Samuel, wanting to have a king "like the other nations" Samuel reminded them that in the past "YHWH was your King" (1 Sam 12:12). Therefore, to have a human king was blasphemy. It betrayed a lack of faith in YHWH. Thus, kingship violated the sacral traditions of dependence on YHWH. It tended to undermine the priestly dynasty which interpreted YHWH's will for the people. It threatened the independence of the tribes to function according to their traditions, customs, and covenant obligations.

We must understand here something of crucial significance about ancient kingship. It rested both on military success and on sacrality. The two functions come together because military action demands our utmost willingness to sacrifice ourselves. It is an inherently religious action. People only fight effectively in a war deemed to be holy. Moreover, they are willing to set aside the usual social relationships, in which power is more decentralized, for a militaristic concentration of power only if this power is constrained by the source of their morality itself. In Israel's terms, YHWH's fighting, like YHWH's law, had to take precedence over the king.

Not only were kings subordinate to YHWH, they were also hedged about by the popular assembly which elected them (2 Kgs 23:30). They were not descended from gods nor were they divine ambassadors. At the most, they simply had "the spirit of YHWH" upon them. They were recognized by the elders in assembly and confirmed by the priests. The basis of the king's election, however, was always an unstable one. Kings could circumvent the assembly, as Solomon did, by appealing to a special covenant with YHWH. However, as his son, Rehoboam discovered, the assembly of Israel could also make and break kings (2 Chr 12).

This limited kingship was rooted in the conditions of Israel's birth as well as its later history. The Hebrews had a very strong memory of their origins as a people bound together in covenant with their god, YHWH. YHWH was the power that had brought them out of Egypt and led them into Canaan. Through the mediation of the prophet

Moses, they had struck a covenant with YHWH which governed their relationships with each other and welded them into a multi-tribal unity. Because of this original pattern, their god was not manifested in a person, such as a king, nor in an administrative center, but in the portable record of that covenantal agreement—the ark.

It was the priesthood that controlled the interpretation of this stable center of an otherwise nomadic Hebrew life. The center of this priestly legitimation of the covenantal order was Shiloh, seat of Samuel, who anointed Saul and later Ahijah, who led the rebellion against Rehoboam. Even when the monarchy established its own priesthood in Jerusalem, the tension between king and priest persisted in subdued form, with the more idealized priestly picture of what kings ought to be finally eventuating in messianic expectation, as with Jeremiah and Ezekiel.

This stress on a limited kingship devoted to covenant law is central to the meaning of kingship in Israel. Therefore, Samuel confirmed Saul as king only within certain covenantal restrictions limiting his power (1 Sam 10:25; cf. Dt 17:14–20). The king, as the Deuteronomist later formulated it, must be one of the people (not a foreigner). He must not aggrandize power (horses, wives, gold and silver) for himself. He must live according to a written code rather than his arbitrary will.

These demands probably reflect deep-seated customary expectations in Israel. However, the tribes were willing to risk their violation in exchange for the military security that could be provided by a monarchy. Both David and Solomon soon violated every one of them. They remained as standards of judgment, but became so idealized that no actual king conformed to them. Nevertheless, under David this transcendent ideal soon became attached to YHWH, no longer merely the warrior but the great King (Pss 68; 72).

In the long run it was this ideal that informed the image of the Messiah, the title given to Jesus of Nazareth. The prophetic figure of Moses and the priestly image of Samuel faded into the far background. Even the union of priest and king in Melchizedek appears only in the Letter to the Hebrews.

When the Jerusalem monarchy tore away from the covenantal limitations based in the northern centers of Shiloh and Shechem, it took up the widespread claim that the king was governed by "wisdom," a charisma transcending the legal formulas of covenant. This wisdom was a core pattern of righteousness infusing the king and his rule. Here we see the predilections of Egyptian and Babylonian beliefs in the king as a representative of a transcendent order. Not only did this crown of Wisdom legitimate the king's individual decisions, thereby giving him immense discretionary power, it also could be called upon to require the king to act rationally and consistently in accord with the collective wisdom of the people. (See the story of the wise woman of Abel in 2 Samuel 20:14–22 for an arresting manifestation of this.)

These two conceptions of royal legitimation—covenant and wisdom—persist throughout the history of monarchy. To covenant accrue the ideas of social contract, constitutionalism, and popular election. To wisdom are attracted belief in the ruler's genius, reason, enlightenment, spirit, and expertise. The first seeks to limit the king through explicit agreement, the second by his education. The way these two themes can be drawn together in our own time around a notion of covenantal reason will occupy us in a later section.

In the royal psalms of the monarchy we see the coagulation of the traditional attributes of kingship. The king takes on the priestly function of representing the people before God. The right order of society and nature revolves around the integrity and stability of the monarch. The monarchical order becomes the model for life and faith. YHWH's relation with Israel is mirrored in the king's relation with Israel. This extends even to his succor of the poor and oppressed—a necessary strategy if the monarch was to develop his own constituency. All the elements of this idealization appear in Psalm 72:

> God, give your own justice to the king,
> your own righteousness to the royal son,
> so that he may rule your people rightly
> and your poor with justice.
> Let the mountains and hills
> bring a message of peace for the people!
> Uprightly he will defend the poorest,
> he will save the children of those in need,
> and crush their oppressors.

With this paean the strains of the confederacy were finally absorbed by the monarchy, but not without rebellion (2 Sam 20) or nostalgia. The formative memories were confederal: the tribes gathered in an assembly of equals to take direct charge of their life under YHWH's covenant. The practical severance from this tradition was clearly remembered: the settlement of the ark in Jerusalem, the building of the temple, the taking of a census, the centralization of judicial as well as sacral and military decisions in Jerusalem, and the maintenance of a standing army.

The tribes in part accepted these developments because they experienced security from potential enemies. Others were cowed into submission through assassinations and military garrisoning of the country. Local prerogatives were slowly absorbed. Order and security were bought at the expense of local participation in decision-making and local control. This trade-off echoes down the long corridors of monarchical memory to our own time.

By drawing on the earlier images of YHWH as warrior, David (or at least Davidic tradition) was able to mold YHWH into a king—an image which would legitimate his own rule in turn. Solomon appealed not only to this Davidic covenant but to rising beliefs in royal wisdom evidently influenced by Egyptian views of kingship. Covenant posed a bigger problem. Here David had to go behind the Mosaic covenant and the traditions of a "conditional" covenant (which we find formulated in Deuteronomy) to YHWH's original covenant with Abraham. The Davidic monarchy re-presents the original unified nation of Abraham. Its survival is coincident with the survival of the people of Abraham. Thus, in the Davidic vision monarchy and people became one.

With the completion of this monarchical edifice under Solomon that the tradition of Israel holds up, we have two fundamental symbol systems and models of governance in ancient Israel: confederation and monarchy. The first was successful in mobilizing a motley group of tribes into a people. The second was successful in securing their settlements in a new land. These were the two sources for ordering Hebrew life from then on. These were the two wells of inspiration available for later Jews and early Christians as they struggled for a form of government that was both faithful and firm.

B.   Kingship in Greco-Roman Antiquity

Our evidence indicates a slightly different meaning of kingship in the lands of the Mediterranean in the first millennium BCE. In Greece and Italy the king emerged as the sacral patriarch. The Greeks knew him as *basileus*, an evidently archaic term of unknown derivation.[3] The Latins knew him as *rex*, from the same root as "to guide" or "direct." The origin of his power and authority lay in his command over the liturgies of the ancestral hearth and the lands and people attached to it. That is, it lay in his power to guide and "divine" the will of the ancestral gods who really owned the land and ruled the house through the present living heir—the king.

This patriarch was heir to the mysteries of the ancestors. He was closest to them, to their graves, to their spirit still present in him. Through him stemmed the power to organize people and maintain the proper order of things. From this ancient tradition stems what the Latins called the *pater potestas*, the absolute right of the father over the household. It was a power grounded in the beliefs he held in common with his subjects, not merely in the coercion he could wield.

The household of this tribal king was an entire, somewhat self-sufficient society. The Greeks called it an *oikos*, from which we derive our word economic as well as ecumenical and ecological. The Romans called it a *domus*, from which we gain dominion. It contained slaves, servants, and other dependents as well as wives, children and relatives. Kingship was the highest office in a social order modeled after the patriarchal household. The *oikos* was sustained as a traditional order based in the will of the original ancestor, who may or may not have been seen as a god. Clans were brought together inasmuch as they claimed the same original ancestor.

Here kingship arose from the tribal household and then developed what we would call a public sphere. In Israel, the king arose in the public sphere and then created his own dynastic house. In Greco-Roman culture kingship normally arose from "nature" or the gods, that is, transhuman forces. In Israel it arose through human choice in response to specific needs. The patriarchs of the Hebrew tribes were never known as kings. They became so by military need. In other lands kingship was already rooted in the patriarchal household and then extended to civic and military spheres.

The founding of ancient cities, as Fustel de Coulanges pointed out long ago, occurred as various kings brought their tribes together and founded a common hearth, whose god would preside over their life together. That is, their intercourse would be controlled by common traditions and loyalties. In effect, the ancient city was a kind of immense household. It also demanded some presiding king who would relate the people to their traditions, lead them in their liturgies, and defend their city.

It was clear, however, that this was an unstable position. The other kings chafed under this pre-eminence. It was not right for sovereigns to be members of another household. Through overthrow or reform, they came to constitute themselves as a council of kings, whose president would be elected or would circulate according to lot—that is, by divine choice.

Within this council we have the first emergence of the possibility of discourse among equals regarding decisions affecting them all. But this discourse was completely immersed in tradition and divination. Moreover, most of the affairs of daily life were still under the control of each king in his own house. The council's main concern was mutual defense or war.

In all the major cities engaged in commerce, various strangers unrelated to the original tribes soon assembled. To these were added loosely attached clients and other dependents who had acquired wealth through commerce (property through land being completely under the control of the patriarchs). A conflict ensued between this class of unenfranchised people and the nobility. To lead them in revolution they appealed sometimes to ambitious kings, as in Italy, or to tyrants, as in Greece, where the king was still too closely identified with oppression.

Here, as we will see in other times, people who sought protection from monarchs or even entry into governing power could appeal to kings themselves to lead them. Thus, at times kings were democratizing influences, widening the scope of participation. However, in doing so the patriarchal and monarchical order of government was also preserved, thus estopping the very participation they served.

The fate of tyrants was mixed. Some, freed from all traditional restraints, ruled with such arbitrary severity that they were overthrown again by the nobility. Others were able to introduce new legal codes and provide a more democratic framework. Both Plato and Aristotle seem to have appealed to such a model, possibly the work of the Athenian, Solon, as the basis of a genuinely stable civic life. However, in both of them we find a deep suspicion of widespread participation in decision-making, fearing its recourse to tyrants. They preferred the stability offered by the traditional council of elders rooted in the sacral past of patriarchal kingship. In the end, as Ellen and Neal Wood point out, they modeled the desirable polis after the well-run household.[4]

Because of this purported stability and because the sacred traditions of the people were rooted in the cult they presided over, kings were always revered even though they might be shorn of their power. Kingship and its patriarchal aedifice remained the nucleus of people's ultimate beliefs about the right order of things. The civic orders that might arise to redress regal abuses did not have the force of ultimacy. Moreover, perhaps most importantly, they were not instilled in and corroborated by people's familial experience. They were not associated with the satisfaction of their infantile needs. They arose from historical experience rather than psychological development.

Nevertheless the conciliar experience of Greeks and Romans continued. The Greek experiments were finally overrun by the Macedonian empire under Alexander in the fourth century BCE, but the Roman senate, through its military triumphs and its method for governing the cities it conquered, survived much longer.

In the corruption or failure of these forms of government people always had recourse to some kind of monarchical tradition. The king, in sum, retained an aura of familial security to rescue people from the vicissitudes of factionalism, clan warfare, and the oppression of lesser lords. He was the epitome of archaic piety, nostalgic perfection, and protectorship. While a savior from chaos, he was always, in turn, unable to found a more expansive public order to deal with the increasing complexity of social life in classical times.

In the face of this frustration Plato developed his plan for an ideal "polity" ruled by a rightly educated ruler and class of guardians. Here we see the Hellenic appeal to wisdom to legitimate monarchy. Moreover, we see sophisticated refinements that persist throughout our history.[5] Plato conceived of the polity as a kind of single being, the great image of a man. The actors within it are functional organs obeying the rational will of its head. The monarch acts like a lens to the cosmic harmony, refracting this harmony throughout the social body. The only way the parts can function is for them to reflect the grand design mediated by the monarch.

Earlier folk believed that through the bond of kinship they were all represented in the king, who ruled them like a father does a household. With Plato's vision the explicit belief in kinship is replaced by participation in some divine wisdom mirrored in the king. Ruler and ruled are one body made visible in the monarch.

Governance of this body occurs through "iso-morphy" (identity of form), that is, through each part's conformance with the ideal in the mind of the ruler. The self, the household, the polity, and the cosmos are all based on the same order of rational rule. The polity is a thinking body whose head is a monarch. This conception of governance, rooted in tribal kingship and cast in philosophical terms, is what I call "body thinking." It has had enormous impact not only in our political theory, but also in ecclesiology wherever appeal to the "body of Christ" has been dominant. This is the sacral metaphysics underlying the unalterable contest between kingship and all forms of political pluralism.

The alternative conception of political wisdom as the consensus of the elders or the citizens has usually been seen as an accommodation to practical necessity. However, Aristotle tended to trust it more as a principle of governance. The many, by each seeing a part of the truth, can come to a better understanding than any one person, no matter how well educated. It is only in the assembly that practical wisdom can arise. This became a root of democratic appeals in later thought.

Let us recapitulate. Greco-Roman kingship was rooted in the sacral chiefdom of the tribes. It underlay the establishment of the cities and was often appealed to in efforts to overcome their corruption. Kings were often conceived of as ancestral divinities and high priests (*archon, pontifex*). However, the functions of priest and king never achieved the differentiation customary in Israel. Their union in ancient tribal chieftainship maintained its grip all the way to the seventeenth century formulations of James I. Moreover, appeal to the special wisdom of tradition or reason shaped the philosophic argument for monarchy even into our own times, where many people believe in government by scientific experts.

C. Kingship in Early Christianity

The followers of Jesus drew on both Hebraic and Greek traditions to understand the meaning of Jesus' presence among them. The evangelists viewed Jesus as a King of Israel or of the Jews. They saw Jesus as the Anointed One who would restore Israel according to the promises in YHWH's covenant with David.

Jesus, they thought, stood as the culmination of a royal cult that began with the praise of YHWH as King during David's reign. The decline and fall of this monarchy precipitated both a belief in YHWH's ultimate royal rule and also the conviction that YHWH would anoint a restorer of the Davidic dynasty. This expectation appeared first in Isaiah's image of "the shoot from the stump of Jesse" (Is 11; cf. Is 9). By the time of Daniel this image of an expected king, now transformed by other motifs from Babylonians, Persians, or Canaanites, attained a more extravagant status as "the Son of Man," "the Ancient of Days," who would introduce a cataclysmic and cosmic renewal of things.

This monarchical image easily takes on the Wisdom motifs associated with royal ideology elsewhere. The final ruler will perfect a governance through wisdom. He will be a king of charismatic intuition. "Wisdom" can supersede custom because it is even more ancient than custom. We see this emerge in the Wisdom literature imputed to Solomon. Indeed, in Hellenic Judaism it is Wisdom herself (*Sophia*) who will be this governor.[6]

At this point the more earthly kingship anticipated under the symbol of David's monarchy begins to blend with the old tradition of YHWH's unique kingship—a kingship which transcends and subordinates all earthly monarchs. Sometimes this Yahwistic kingship can be appealed to as a legitimation of earthly monarchy, as with David. Other times it opens up the possibility of other forms of right order, principally of the confederal union of the tribes under charismatic and priestly leadership.

It is this strand that the Maccabean revolutionaries against Syrian rule revived in the second century BCE. While drawing on and intensifying the expectation of an imminent Messiah, they appealed almost exclusively to the confederal priestly traditions for legitimation (1 Mac

2; 14:4–15, 41–49). Judas Maccabeus, member of a priestly family, was known as "the savior of Israel" (1 Mac 9:21). His brother and successor, Simon, was called "the great high priest and commander and leader of the Jews" (1 Mac 13:42). The account of their rebellion revolves around restoration of the law and sanctuary. Like a meteor from an earlier system the priestly warrior appears to fight against oppressive kings in order to liberate Israel.

Judas Maccabeus evidently admired the Roman's senatorial government and appealed to it for aid against the Syrian monarchs (1 Mac 8). This preference for conciliar rule resonates in the vision of restoration typical of the confederal tradition:

> He established peace in the land,
> and Israel rejoiced with great joy.
> Each man sat under his vine and his fig tree,
> and there was none to make them afraid.
> No one was left in the land to fight them,
> and the kings were crushed in those days.
> He strengthened all the humble of his people;
> he sought out the law,
> and did away with every lawless and wicked man.
> He made the sanctuary glorious,
> and added to the vessels of the sanctuary.

(1 Mac 14:11–15)

Thus we have several traditions informing the Messianic title attributed to Jesus: the earthly king of the Davidic monarchy, the transcendent monarchy of YHWH's kingship, and the warrior liberator of the priestly confederacy.

We can only conjecture why the disciples of Jesus chose the monarchical rather than the confederal understanding of the Messiah. It is not enough to point to the genealogy in Matthew and the citation of Jesus' membership in David's house found in Luke (Lk 2:4; cf. Acts 13:32–39). Luke clearly has to labor, no matter how poetically, to place Jesus's true home in Bethlehem rather than Nazareth. John's only reference to Jesus' Davidic lineage is simply to air the obvious dispute that surrounded this attribution (Jn 7:40–44). Paul simply accepts the tradition that Jesus was descended from David (Rom 1:2; 2 Tim 2:8), but this claim plays no part in his theology, since it is entirely severed from Palestinian Messianism.

Clearly, the Davidic titles for Jesus resulted from a decision people made about Jesus rather than from any genealogical fact. It was a decision to interpret the significance of Jesus in a particular way. Why, then, did the first Christians decide to interpret Jesus within the framework of Davidic Messianism rather than confederal liberation? Why did David (but not his son Solomon!) loom larger than Moses, Samuel, and Maccabeus?

This is a largely insoluble question. Simply to raise it is to recognize that Jesus, as God's anointed and chosen one, could have come to legitimate other governmental forms than monarchical ones. Indeed, it is to these other traditions that later Christians had to turn in contesting the dominance of monarchy in Christian symbolism and political ethics.

However, some clues to an answer are evident. First, the revolutionary ideals of independence associated with the Maccabees made it extremely dangerous to entertain their leading symbols of priestly warrior and liberator. It was a recipe for death—a death that Jesus suffered anyhow, though with the title of "King" rather than "high priest and commander." The only way to save Jesus' political radicalism and also to survive as a community was to choose the more ambiguous title of "King."

On the one hand this could preserve the expectation of some kind of restoration of Israel's integrity. This was its radical side. On the other hand, it could refer to an a-political, transcendent "kingship of YHWH," which posed no immediate threat to the status quo. Moreover, even if it did gain some political realization, kingship was not really a problem for the Roman Empire, since it governed through treaties with local kings. After all, its ruler was an emperor, not a mere tribal king.

That Pilate's attribution to Jesus of "King of the Jews" expressed an exasperated contempt for Jewish controversies merely reinforces the evidence that the Romans were unperturbed by these Jewish monarchical claims. Indeed, they seem to have perceived Barabbas, who was probably closer to a Maccabean position, as a more dangerous person than Jesus. In this they were probably correct, for a collectivity of semi-autonomous tribal councils would be much more difficult to control and administer than a centralized monarchy.

Clearly other considerations also must have played a role, especially in the relation of the early followers of Jesus to the existing Jewish movements, institutions, and factions. The interaction with Roman-imposed conditions played a key role in this development. Jesus took on the title of *Basileus* (King) in the ancient world. Though Palestinians may have carried over some of the earlier attributes of the Hebrew *Melek* (King)—the elect and anointed charismatic warrior—the connotations of Basileus inevitably conveyed an image of Jesus Christ as the heir to a patrimonial cult safeguarding the household and the traditions of the polis. This conception of Christ's followers would have made it possible for Rome to legalize its relation with them as one of these ethnic cults.

Before we turn to the way Jesus as *Basileus* was taken up in Roman Christianity, we need to examine the significance of the household for early Christian development. The central point here is that kingship and household were not antithetical in the sense of our modern distinction between public and private. Kingship represented the apex of a household pyramid. A king was essentially the Great Father, the living presence of the Founding Father. A monarchy was essentially a vast household controlling land, people, and cultural norms. At its center was the ancestral cult rather than the army. This was the real source of its power.

Monarchy and household patriarchy were thus the same thing on two different scales. Therefore, Christians could worship Jesus as Basileus and also form themselves in household assemblies. Their actual character as public assemblies had to act itself out in a domestic forum by necessity. Ultimately, as Elisabeth Schüssler Fiorenza has shown, the household-monarchical structure won out over the voluntary public assembly of equals, preparing Christianity for its chief role as legitimator of empire and monarchy for the next fifteen hundred years.[7] The warrior-king of ancient Israel's assembly was domesticated into a household patriarch mirroring the kingdoms of this world.

Even this Roman and European development was not without its ambiguities and turnabouts. To understand what was at stake in Christianity's fateful union with empire and monarchy, we need to understand the Roman situation into which the early Christians entered.

D. Roman Empire and Christian Kingship

Kingship as hereditary tribal rule was shared by Greeks and Romans. Both experienced the royal oligarchy of rule by an assembly of such kings. Both had appealed to kings to admit strangers into the civic order. The crucial difference between them seems to have been in their principle of expansion.

The Greeks pursued primarily two means. In the first case they formed alliances among cities, the most famous being the Boeotian amphictyony (confederation, league). The failure of those confederations lay simply in their inability to act decisively to defend themselves. Moreover, they were confined to Hellenic cities. The second, under Philip and Alexander of Macedon, was to conquer non-Greeks with a mighty army and then seek to rule these lands directly rather than through client kings. While these monarchs were enormously successful militarily, Greek rule, with its need to set aside the kings and cults of the defeated, was not. The household principle of kingship was not adequate for rule beyond tribal boundaries.

The Romans followed a different course. Their army of conquest was sent out by an assembly of royal descendants (the senate), but was not led by them. They were simply directed by commanders (*imperatores*). Having conquered, the Romans had no need to replace the native kings and cults, because they did not seek to incorporate them into their tribal household. They formed a relationship of treaty with them, allowing them a good deal of autonomy in exchange for taxes, soldiers, and passivity. Eventually, some residents of these colonies would settle in Rome and add their cult to the pantheon of acknowledged tribal deities. The household principle of monarchy was accommodated to the assembly of gods under a common treaty law.

In this stable and successful situation the army eventually became a standing assembly of its own with enormous power. Through its insistence on participation in decisions, the masses unaffiliated with an ancestral hearth eventually found their way into the highest Roman offices. Under these conditions the earlier senate of elders was transformed into the open assembly of the Republic. The governance of Rome and its empire were by the Senatus Populusque Romanus (SPQR), the senate and people of Rome. The cities and tribes related through conquest were not a vast household (*dominium*), but an empire (*imperium*, command).

In this situation kingship referred to the tribal leaders within the empire or to the ancient though now superseded ancestral founders of Rome. Kings, though wreathed in nostalgia, were naked of power. Therefore, when the increasingly powerful army finally overwhelmed the senate, its leader did not become king, but remained *imperator*, that is, emperor. In order finally to take over the cultic presidency essential to legitimate rule, Julius Caesar and his successors absorbed the title of *pontifex* (or *pontifex maximus*) rather than *rex* (king). Thus, in the words of Henry Myers, a "less than king became more than king."[8]

When Christians, with their worship of Jesus as Messiah and *Basileus*, entered into Roman culture, they had to decide how they would translate this Greek term. The title of Messiah (now in Greek as Christ) was already lost on Greek Christians and could be preserved as an element of an almost tribal cult. However, to translate Basileus as "imperator" would have posed a direct threat to Roman rule. Indeed, it was only radicals like Tertullian who referred to Christ as emperor in order to hold earthly rulers in contempt. It was only after Constantine that imperial designations were widely used for Christ. King was much safer. It brought with it the sense of ancient household worship, archaic wisdom, and cultic preoccupation without the authority attributed to *imperator* and *pontifex*. Jesus Christ, in Roman eyes, could take his place beside the other ancestral god-men.

Even at the earliest time it was almost impossible for Christians to link themselves to republican Rome. That era was decisively past. It would be centuries before its memory would be revived in Renaissance conciliar movements. Moreover, Christians were already wed to Jesus as Basileus—a king who also absorbed the charismatic power of the prophet and the cultic authority of the priest. The three offices of prophet, priest and king came to be united in the bishops of the Church just as they had been fused in the kings of the ancient household.

When Constantine turned to Christianity as the source of his authority, he was dealing with a movement that had already absorbed many of the features of antique Roman religion, but without its direct association with its ancestral cults. By his conversion he saw himself as the "servant of God," executing his will according to Divine Providence in order to secure the concord of all peoples. His rule could find a brilliant mirroring in the Christian monarchy of God, of Jesus, and his heirs, that is, the bishops. The monarchy of God reinforced the monarchy of the empire. In the words of Eusebius, Constantine's obsequious admirer and extremely influential interpreter:

> . . . invested as he is with a semblance of heavenly sovereignty, he directs his gaze above, and frames his earthly government according to the pattern of that Divine original, feeling strength in its conformity to the monarchy of God. . . . [9]

Here again we see the "causal isomorphy" in which material and human order is preserved through a hierarchical mirroring of the purer images above us. This isomorphic rule by imitation of higher forms resonates strongly with the transmission of rulership by hereditary descent. In procreation we find the causal principle of rule in the generation of like by like. Here is the principle tying together science, domestic life, and political rule. The obedience of monarchical rule echoes in the causal relations of matter and the generation of progeny.

Not only did Constantine provide the model for Christian kingship, he also established the basilica as the normative pattern of Church architecture. [10] Hitherto Christians had assembled in houses or rented halls. It was there that the initial thrust toward public preaching, witness, and open assembly was domesticated in accord with the model of

the patriarchal household. Now this organizational model could once
again go public, this time in the basilica.

The term *basilica* was a Latin derivation from the Greek for king.
Essentially the basilica was the palace, especially the audience hall, of
the king. It was also a place of public assembly for business, funerals,
and observance of the king's cult. By the fourth century the emperor's
statue occupied a central place. It was a throne room, the house of God.
On this throne sat the judge, the ratifier of contracts, the teacher of wisdom. The royal ideology of the wise ruler we found earlier in Solomon
finds full flower here. In the basilica the throne takes precedence over
the altar. Eventually it became the model for the episcopal cathedral,
the bishop's throne room.

Thus, Christianity's emergence as a fully public assembly occurred
within the framework of imperial monarchy. Church organization under the bishop increasingly mirrored imperial structures under the emperor. Both of them reflected the divine monarchy of God in Christ.
The Church became public under the condition that it be monarchical.

Subsequent Church leaders moved away from Eusebius' flattering
portrait of Constantine as the vicar of Christ, but his image exercised a
decisive impact on later centuries, especially under the Carolingians in
the ninth century. The mirroring dynamic between Church and empire
became entrenched. Soon after Constantine the emperor Gratian assigned the pontificate to the Bishop of Rome, thus solidifying the pattern of distinguishing between cultic leadership on the one hand and
civil governance on the other.

Moreover, the bishop, with his ecclesial "family," begins to take
over the earlier function of the kings of local civic hearths. Bishops occupy the local thrones, maintain the central cult unifying the people,
and even dispense justice. It is they who eventually control marriage—
the key to tribal power and authority.

Thus, the new configuration of emperor and bishops still preserves
wide play for local rule under various forms, whether by assembly, by
noble family or both. The emperor preserves order, the Church preserves the cultural frame of reference, and the cities attend to local affairs.
This is essentially the Roman heritage: patriarchal order in all institutions, imperial peace, Church hegemony over culture, and local government through princes and advisory councils.

Before assembling the implications of our brief survey, we need to
see how this pattern adjusted to the impact of Teutonic and English patterns in subsequent centuries.

E. Kingship in Christendom

The peculiar amalgam of Church and government we now call Christendom was not merely an extrapolation of the Constantinian model. It arose in the further engagement with Teutonic, Celtic, and English kingship. It was in this context that distinctive biblical themes re-emerged and fused with actual institutions. To grasp the significance of these developments we must attend to the decisive turning points in this story.

Henry Myers points out that the Germanic kings bore two different titles—*thiudans* and *reiks*. The thiudans was a sacral representative of the people. The reiks was king by charismatic prowess in war. The *thiudans* was rooted in archaic tradition, the *reiks* in present achievement. At various times one or the other of these aspects came to prominence in the exercise of royal leadership. In any case their kingship was exercised over and within a tribe, though it was not necessarily hereditary. Kingship in the Germanies always rested on the approval of the elders. The concept of emperor was foreign to them.

When the Goths moved into Italy they brought their kingship terminology with them. Theodoric, the great Western emperor of the sixth century, took the title Flavius Theodoricus Rex. Though called king, he actually functioned as emperor. Over the centuries the disdain for kingship gradually waned and in most people's minds kings merged with emperors, the only differences lying in function and method of selection.

In the three centuries after Constantine the effective armies of the region fell to the leadership of first the Goths and then the Franks. The Bishop of Rome, however, maintained the legitimating authority of ancient tradition as Pontifex Maximus.

It became increasingly difficult to continue the Greco-Roman patterns in this new situation. First, Rome had to shift allegiances from time to time in order to ally itself with the tribe most likely to protect it from other tribes or the Eastern empire. Second, the northern tribes had peculiar conceptions of kingship which could not be easily reconciled with those emerging from Roman history. Third, the cultic components of royal legitimation were inevitably refined in a more distinctively Christian direction.

These three factors really began their work when Rome turned to the Franks in the seventh century to defend its interests. One could also say that Clovis, the Frankish ruler, turned to Rome to legitimate his power. In any event, we find in his conversion a distinctly new development. First, we see a close union between baptism and royal consecration. In effect, his conversion was his consecration. Baptismal motifs and the higher call associated with baptism began to flow into the royal mold. The sense of personal vocation felt by Constantine now became attached ritually to kingship. Constantine himself had delayed his baptism till death, associating it with preparation for the next world rather than conversion in this one. Future emperors came to claim its powers for their earthly rule.

Clovis, moreover, was anointed with oil at baptism, an ancient rite which originally was connected with kingship (as with Saul). Later, Pippin and Charlemagne would be anointed with oil at their coronations. Increasingly the motifs familiar in Hebraic kingship gained expression. The early Carolingians spoke of the Franks as "the people of God." Their kings felt that "it is quite evident that Divine Providence anointed Us onto the throne of the kingdom." Their vocational ideal was not merely based on Constantine but even more fundamentally on David. The Franks became the New Israel. Hebraic kingship began to mix with Roman emperorship.

With this messianic conception the king became the instrument of God, revealing wisdom, making laws, enforcing justice, and bearing the destiny of the whole people in his person. Kings exulted in victory but also did penance in defeat. Mighty warriors in battle, terrible judges in their court, they were also humble children at their Church's feet. This infusion of Christian motifs was reinforced by tribal traditions. Both Germans and Franks had a charismatic view of kingship as something bestowed by God, whether in battle or in miraculous powers. Both realized that this charisma could be taken away as mysteriously as it came. The Germans always had a more elective tradition of kingship, with local leaders having much more control. The Franks tended to see kings coming "from above," but realized that kings and dynasties could fail.

Along with this charismatic awareness they saw kings possessing miraculous powers. The *Heil* associated with the German king was also a healing power, a belief shared with the Franks and English. People came to the kings, not merely for wisdom in dispensing justice, but also for healing. The rectitude inherent in the consecrated king also flowed into those he touched, that is, those who were "kin" with him.

In the tribal perception the king was one blood with his people. He was in that sense married to them and, especially among the French and English, to the land. This primitive sense of co-inherence could easily lead to seeing the king as a kind of priestly representative of the people. The king was the unifying head of the body of the people. The existence of peoplehood became identified with having a king. To some extent the

Church fostered this but it also had to limit it to a lay piety focused on healing.

The crucial Church concern lay in the disposition of the emperorship. Through the emperor the Church could establish a defender, especially of Rome's interests. It also could find a way of bringing some peace among warring kings as well as of defending the West against first a Christian and then a Muslim East. In order to secure this it was important that the emperor be even less hereditary than kingship. Otherwise, the Church's interests would be bogged down with local considerations and the vicissitudes of specific dynasties.

The empire was the Church's effort to preserve and extend the sense of a Greco-Roman *oikoumene*, literally a world household, in which many features of republican citizenship and local governance were sheltered under an over-arching patriarchal power. Outside Roman culture it at least hoped that the tribal loyalties attached to kingship would be transferred to the emperor, thus ensuring a unified Christendom which could be permeated with Christian faith and morals. In fact, the Church had to settle for even less.

The election of the emperor under Church auspices began with the traditional Roman acclamation, as with Charlemagne, who was crowned emperor in Rome on Christmas Day, 800. Later, however, when the emperorship shifted to the German kings, the election process, which was anyhow more familiar to German kings, became rooted in the electorships north of the Alps. This meant that election by lesser royalty underlay the empire, while inheritance and designation "from above" remained with kings. The emperor, even though appointed for more universal functions, almost always lacked the stronger and more primitive loyalties of ancient tribal kingship.

Without giving up its efforts to mirror the world emperor with Christ, the Church therefore had to attend primarily to the legitimation and limitation of the local kings that actually dominated local life. It did so by appropriating control over marriages and establishing the terms of kingship through consecration ceremony and education. In Carolingian times we already have the production of literary "mirrors" for the ideal king, as in this widely echoed formulation:

> Eight pillars support the rule of a just king: the first is truth in the exercise of kingship; the second, patient forebearing in conducting all his affairs; the third, generosity in rewarding service; the fourth, a convincing way with words; the fifth, correction and restraint of criminals; the sixth, elevation and

public praise of good men; the seventh, lightness of taxes levied on his people; the eighth, equal justice to rich and poor.[11]

This is "limited kingship," but it is limitation by education and moral suasion, not by countervailing power. It relies on the power of cultural belief rather than independently codified law. It is still monarchy, indeed, "constitutional monarchy," in the sense that there is a decided form or constitution to it. But it is still monarchy; that is, all the legitimate powers of government are in one person. With one or another modification this became the pattern of Western kingship down to modern times.

Before moving to the final stage of kingship conceptions, it is important to highlight the significance of the eighth pillar—the equal dispensation of justice. While kings were more parochial than emperors, they were more universal than the lesser nobility. These had actual control of the land and its workers. The king represented a more expansive justice.

First, his justice extended to all those who were not bonded to the land and its lords, that is, to merchants and travelers. Pilgrims and free men of all kinds turned to the king for protection and adjudication of disputes. Recourse to the "king's peace" was essential to any commerce or communication.

Second, in order for the king to extend this service, his judgments had to be delegated to representatives. This required written codification of laws and decisions in order to ensure consistency. It also required a uniform training of these royal delegates.

Finally, the king's justice infiltrated between lords and vassals, between greater and lesser lords. Already with Charlemagne we see bonds developing not only among lords and vassals but between each one of them and the king. This is the actual web of covenants which liberated individuals at the same time as it elevated the king. Through kingship people began to escape the arbitrary power of their immediate lords. Kings became the saviors of the little people of the highways and the land.

This is why kings, especially in the eighth to fourteenth centuries, were more likely to be seen as liberating, redeeming figures than as oppressors. Their interests were tied to those of the Church, merchants, and all those displaced from feudal bonds. They represented an ultimate recourse from the arbitrary tyrannies of petty princes. Little wonder that the mantle of Jesus came to fall so heavily on their shoulders. Little wonder they embraced it so in their struggles with the princes. And, ultimately, little wonder kingship fell upon such crippling abuse.

F.   The Apotheosis and Collapse of Kingship

Two factors came together to elevate kingship to a position of absolute supremacy. The first, more associated with France, was the centralization of legal, financial, and military power in the crown. The second, more typical of England, was the increasing arrogation to the king of properly ecclesiastical powers. The first is epitomized in Louis XIV and XVI, the second in Henry VIII and James I. To understand these dynamics is to begin to unravel why such a symbol as "kingdom of God" could have gripped the hearts of Christians so long after monarchy's actual power had ended.

The first dynamic, that of centralization, lay in the extension of the king's justice to merchants and other free (i.e., non-landed) men. The interests of nascent capitalism lay with kings, the higher the better. The bond of king and merchant tended to dissolve the feudal ties that kingship originally was rooted in. Land which had been inalienably bound to personal fiefs was willed or sold to people who were "owners" rather than "lords." The land and the services of people tied to it began to enter the money economy. Kings came to charter merchant corporations to secure the common good, or at least the national wealth.

This meant that the king, when he had run out of land to grant as benefices to helpful lords, could turn to money taxes to raise a mercenary army apart from the webs of mutual obligation typical of feudalism. The king began to move from being a "lord of lords" dependent on land control to a "crown monarch" who headed a "state" based on taxation and a standing army. The modern state, with its unification of power and its alliance with mercantile interests, arose in this way. Absolute sovereignty it derived from monarchical tradition. Absolute power it derived from the monopoly tendencies of capital economy.

These tendencies crystallized in the so-called mercantilism of the era of Louis XIV. The state not only lived from its money taxes but also centralized and directed the economy and oriented it to centrally determined goals, both foreign and domestic. At this point rational administration practically replaces sacral charisma. The king disappears behind the crown, and the crown is swallowed up in the state. The Church is left with regal mystery but no effective tie with government, either in its monarchical or its republican form.

In England, beginning with Henry VIII and Elizabeth I, we find a similar monetization of the crown and the rise of a tax-based military, but a lesser degree of centralized power. However, the king is imbued with more sacral authority, like the ancient Germanic *thiudans*. As William Chaney so thoroughly shows us, the ancient Anglo-Celtic king was a typical sacral ruler of the tribe.[12] In his conversion he led his people like a shepherd (*pastor*) into the Church, which he was to protect and extend. The power he once had through hereditary charisma he now had through election by the people and consecration by the Church. However, he was still a highly sacral figure. This, coupled with his unique position on the island, always tended to draw sacral authority to him, just as his need to countervail the power of the lords drew him close to the Church.

It is in this period between the Reformation and the first revolutions that the idea of the divine right of kings achieves its final condensation. The elements of this theory, which we have in different forms from James I and Robert Filmer, were ancient. Their absolutist conjunction arose from historical circumstances.

What James I did was to complete the long process in which characteristics previously vested in the emperor were transferred to national kings.[13] The universality of the emperor became the king's universality of rule within his realm. The special role of the emperor as *alter Christus*, or "the regent of Christ by grace of God and by Providence," fell to the king. Imperial consecration and anointing by the Church had made the elected emperor's authority inalienable. Now this inalienability came to reinforce hereditary succession through the eldest (as if only) son. Heredity replaced election. Patriarchal nature, as Filmer contended, replaced popular will. Thus was the imperial crown of Christendom swallowed up by the royal crown of England.

These absolutist claims arose to defend the precarious monarchy of the Stuarts in the face of the rising strength of the parliaments. Moreover, these monarchs could no longer rely on the power of the empire or the authority of the Roman Pontiff. They had to stand on their own directly under God. Ironically, they claimed for themselves a right of kingship analogous to the rights of conscience claimed by Protestant radicals. Both appealed to the sovereignty of Christ, but reached opposite conclusions. To live within this contradiction, kings would henceforth have to rule with parliaments or rule not at all.

Germany presents yet another scene, since the power of local kings and nobility prevented the development of any central kingship. Any efforts toward unity were drained off into the maintenance of an increasingly illusory and ineffectual Holy Roman Empire. Neither monarchical unity nor an elevated conception of kingship could develop under these conditions, even though its cultural components lay deep within the ancient Germanic roles of *thiudans* and *reiks*.

Late kingship in France and England was thus composed of immense contradictions. On the one hand kingship progressively allied itself with capital over against land and personal bonds. On the other hand capitalist groups increasingly resented the aristocratic prerogatives hampering their development. The rationalism, achievement-orientation, individualism, and utilitarianism of the merchant class found no resonance in heredity, status ostentation, paternalism, and regal mystification. Both sides fell into increasing tension, with ambivalent and fluctuating appeals to the rapidly marginalized lesser nobility. The outcome, as Marx so concisely depicted it, was the bourgeois revolutions of the seventeenth to nineteenth centuries.

In the wake of the revolutionary overthrow of monarchies the Holy Roman Empire came to an end. Officially it ended in 1806 with the abdication of Francis II. Culturally it incinerated itself in Napoleon's self-proclaimed descent from Charlemagne. Napoleon was, in fact, the last to draw on this imperial heritage to create a trans-national empire administered according to a rational legal code derived from Roman tradition. With the failure of his own over-reaching absolutism the imperial memory went the way of monarchy, leaving the Western world a congeries of states in search of a new principle of concord. Both Hitler's and Mussolini's attempts to recover its forms took bizarre forms and ended in catastrophic human suffering.

In this process of magnification and collapse, what happened to kingship symbolism? We find a number of intermingled threads. First, among Anglophones mercantile and artisan groups seized on the King James Bible with rationalistic and literalistic hands. With eyes of reason and ears of legalistic constitutionalism their heads absorbed the patriarchal and monarchical ethos so prized by James' translators. The Bible, their spiritual magna charta, answered their republican aspirations with monarchical anointments for their individual consciences. With one eye clear, the other blind, they sought to navigate a new uncertain sea.

Second, the memory of the royal alliance still left a warm nostalgia. The justice, peace, and mercy of the king's ideal still appealed no matter what the context. Moreover, the now displaced nobility would rather return to feudal bonds based in land than calculate the pound, dollar, and franc above the factory floor. They would rather chase game in the Lord's domain than earn the salvation of the industrious saints.

Finally, and most important, with the rise of the bourgeois corporation the whole edifice of kingship shriveled back within its household womb. The bourgeoisie retained Christian kingship by enthroning it within the home.[14] Christian kingship became a model for ruling the passions rather than the people. The cultivation of Christ's rule became a domestic function cut off from wider public life. Greco-Roman republican architecture governed the public realm, Gothic and Tudor manorialism the private. All that remained of kingship was a patriarchal core to legitimate the parental hierarchies of the private realm. Kingship, like religion, returned to its original hearth, only this time the castle was a retreat from rather than the keeper of the public realm. Under the banner of kingship both Church and home retreated from the sphere of republican aspiration and achievement.

One of the chief reasons that kingdom symbolism has persisted so long in Christian circles is because it helps resolve a deep and uneasy tension between the private interests of our households and the corporate interests of an alien state and industry. In invoking "the kingdom," religious people express an inchoate yearning for a more satisfactory reunion of household and public life. It is not that we would like to return literally to Constantine, Charlemagne, or James I. We simply have no other way to dream of the future than by nostalgia and recollection. Both our Bible and our cult have crystallized and sacralized kingship as redemptive agency. However, our commitment to kingship symbolism is only a symptom of our public impotence rather than the catalyst of our liberation. We can only wake from this trance by recovering other elements of our heritage and taking a fresh look at the captivity we actually face in household, industry, and public life.

The attack on sexist symbols in christian faith and worship strikes at the center of this nostalgic union as well as at the isolation of family and Church life from the public world. The overcoming of sex discrimination is linked with the reconstruction of the relationship of the private and public dimensions of life. It is in fact a call to a new public order and a new relationship of the Church and family to public life.

Before we turn to the threads of republic and covenant that proffer an alternative vision we need to gather both the wheat and chaff of kingship. What ongoing needs did kingship serve? What enduring values can we harvest from this long experience? What elements must we decisively reject?

II.   The Kingdom Harvest

Our long experience with kingship in the West leaves us with the straw of bitter memory as well as the grain of partial victories. Kingship was a response to fundamental human needs as well as an expression of arrogant power. In order to lay the religious foundations for a different approach to our common life, we need to take stock of the positive achievements of kingship as well as its limitations and inappropriateness for our situation.

We need to remember four achievements of kingship:
(1) as a response to needs for survival and stability,
(2) as a means of socialization,
(3) as a means to wider justice, and
(4) as a form of elected and therefore limited rule.

After examining these four achievements we can rehearse the inadequacies that force us to another symbolic model for human affairs.

A. Survival

Kingship was a response to survival needs in two ways—military and civil. Leadership of military forces was the primary function of early Hebrew kingship, drawing on the Babylonian model. Kings evoked strong loyalties and could bind warriors together for the ultimate risk of warfare. Kings were kings because they seemed to be more than mere men. Their military status, in turn, heightened their ability to awe people with victory and the blessing of the gods.

Civil survival meant, above all, social stability. Kings were, in some way, the presence of a principle that transcended the vagaries of human action. They represented nature, God, Wisdom, or the sacred, unchanging past. They were the basis of social order, not its product. As in Hobbes' *Leviathan*, people surrendered their freedom to the king in exchange for security. The king was a fulcrum by which to move human beings by necessity in order to secure their freedom.

To secure long term survival kingship inevitably gave rise to a pattern of hereditary succession, thus lessening the conflict over selecting a king. The hiatus of death was absorbed in the continuity of procreation. Kingship represented right order grounded in a supra-human source. The conventions of human life could be rooted in a nature that transcended them. This nature was God's creation. An alternative to kingship symbolism would thus demand a different understanding of God's creative activity and relationship to the foundations of political order. It is to this point that we will return with the concept of covenantal reason and public discourse as the cradle of truth.

Kingship was a way of dealing with defense and death. It did so by posing as a bridge between this mortal realm of change and the immortal realm of permanence and peace. This is the common thread running through its function in warfare, rule, and succession, whether this consisted in appeal to *maat*, YHWH, Wisdom, Reason, or Nature. Kingship spoke to a question embedded in the human condition.

B. Socialization

Not only did kingship have a directly societal function. It also provided a path for leading people from familial infancy to maturity in large-scale institutions, such as the city, army, and, with Christ's kingship, the Church. Just as the king could relate an uncertain people to a transcendent, certain world, so he could also relate active adults to their infantile satisfactions. The king was a bridge between household and universe. Kingship was a powerful vehicle of socialization.

In most traditions kings were sacralized representatives of the household and its founder. The king emerged as the chief elder of a powerful *oikos*. With king came house, land, and cult, all tied together as the basis of life. People could be led beyond this little economy by extending its principles to the wider household of the kingdom. In a kingdom people had a place through a fictional adoption by their father—the king. The king made them kin, the kingdom was his kind. Kingship was the principle for expanded ethnic organization. Kingship ruled nativity just as nativity governed the emerging sense of nationality.

Kingship could therefore appeal to very deep motivations. Not only was there the extrapolation of the bond between father and child. There was also the royal replication of familial unity in the face of the inevitable pluralism of clans, tribes, classes, and interest groups. Kingship provided a comforting sense not only of unity, but of familiar unity.

By being a big family, a kingdom could induce the participation and cooperation known in the household. The king was the coordinator of the people's entire economy, including the conservation of their land. It included everyone affected by this *oikos*, though in the way of a family, where the parents provide for the needs of the members subject to their care.

This sense of participation depended on the belief that the monarch incorporated everyone within himself and would therefore care for them even as he would his own body. Moreover, even if he died, his immortal body, the crown, would carry on this task. The king, as Ernst Kantorowicz has pointed out, gained two bodies—one temporal and one immortal. The duality of Christ's nature became his.[15]

This sense of representation by the king was actually a two-way street. The king had the authority to act on the people's behalf. This is the paternalistic as well as despotic outcome of his representativeness.

Similarly, however, the king was also represented in the people. His victories as well as his failures were theirs.

This reciprocity had a very important outcome for our purposes here. It meant that in the medieval Christianizing of kingship the "dignity" of the king was gradually bestowed on the people by their common sharing in baptism. Baptism, with its anointing, was always closely connected to Christ's royal office. In baptism an individual became in fact a person, a subject of the realm, and in later times a citizen. Over the centuries the authority, sacredness, wisdom, and dignity associated with kingship accrued to every Christian and, finally, to every person. In this respect, kingship ultimately dissolved in universal citizenship, a process reinforced by the republican currents we shall examine shortly.

C. Transcendent Justice

Kingship's capacity to lead people to wider loyalties than the clan rested on realities of power as well as culture. Kings and dynasties survived only as long as they could elicit obedience and consent. Over and over again monarchs enlarged their constituency by defending the claims of marginal groups—the demos, plebs, clients, vassals and merchants. This struggle to augment their power in the face of the aristocracy could find legitimation in appeal to a justice that transcended the prerogatives of patriarchs and ancestral clans. The law of the lesser households, which also excluded aliens, newcomers, and the disinherited, was superseded by the justice of the king. The debilitating warfare among clan lords was overridden by the king's peace.

The expansionist strategies of kings thus fostered a sense of a more universal justice. When kings were unable simply to isolate and subdue lesser lords, they had to cooperate with them as an assembly of equals. Basic decisions had to be shared and discussed. Arguments had to appeal to common convictions and reason. The king was only able to be king in council. Kings had to operate within a wider covenant with God and Church. Rather than acting by his own wisdom or power, he had to operate within an overarching consensus of right shared by the leadership elite.

Thus, both the expansionist dynamics of kingship and the accommodation to councils and assemblies promoted a sense of a more transcendent justice. Kings used it to legitimate their rule. It was also used as a popular and aristocratic lever against them. Regardless of the motives of the carpenter, the plumbline still hung straight.

D. Elected Kings

The concept of election has always been closely associated with the development of Christian theories of kingship. Election has meant two things: (1) kings are specially appointed to their task by God, and (2) the king is elected by the assembly of the people.

In the Bible divine election is rooted in the charismatic kingship of the warrior. God's election is an important component in legitimating kingship. We see it in David, we see it in Constantine's appeal to Providence, and then in numerous successors. This augments royal power but also limits it. The election is for a specific task. The king, in Constantine's phrase, is a servant. Election reveals God's appointment of him to this task. His legitimate authority is limited to his divinely appointed tasks, tasks which became more and more clarified in the "mirrors" of the king. Divine election limited as well as legitimated the king.

This charismatic approach to divine election was always curbed or complemented by election through the traditional sacral leadership. Kings could rarely appeal purely to charismatic election. They had to appeal to the sources of traditional legitimation as well, namely, the priests and the patriarchs. The patriarchal leaders of the nobility often had the power to elect him. The priests, that is, the bishops and the Pope, augmented this power with their authority over souls.

Even with the practical apotheosis of the Roman emperor the Church always sought to preserve this crucial distinction between ecclesiastical authority and royal or imperial power. This distinction reflects the difference between the abiding culture of a people and the power configurations of the moment, between fundamental consensus and executive action. On the one hand we find the settled customs, consensus, beliefs, and conventions that enable people to live together in social order. These the Church came to champion. On the other hand we have the exigencies of military defense, economic survival, and the ever-renewed struggle for power among individuals, families, groups and classes. These forces were channeled into monarchical establishments.

The Church sought to use monarchs to preserve the peace and advance this common culture of Christendom, thus making possible a wider civil order. Monarchs and emperors tried to use the Church to legitimate their own power and secure its transmission to successors. The ever-changing shape of this symbiosis frames the whole history of the Holy Roman Empire to its final expiration. The search for God's election fell from both their hands into those of "the people," where the grain of divine covenant was often trampled in the mud of private interest and opinion polls. Recovery of this wider concept of election will become an important theme in our appropriation of the symbol of God's Federal Republic in our own time.

Behind this ecclesial defense of a basic culture limiting and sustaining kingship lies another component arising from biblical concepts of election. That is, election always implies a covenant between elector and elected. God makes a covenant of election with David. Even more importantly, God elects a whole people and binds them in covenant. This covenantal model first arose with the Hebrews, was taken over by the Church, borrowed by the Franks under Charlemagne, by the English, and, as we shall see later, by English Independents, Puritans, and Presbyterians.

Thus, there was always a drive to envelop kingship in a network of promises, pledges, and laws resting in the covenant of divine election. Kings constantly tried to escape this with appeals to direct charismatic election by God. Though often shattered in times of crisis this constitutionalism continually re-emerged in more settled times to become an underlying assumption of all governance.

These four achievements of kingship—survival and stability, socialization, wider justice, and limited rule—were achievements in the face of social disintegration, clan isolation, household rule, and arbitrary dictatorship. Kingship had a merit in its context—a merit recognized and advanced by Christians, though often in ambiguous and ambivalent ways. Kingship came to provide the overarching construct for governance and for symbols of an ultimate justice and peace beyond the brutality and evil of our historical experience. It was with these achievements in mind that most Christians and Jews have looked forward to the kingdom of God.

III. The Limits of Kingship

Christian kingship was not only a theory of limited rule, it was also a limited theory itself. Some of its limits arose from the sacred traditions of kingship—its limitation by tradition, by the specification of task inherent in election, and its close tie to a specific people and their land. Other limits, however, were actually brought *to* kingship—the authority of assembly, people, and Church being primary among them.

Inherent in these limiting groups and their ideas were other conceptions of governance, specifically those of covenant and republic. In the light of these alternative approaches we can see some inherent deficiencies in kingship. We criticize it not merely because of its excesses, but because its structure presented people with relationships inappropriate for a fuller realization of the impulses of their humanity. Not only was it patriarchal and hierarchical, it literally deprived people of a public life.

We criticize kingship for its status hierarchy, its elevation of biology over politics, its confusion of cultic legitimation and social task, and its reduction of the public realm to household management. The first three all flow from the last. The injustices perpetrated by kingship arise from its inappropriate use of household values, concepts, and practices to deal with the dynamics of interaction among independent adults.

Once you conceive of the household as an estate composed of property first awarded to a founding individual, then the larger conception of the public order is set. It shall be characterized by *status hierarchies*, that is, distinctions of power among people that run across the whole spectrum of relationships. In a status hierarchy, the inequality with regard to economic control is carried over to religious, political, sexual, and cultural control. The two parties are unequal in the same way in every respect, because they are permanently assigned to different, unequal levels. The inequalities are not limited to specific institutions, tasks, or functions. The natural inequality of parent and child is extended to all relationships.

In a society where the parent-child relationship typifies all relationships, biology has overwhelmed all other bases for interaction. Cooperation, rotation of leadership, assignment on the basis of ability, and decisions based on reasonable argument are hardly possible. Moreover, this model undermines the ways that various publics can join in association with others to form a complex web of mutual obligations and benefits. The lateral relations of equal publics are subverted by the hierarchical commands of dependency and obedience.

Finally, by taking on the aura of parental control kingship inflated its claims to allegiance by appealing not only to people's infantile fantasies and needs but also to their need to have an absolute which could justify the sacrifice of their very lives in battle. Kingship was the extension and remnant of the ancient worship of the hearth. Its unity of holy awe and domestic sovereignty remained its decisive characteristics throughout its development and arrogant decline.

The problem with kingship lies in the way it obstructs the development of a truly public realm in which people are bound together in arguments, promises, reasons, and convictions about their common life and the world they inhabit. It seeks the order of the household rather than the clamor of the fair, the silence of Father's final word rather than the many words of citizens in argument, the inequality that makes possible coercion rather than the equality that demands respectful reasoning.

These alternative values and conceptions are not simply new discoveries made possible in our own time. They have ancient roots which competed with and altered monarchical institutions. It is now time to turn to the illumination of these "public things."

3 | The Republican Heritage

If the republican alternative to kingship is to remain viable it must serve the functions traditionally met by kingship or find congenial partners to meet these needs. Moreover, it must further ground its claim on us in our basic tendencies and aspirations. The purpose of this chapter is to fill out the meaning of this heritage so that republic emerges more clearly as a symbol for a way of ordering, understanding and energizing our lives. Such a history does not "prove" its symbolic priority but enables us to put it on and live into its power. It enables us to sense this governing symbol as a memory and as an earnest of our ultimate end. The recital of its history can reveal its limitations as well as its power.

I. The Classical Origins

The republican vision arises in the Greek experience of the *polis* and the Roman conception of the *res publica*. Though it emerged in revolutions against monarchy, it was not originally antithetical to kingship. The polis was a sphere of action in which many could participate in governance. In Roman terms, it was a means for securing the common good of the many rather than the private good of the few. Kings could exercise the function of preserving this structure, especially through military action. They could play an essential but limited role in the life of a people engaged in "political" or "public" activity.

The innovation inaugurated in the polis was a form of governance based on mutual consent among equals rather than obedience to a natural superior.[1] It was more than a city, it was a way of life. It was a

54

cultural artifice which walled off the rulership exercised in households so that decisions could be reached through persuasion rather than force. In this sense, it was a realm of equals, though this egalitarian root existed more in germ than flower.

With the polis and the pursuit of what the Romans called "public property," (*res publica*) or public affairs, people broke through the organizational forms rooted in biology and family. They created a frame of interaction which assumed they all were adults. The bonds of nature erupted with the freedom of the spirit. A center of loyalty beyond family, tribe, and clan began to galvanize human action. People were no longer only property of their fathers and their fatherland, as Cicero said, but of a public realm.[2]

In the revolutions against monarchy experienced in Greece and Italy between the seventh and the fourth centuries BCE, a number of themes emerged which have formed the main outlines of republican thought and action ever since. They are *publicity, stability, equal participation*, and *persuasion*. These essential principles of republican theory lost their material basis with the rise of Julius Caesar. They lay dormant and distorted under the impact of Augustinian otherworldliness and the medieval commitment to kingdom and empire. However, some memories, especially that of governance through councils, remained alive to emerge with vigor in the fourteenth and fifteenth centuries. With the advent of the new republican era in the seventeenth and eighteenth centuries, the classical themes received new formulations which were embedded in the English, American and French revolutions. Since that time republican symbolism, thought and practice have circled the globe, but not without manifesting some fundamental limitations and deep ambiguities in practice. To grasp the essentials of this long development, we turn first to its Greek and Roman founders.

A. *Polis* and *Res Publica*: The Central Themes

The Greek *polis* and the Roman *res publica* nourished a family of themes which endured long after their ancient buildings crumbled. I have assembled them under the general notions of privacy and publicity, stability, equal participation and persuasion.

1. Private and Public. Originally towns were artificial households held together by loyalty to a common "hearth," whose fire was drawn from the founder's home. The patterns of governance were drawn from those of the household. The king of the city presided over this cult and ruled the city like a father, whether for good or for ill. When the heads of the other households in the city rebelled they established a *civitas* or *polis* whose principles developed around agreement among equals about the matters affecting them all—the *res publica*.

The matters of the hearth became *res privata*, private matters. The world based on ancestral ties, familial bonds, blood, and fatherland began its gradual contraction within the household while more and more decisions were taken over by an expanding public arena.

However, the myth of common ancestral origin still operated powerfully to define membership in this *civitas*. Even when aliens were finally granted a place in the public, the founder's cult still defined the shape of morality, the bounds of friendship, and the character of the people's ethos. It provided the cultural base of common assumptions which made public argument possible.

Thus the artificial public world of the city was grounded in the religious orientation provided by the official cult. These cults were in turn permeated by natural biological assumptions about human origins, dependency, and relationship. The legal world of the public stood on the cultural world of archaic religion. Archaic religion in turn was the symbolization of patriarchal householding and family.

As Hannah Arendt has so magisterially described it, this public world of the city presented the possibility of a wider existence, both in space and time, that could not be realized in the restricted circle of the home. In the public realm people could act before many others and seek a memory that was potentially immortal. Engagement in public affairs offered the possibility of glory, greatness, fame, and dignity.

Life in the home, though intense and immediate, could offer only a limited audience. One's acts were easily forgotten in the endless cycle of the generations. In Arendt's incisive categories, the public offered the possibility of action, the home only that of labor. Labor could yield only the faithful repetition of the cycles of life, while public action was sheathed in a linear arrow of immortal destiny. The patriarchal heads of household formed and occupied this public sphere. Women could only gain completeness through replication of household roles, while men became the rocks of monumental memory. The earnest of a public world open to everyone slept fitfully until our own time.

This salvation through immortality offered by the public, however, was attractive only if the public itself could guarantee its own endurance. The world, with its endless cycles, had appeared immortal in the face of human death. Now people confronted a human world which could conceivably endure through the preservation of its chronicles, monuments, history, and religion. The struggle to preserve the city in the face of corrupting forces became the highest ideal of its members. Loyalty to the city transcended bonds of family and the natural instinct for self-preservation. One's strength as a man (Latin *vir*) was manifested by one's heroic devotion to the public realm (*virtue*).

The search for some means of making the public realm durable became an obsession among philosophers and citizens. Plato's *Politeia*, Cicero's *De Re Publica*, and Polybius' *History*, as well as the works of Aristotle, were all responses to this question. In each case, though in different ways, they tried to find the principles of the immortal nature around them which could also be applied to public affairs. In approaching politics as a kind of "nature" they might unlock the clue to its potential immortality. The city had given them the tantalizing taste of a human reality more durable than the family, one approaching even that of nature. By examining the events, history, and structure of politics people might find out not only how to achieve its public values of justice but also of eternal endurance. The discovery of public life led to republican science.

2. Stability. In his history of the Roman conquests of Greece in the fourth century before Christ, Polybius articulated both the classical form of the problem and what became its classic solution.[3] Like others of his time he believed that civic life inevitably passes through phases created by the strengths and weaknesses of specific principles of governance—monarchy, aristocracy, and democracy. Each of these principles takes specific forms, with different virtues necessary for preserving the *res publica*. Each form has its typical corruption. Monarchy degenerates into tyranny. Aristocracy deteriorates into oligarchy, democracy into anarchy. Each form can serve the public good, but each form has a typical corruption to the private interests of its advocates.

The solution to this "revolution of polities" would be to bring all three principles into a simultaneous, balanced interaction. The strength of each would forestall the corruption of the others. This achievement, Polybius claimed, was the source of Rome's great strength and endurance. His argument for a mixed polity dependent on kings, aristocrats, and the people became the core of republican thought down to the American Revolution. Mixed, or balanced, polity and republicanism became practically synonymous.

What crucial element did each component contribute to this harmonious whole? What crucial functions could political philosophers discern beneath the multiplicity of personages and offices of the city?

The kings, as we saw in the previous chapter, contributed not only a sense of the people's common heritage, but also unified leadership in military action. The king could be both high priest and chief executive, founder as well as defender of the *res publica*. As such he could be known as *Basileus, Strategus* (General), *Archon* (Chief), or *Polemarch*. The king, when in concert with others, could be a support rather than a threat to the public.

The aristocracy, as we generally might call it, was composed of the elders of the established houses. They were the "old ones," the *senectus* in Latin, from which we derive our word "senate." They were the few who were distinguished by noble birth or virtuous achievement. They were those who had acted generously and heroically on behalf of the *res publica* or *polis*. They had exhibited, as the Greeks would say, *arete* (virtue), from which we derive our word "aristocracy."

These few assembled in council or senate. It is in their deliberation that collective wisdom could be brought to the difficult decisions engendered by public interests and needs. Typically, the senate or council drew up the proposals offered for popular vote. They also handled all extra-mural affairs.

The "people" were simply the members of the households of the city (the *demes* in Greece, the *plebes*, or clients, in Rome). In Greece, they came together in assemblies (*ecclesia*). The word *ecclesia* means literally "called out." The citizens were those called out of their households into the public realm. The basis for their participation in public affairs was neither the noble prowess of the king nor the virtuous wisdom of the elders, but their indispensability to the city, whether as workers or warriors. Without their consent neither the economy nor the military could function.

Of course, "the people" did not comprise all individuals in the city, but only those touching on the common world of the public. They were farmers and artisans who sold their surplus in the market. They were men who could shoulder arms in battle. The rest—women, household slaves, and children—rarely participated in the popular assembly. Occasionally, under extraordinary circumstances women of exceptional courage and skill broke through their domestic walls to influence or lead the city, but these were clearly exceptions rather than the norm. "Democracy" did not liberate people from domestic privation, it only enabled public men to share in government.

Classical thought as well as its later revivals assumed that the strength of a republic would depend on the proper balance among the virtues associated with each group. Political stability depended on the presence of regal oversight, aristocratic wisdom, and popular bravery. The stable polity is one in which these three groups are "represented" in the sense that their virtues are well-actualized by those in power. "Representation" pointed to the way government pursued the common good rather than to the actual participation of all the members of the represented group. At this point the preservation of the public realm took precedence over everyone's access to public activity.

The belief in republican balance, whether in terms of Plato's organic hierarchy, Aristotle's middle-class constitution, or Cicero's aristocratic leadership, became the classic answer to an essentially religious question: How can we create a stable, everlasting order in which we can achieve the good life? How can we enjoy all the rare pleasures of public action without suffering its seemingly intrinsic fragility, uncertainty, and tumultuous change? The republican answer was a theory of balanced representation.

3. Equal Participation. The stable republic was not in itself egalitarian. Its first concern was civic preservation. Only then could it turn to wider questions of participation. Republican thought has always strained toward an equality of participation, but has usually focused on some kind of representative participation. This representation itself has often been more concerned with the public presence of groups than of individuals.

Aristotle saw that the components of republican balance had to reflect the composition of social forces in the city. Where the masses were stronger, especially through arms, the polity would be more democratic. Where a wealthy few exercised actual power, the polity would be more oligarchic or aristocratic. Groups had to be able to participate commensurate with their actual power. The republic's authority depended on its structure of participation.

Even granting the inequality presupposed in this ceaseless jockeying for power, a genuine polity contained intrinsically egalitarian strains which would work themselves out in a variety of ways over the next two millennia. Participation by a plurality of groups opened the door to a greater sense of individual participation and equality.

The first thrust toward greater participation and equality arose from the search for stability itself. A balanced constitution ensured, among other things, that no one group would be so disadvantaged that it would seek to overthrow the existing order. As Aristotle argued, this implied that the more power was distributed among a large "middle class" the more stable the regime would become.[4] Equality, therefore, cultivated stability. The desire for stability encouraged equality.

Equal participation, however, could not be guaranteed by a political arrangement itself. Both Aristotle and Polybius after him argued that some kind of economic equality, such as that of Sparta, was a necessary bulwark against the inequality of unstable regimes. Principally, this could be gained through equal distribution of land or of arms.

Landed equality depended on withholding land from marketplace dynamics. Military equality demanded not only an armed citizenry and low-technology weapons, but the exclusion of mercenary soldiers, whose interest would always be a private and never the public good. Both of these egalitarian currents flow through republican literature to the present day.

The character of public life as an effort to pursue the common good also had a certain leveling effect. People's relative goodness as individuals need not carry over, as Aristotle observed, into their action as citizens. With regard to that which affected all, all had a certain degree of equality.[5] They interacted as citizens devoted to the same end rather than as household members subservient to particular needs of children, women, men, fathers, mothers, and slaves.

The justice of the public realm strained toward some kind of equality, whether it was an arithmetic one of balloting, or a proportional one of assigning rewards and sanctions strictly according to impartial rules. To the degree that political life created a new kind of justice appropriate for free and equal persons, even though small in numbers, it introduced a strain toward legal equality.

Political life was always conceived as life according to general laws established for common or public matters. Life in public was not one of subordination to arbitrary decrees, no matter how well intentioned they might be. The law in this sense was a great leveler of inherited status or acquired power, even though the structure of governance itself might be characterized by many inequalities of office.

The idea of law among these thinkers was inseparable from that of reason. The laws were the product of an interest in achieving the common good, whether set forth by a lone legislator, such as the great Solon of Athens, or by an assembly. Not "respecting persons," they must overlook people's peculiar differences for the sake of a public uniformity and dependability.

Now reason, as a trans-personal structure of thought, accompanied and undergirded an effort to establish laws that would take account of contingencies ahead of time and lead people to the common good, often in spite of themselves. In order for people to be led by reason rather than force, coercion, or biological necessity, they had to be persuaded by arguments. Rational argument for the formulation of public policy, though it creates new hierarchies of skill and knowledge, can be learned by most people, whereas correct birth, physical strength, and other "natural" attributes cannot. Dependence on reason undercut the claims of raw power in order to promote individual judgment.

Finally, even though the early republics had a restricted membership, the experience of argument among equals did gain a place in human memory and aspiration. It was an ideal that could be shared and was shared as more and more people—artisans, aliens, farmers, soldiers, and even women—sought to enter it. The circle of public debate could and did grow wider, even as it was often crushed by force or natural disaster.

In all these respects the early publics, both Greek and Roman, contained strains toward a more democratic participation. The opposition between democratic and republican ideas which we often hear today has always been a distortion. The idea of a republic offers a structure for preserving genuine public action. That of democracy points to the strain toward wider and wider participation in that public sphere.

4. Persuasion. Publics could include more people only if they cultivated symbols, rituals, language, and a world outlook common to the variety of participants. It was not merely a case of pretending they were all from the house of the founder. This they did by paying homage to the ancestral hearth and its cult. It was not enough to speak the same language. They had to see, in the words of the Stoic philosophers, that the whole universe was their hearth, their *polis*, their *civitas*.

The best expression of this desire for a common world was the search for a common law governing the actions of all. This law had to be more than the customs of any one family, clan, tribe, or people. It had to be rooted in the nature of a life shared by everyone. Here we find the origins of "natural law."[6] Natural law, from its Stoic founders down to the present, is not necessarily an effort to derive human laws from the patterns of biology or physics. It can be seen as an effort to base people's mutual expectations on something transcending their particularities and yet also be accessible to their inquiry.

A public order required a dependable system of reciprocal rights and duties. People had to know what to expect when they agreed to a contract or became citizens of a city. This pattern of law could not be arbitrary, could not depend on individual or even group caprice, and had to be intelligible and understandable to the average person. This is the universal law underlying the expansion of a public order.

Without this sense of a natural law binding all rational beings together people could not seek to persuade each other rather than rely on coercion. Persuasion depended on the possibility of arguing back to commonly held beliefs, assumptions, and purposes. The common belief that these existed made discussion, argument, and persuasion possible. A public order could therefore be expanded beyond tribal boundaries. The arts of rhetoric indispensable to this process were not simply oratorical flim flam but the rehearsal of the full panoply of symbols and logic that knit together the public sphere. The recovery of such reasoned discourse from an objectified science and technology in our own time is essential to the development of public life.[7]

Initially the tribe had provided this web of mutual sympathies, beliefs, and outlooks. Now this was taken over by the law. The philosophers generally sought to ground this law in reason and nature, but still had to find some way of making it visible, impressive, and tangible for the people. At this point they frequently turned to kings and aristocrats to personify this law, mirror the cosmos which it supports, and make it concrete through their own conduct, decisions, and government.

Here again, kings were often sought because they could provide the cultural cement underlying the cool stones of the public arena. Kingship, but not tyranny, often became the religion of republican order based on natural law. This was not the only way the culture necessary for public life could be grounded, as we shall see, but it became dominant as the possibilities of a mixed polity within a small city eroded under the spread of Roman power and authority. The theory of "covenantal reason" developed in Chapter Five takes the place of this natural law in the more voluntary setting of the modern republican ideal.

B. From Republic to Empire

People have usually attributed the fall of the republican order in Rome to the corruption of senatorial virtue and the expansion of empire. Senators came to seek only private interest in their public office. They neglected the unifying worship of the ancient hearths. They convulsed the republic with factionalism and civil strife. The republic collapsed through loss of virtue—the courage to sacrifice for the public good.

It was also clear that the expansion of Rome's imperium ruined the republic. It introduced foreign elements into Rome's culture and bloated it with riches. It created an enormous standing army, not of citizens defending their land but of mercenaries loyal to their commander. Finally it was the commander Julius Caesar who completed the transfer of authority from senate to emperor. Caesar Augustus consolidated his work, creating, as later Christians would recite, a cradle of peace for the spread of the Gospel of Christ.

We could also say, transforming a note from Polybius, that the Roman republic failed because of its repudiation of the principle of confederation. Polybius had explained Rome's victory over the Greeks as a victory of the mixed republic over the fractious confederation. We could also say that the fall of the Roman republic was the collapse of republican order under the centralizing tendencies of empire. If the corruption of the senate and the ascendancy of the emperor were both due to the effects of centralized empire, then this collapse was promoted by lack of a confederal principle which would have decentralized power and authority. Without an adequate principle for sharing power the republic was doomed by its own imperial success. Without a confederal principle the republic was devoured by empire. This is the lesson to be remembered from the death of the political order that first made republic a noble symbol of political justice.

C. The Classical Coda: Councils

The experience of *polis* and republic left a lasting memory regardless of how people evaluated their successes. It was a remnant with revolutionary impact in later eras. However, the symphony of republican instruments did not end with a crashing crescendo. There was one note held when the rest of the chord had died away. It was the note of conciliar form, played by two instruments—town and Church.

Councils were such a natural form for small cities and towns that they continued a strong though intermittent existence even under empire and feudal hierarchy. Sometimes extinguished by tyrants or exploded by corrupt oligarchs, they continually re-emerged, especially in Florence, Milan, Venice, and many Greek settlements. They also had a subordinate existence for governing ethnic communities in alien territory, as with Jews in Alexandria. The conciliar experience of the towns was to re-emerge with explosive force in the fourteenth century.

Christianity as well as Judaism preserved conciliar forms in its corporate life. The Greek word for meeting, especially the meetings of members of a confederation, was synod. Synods of Church elders were a widespread feature of Church life, though the practice became attenuated in the imperial West. The related term, synagogue, became the main organizational form for Jews after the destruction of the temple and the end of possibilities for an effective territorial government. Politically, the synagogue, along with the covenantal idea we shall examine in the next chapter, were the main Jewish contributions to the political theory of the West.

The Church also took up some of these elements into its language and practice. The Church called itself an *ecclesia*, a public assembly. So powerful was this political concept in early Christianity that the word was simply carried over into Latin. The character of the Church as a public assembly with roots in the Greek *polis* remains to this day a common bond of union between Eastern and Western Christianity—a bond whose resources have yet to be realized.[8]

Moreover, in the first five centuries councils, or synods, whether local or "ecumenical," provided the means for resolving disputes among the churches. The pattern as well as the language was drawn from the culture of the polis. Gradually, of course, this ecclesial polity waned as emperors like Constantine assumed the authority to call councils, and later Bishops of Rome, having assumed the Roman title of Pontifex Maximus, acted totally apart from them. Like their civil counterparts, however, they continued as living memories, only to revive in the fifteenth century.

The republican city sank beneath the imperial waves, but even then it left spires to snag those kings who thought they could sail at will wherever they wished. It left the legacy of government under a higher law as well as the claim that the king existed only to preserve the common good. Not only was the king the upholder of the higher law and the common good, he could only do this most effectively and legitimately when acting "in council." The king in council became the norm for kingship in the West, to be transgressed only at the peril of losing crucial legitimacy.

For Christians as well as for most of European culture, this classical heritage and its theological meaning passed through the gate controlled by Augustine, bishop of Hippo and protégé of Ambrose of Milan. To understand our received notions of the relationship of politics to faith we must see how Augustine handled political symbols in his monumental treatise, *The City of God*.

II.   Christ the King over the Christian Republic

Augustine wrote the books compiled as *De civitate Dei* some four centuries after the advent of empire and in response to immediate signs of its collapse. It is an apologetic for Christian faith and a polemic against the old Roman religions, whose error and idolatry, he claimed, lay at the root of Rome's ruin. In constructing his argument he forged the instruments of thought and debate for the next thousand years. It was in bulk an arsenal against a political and republican conception of Christian faith.

Augustine's argument contained four major components. First, he had to take up the republican argument, originating with Cicero, that Rome's decline was due to the abandonment of its republican forms. He did this, not by arguing the merits of the republic over the empire—that is, with a political argument—but by claiming that "Rome never was a republic, because true justice had never a place in it."[9] By emphasizing Cicero's claim that a republic exists for justice, he turned to an ethical argument that all forms of government are equally corrupt and therefore equally irrelevant, whether they be republics or empires.

Moreover, once having taken justice as his criterion he turns, not to an examination of its forms, but to its religious basis. Roman justice could not even be justice because it was falsely grounded in error and idolatry. Rome's religion, far from protecting the *res publica*, as Polybius and so many others had argued, had always failed it. Christianity arose, not as the opponent of justice but as its only adequate base. "True justice has no existence save in that republic whose founder and ruler is Christ, if at least any choose to call this a republic (*res publica*); and indeed we cannot deny that it is the people's weal (*res populi*)."

Here we see that Augustine is not in principle opposed to the use of republican symbolism to articulate the concerns of faith. However, he uses the symbol of Christ's republic not only to denigrate the republic of Rome but also to draw us away from the whole set of arguments by which classical authors tried to wrestle with the definition of the good life and its practical framework. "Republic", thought Augustine, is so redolent of that enterprise that it is best simply to discard it altogether. Augustine continues,

> But if perchance this name, which has become familiar in other connections, be considered alien to our common parlance, we may at all events say that in this city is true justice; the city of which Holy Scripture says, 'Glorious things are said of thee, O city of God.'

Refuge in the Scriptures seals the case against even the use of republican and Greek political symbolism, much less the thought patterns it contained.

Ironically, in taking the symbol of city Augustine inadvertently revives the most archaic of Roman traditions—the city is founded and ruled by a king. Christ replaces Romulus. The ancient traditions of the seven hills yields to the eternal vision of the heavenly Zion. A resurrected Jerusalem rises above the ashes of Rome. The Davidic shadows behind Jesus overwhelm the flickering lights of the *ecclesia Christi* in the *res publica Dei*.

Augustine diverts the civic imagery of the republic back to the model of the royal city. Jesus is the Christ, he argues, and Christ means Messiah, Anointed One. To be "anointed" is to be king (XVII.10). The City of God is a city ruled by Christ the King (XIV.13). Augustine was still enough of a classicist to hold to the symbolism of the city, authorized as it was by Scripture, but future generations far from Cicero's world would replace Christ's city with a kingdom, yielding an empire on archaic royal feet.

The second component in Augustine's argument drew on widespread Stoic and neo-Platonic conceptions of the two republics—one ideal, the other actual. One was composed of the various cities and republics of the political landscape. The other was a transcendent republic of the cosmos, ruled by the pure law of nature and nature's God. Most classical authors saw the many cities of this world as merely an imperfect realization of the cosmic city. The politician of one's native city was an earnest of the cosmo-politan of the perfect realm.

Augustine took over this idea but recast it as an opposition between the heavenly city and the cities of this world. The two cities were antithetical rather than compatible. This city, in any form, operated from the love of self, the heavenly city from the love of God. The earthly city was caught in sin, its king was the devil. The heavenly city was redeemed by grace, its sovereign was Christ.

Moreover, these two civic orders were not merely cast in an eternal opposition. They constituted the warp and woof of history where people shuttled forth a pilgrim's coat reflecting heavenly warmth and satanic cold. In the argument between them Providence proceeded to its predetermined goal. The mesh between the cities drove the medieval conception of history. It was a history in which God redeemed believers in a perishing world. It was not the story of the world's perfection to a higher form of governance. It was a history of providential redemption. It was the story of our longing for "felicity"—a felicity gained by souls in another realm.

Not only was this an historiography of pilgrimage from this city to the next, it was an historiography cast in terms of genealogy. It was a story of patriarchal descent from Adam to Christ. Just as the republic had been swallowed up in kingship, so history was swallowed back up into familial inheritance. Just as the ethos of the household would gradually reshape that of the royal city, so the ethos of the family would reshape the notion of historical relationship. Thus, "original sin" was transmitted through intercourse, the product of sexual union was inherently corrupt, and redemption from sin and injustice inevitably implied release from sexuality altogether. The theory of original sin was the theological linchpin for the reduction of politics back into patriarchal order.

Thus, a concern that began with the failure of political justice eventuated with a fixation on personal purity. Here again Augustine's seeming religious progress is in reality a reversion to the patterns of the ancestral bond and the religion of the fathers. The difference is that the household has been replaced by the Church, the patrimonium by the deposit of faith.[10]

This genealogical frame of history reinforces the third component of his thesis, that the goal of history is felicity, or peace. The goal is that tranquility of mind which most people seek in the safety of their home, but which is even there a specious lure. Only philosophers have a taste of it. It is a unity of consciousness forged by a single-minded bond with God, undistracted by any other relationships. This is peace, the goal of all human effort. It is the peace Augustine tasted in reunion with his mother at Ostia.[11]

All human beings seek this peace, but in their sin they seek it through war, argument, and fortification. They seek it through politics and rule. All of these, however, are factious and fractious. They divide rather than unify. They are rebellion rather than obedience, disorder rather than order. True peace finally demands removal from the plurality and division of this world. The most that governments can do and that Christians can expect is to secure a civil peace in which the Church can spread the Gospel and people can meditate on it. Peace, order, and unity are the goals of government. The wider concern to cultivate a public realm for the purpose of realizing the good life is subordinated to the principles of household order. The well-ruled city is like a well-run household. The impersonal standards of justice yield to the personal exercise of charity. The search for gloried memory yields to gratitude for parental care.

Augustine's overarching preoccupation with the felicity found only in the city of God obliterates any interest in the various forms of civic life. While nurtured on classical categories, he regresses from them in the face of their practical collapse and raises up a repristinated pattern of parental authority that shaped what we have come to call the Middle Ages. Augustine was its midwife if not its author.

Instead of the argument over public form Augustine focused on that of psychological orientation. The classicists had argued over the virtues and their corruption. Augustine expounds on our loves and their objects. He replaced the search for public glory with a psychology of individual desire.

We are governed, Augustine holds, by our inclination to be attached to some object that satisfies our basic need for peace. We seek this peace through attachment to friends, lovers, family, city, wealth—any object in creation. The only object that can truly satisfy us is God, the Eternal One.

This assumption meant two things: our desires should be focused on an otherworldly object of contemplation, and the proper relation to this satisfying object is one of humility, obedience, and subordination. Augustine's psychology produces a model of contemplative subordination. This psychology, being fundamental to both his theology and his ethics, permeates his thought. It sought to overturn, though he thought it was just rebalancing, the classic preference for the active life lived in relationships of equality. Augustine's psychology not only undermined classical political theory but reinforced the familial models of rule which were to be associated with kingship for the next fifteen hundred years.

These four poles—the royal city, the genealogical history, the primacy of peace, and the psychology of desire—lifted up a house that survived the many waters of change that were to sweep over Europe in the next centuries. They are popular even into our own time under many forms. Yet within this mighty edifice there have always been peculiar strains, present already in his own writings. While extolling the goal of individual contemplation, he also never completely relinquished the claims of social relationship. While lifting up Christ the King he never entirely lost the civic tradition. While subordinating justice to faith and finding all efforts at perfection in justice to be vanity, he also preserved justice as the plumbline of rule. The coat of civic republicanism became the rags around the feet of empire—stockings for a pilgrim journey. They stayed on in vestigial and essential form throughout the days of Christendom.

III. The Republican Remnant

The ethos of polity and republic survived in many-colored remnants. Even in the seventh century Gregory the Great could speak of "the society of the Christian republic" (*societas republicae Christianae*).[12] Though dwelling in the tents of kings it still warmed the hearts of many. Its conciliar stump emerged not only in towns but also in the colleges of the universities, especially at Paris. It found voice in the guilds of craftsmen and merchants as well as in monastic chapters. In the fourteenth century, for a number of cultural as well as economic and military reasons, it broke through again in new forms, especially in Florence.

In the thirteenth century Florence had already raised up an eloquent champion of monarchy in the figure of Dante, whose thought was firmly medieval even though his language was the modern vernacular. However, his advocacy of the vulgar tongue, with its democratic bias, finally swept even monarchy before it in the person of Leonardo Bruni, Florence's great historian.[13]

Dante had put Brutus and Cassius, the murderers of Caesar, in the depths of hell for their attack on the founder of the imperial order that nurtured Christ and his Gospel. Bruno reinstated Brutus as the defender of civic virtue before a tyrant. The republic was exalted above empire, Brutus' crime renamed tyrannicide. Moreover, Bruno traced the origins of Florence not to Caesar and his army but to a colony formed during the years of the republic. In short, republican traditions should be placed at the heart of Florence's memory and aspiration.

Savonarola, Florence's radical prophet, picked up these republican themes and recast them in an apocalyptic frame. Augustine's legacy had become an otherworldly eschatology irrelevant to institutional change. Savonarola's commitment to justice, however, was so strong that he united history's goal with worldly action—action that could best be accomplished in the founding and preservation of a republic.

Savonarola is best known for the extremes he went to in demanding the kind of personal character necessary for republican life. He raised the question of virtue, but still within an Augustinian psychology, recasting it in the service of public action. He still held that Christ exercises kingship over us, but, in an ironically Augustinian manner, he psychologized this monarchy, holding that Christ exercises this monarchical rule over our passions so that we can achieve the self-restraint necessary for republican government. Rather than be ruled by monarchs from without we are to be ruled by one from within. The political republic rested on a psychological monarchy. This rearrangement of the relations between republican polity and Christ's kingship became the keystone of Christian republicanism in the early modern era.

It was Niccolò Machiavelli, though, who became the intellectual founder of modern republican theory. Christian apocalyptic and Augustinian psychology gave way to "secular" political science as he tried to set forth the basic principles for establishing and preserving republics. Machiavelli renovated the classical quest for the stable republic, if not for the sake of salvation, at least for the sake of justice and dignity.

Machiavelli, who exerted an enormous impact on subsequent republican thought, returned again to the problem of founding and preserving a stable public order.[14] Rather than draw on the traditional appeal to monarchic order, he picked up the ancient Polybian theme of the balanced, or mixed republic. Through the presence of prince, aristocracy, and people a public order could survive and flourish. It could gain a stasis in a world caught in the wheel of fortune. Because of his emphasis on this kind of "stato" he became the author of the peculiar term associated so widely with government and the public order in later thought—the state.

This state could escape the endless cycle of revolution by being grounded in the initiative of public-spirited citizens. The importance of the prince lay not in his coercive rule but in the courageous initiative he should take to preserve a city that included popular as well as aristocratic support. By appealing to people's willingness to risk themselves for the public good, the prince could rescue them from revolution and blind fortune. In this exodus from caprice and powerlessness the prince could lead them into historic meaningfulness before a providential God.

This emancipation into historical action for the sake of the public realm demanded a change in political psychology as well. With Machiavelli and the Renaissance humanists we finally break clear of the Augustinian preoccupation with the psychology of pride and the fixation on humility as the key to Christian virtue. Augustine had left a legacy of Christian thought and spirituality buried in the problematic of pride and abasement, culminating later in Luther's agonized affirmation of God's grace in the face of our sin and despair.

These civic humanists turned to a different understanding of the self, which rescued the classical opposition between a life of glory and one of privation.[15] Only a call to seek a glory remembered by the city could draw people into self-sacrifice for the common good. This call to glory, far from unleashing destructive tyrannies, evoked true self-sacrifice, for to be glorious one had to perform noble deeds worth remembering by the people.

It was only through this kind of appeal to the people that personal glory could be achieved and the city preserved in liberty. This was "virtuous" activity—the performance of a public person seeking the common good through risky initiatives.

Machiavelli sharply formulated the conditions for public life in the Italian cities. Republican life demanded leadership and popular appeal, especially to a citizen army, in the face of resignation to fate, fortune, and self-abnegation. With this upheaval in political thinking and psychology, the public order was decisively rescued from mindless fortune and thrust into the hands of Providence. Public action was thenceforth never again to fall into the obscurity of religious censure. The idea of fortune, meanwhile, left political speech and became equated with wealth and money, whose coming and going increasingly rose from the mysterious forces of the market.

Though the city was now to be upheld by a mixed constitution and public virtue rather than by kingship, it was still open to devastation from enemies. The only solution to this was the ancient recourse to leagues and confederations. Florence, like its neighbors, had to become a "free people federated in equality."[16] Thus, once again, the rise of the ancient republican ideal brings with it the need for some kind of covenantal structure to link the republics together.

This civic humanism left us with a repristinated ideal of public action torn from the old assumptions of natural hierarchies, monarchic order and cycles of decay. Not only did this generate a new sense about time, action, and human psychology, it also gave birth to a whole family of conciliar movements in towns and churches. This conciliar explosion carried many of these republican notions deep into the bosom of the Church. The sense of a city having a providential historic destiny eventually migrated to American soil in Puritan boats.

Machiavelli had seen clearly the importance of traditional religion in undergirding public order, not only as a frame of common reference for public discourse but as a discipline for training individuals in a life of virtue. The problem of pluralism, that is, of a multiplicity of worlds of reference, never occurred to people rocked in Christendom's cradle. The problem as they saw it lay in energizing people to form and preserve a public. For this, traditional monarchical religious conceptions, when anchored within the soul's kingdom, still had their appeal. However, with the rise of the conciliar movement in the churches in the fourteenth and fifteenth century, republican thought started to transform first ecclesiology and then the theological roots of faith itself.

IV. The Conciliar Revolution

The civic republicanism nurtured in northern Italy soon found a lodging in the Church, where it picked up models of the early Christian community as well as the organic social thought being nurtured in the universities. As papal authority eroded in scandal and schism, ecclesiastics and princes sought a conciliar mechanism for reforming the Church. First at Konstanz (1414–18) and then at Basle (1439–48) they hammered out theories of conciliar government which, though they proved finally unsuccessful in ecclesial reform, spilled back out into the republican tradition.

In the work of Marsilius of Padua, Juan de Segovia, Nicholas of Cusa, Jean Gerson and Pierre D'Ailly we find a rich tapestry of conciliar ideas as well as their practical implementation, especially at the Council of Basle. Here we find the further development of a republican theory of the Church, of consensual decision-making, and of authority through public participation. Using the recent essay by Anthony Black, let us examine this development as well as its limitations.[17]

Andres Diaz de Escobar, one of Basle's leading theorists, held that

> the Church is a kind of mystical body, and a kind of republic
> of the Christian people. . . . That most holy republic is the
> universal Church . . . and therefore it is a common affair of
> the Christian people. . . . [18]

This remarkable affirmation found many echoes, as in Juan de Segovia's frequent use of "presidency" to describe ecclesiastical leadership. Conciliar leaders were to be "ministers of the republic" who are "common persons" seeking and reflecting the common good as ultimately found in conciliar discussion.

What made the council authoritative in the first respect was that it was a "mystical body" ruled directly by Christ, who animated each participant through the Holy Spirit. In Black's words, "the Holy Spirit was the true president of the council and inspired its acts." This idea of a mystical body was nurtured by the practices of the university "colleges" who had their independent charters, originally granted by the bishop of their cathedral. Rather than this "body" being construed as a hierarchy in which the head (that is, the Pope, the Vicar of Christ) rules the members, it was an organism permeated in every part by the Spirit. Thus it was a more democratic conception of corporate existence. It was organic without being hierarchical.

Many conciliarists still lifted up the ancient theory of the mixed constitution, translating it into governance by Pope, cardinals, and council. They sought an organic balance among these elements of the Church polity. The radicals, however, equated the body with the council, whose organs might be Pope, cardinals, and priests. It is this radical conciliarism that most interests us, since it reintroduced a democratic, participatory thrust into both ecclesiastical and secular government.

This organic conception of the council also underlay its capacity to represent the whole Church. It represented it essentially as a microcosm of the extended body of all the faithful. As long as all the organs of the Church were represented, that is, typified, in the council, it could speak for the whole. It did not represent their immediate wills, wishes, and interests, but replicated their function in the larger body. In practice, however, this representative theory itself was limited in favor of ordained ecclesiastics. Laity were excluded from Basle's discussions. It was a democratic council of the ordained, but not of all the baptized.

One of the main reasons this closure was necessary was to guard against manipulation by the princes. Ultimately this exclusion undermined the council's own existence as the alienated princes went off to Rome to establish concordats with the Pope. Another reason for excluding laity was that high theological standards for council membership were necessary in order to engage in the free and open discussion among informed equals that had to characterize its processes.

Conciliar action demanded freedom of speech (even from so-called heretics), full discussion, equality of voting power and a committee system designed "so as to arrive freely at the common consent of the fathers."[19] Segovia emphasized that the council's authority springs from the truth it can find through the wisdom attaching to such discourse, even though the participants individually are not particularly wise. Truth would be found through public discourse—at least the truth of Christ.

This discourse had to be rooted, however, in a common faith. Like any polity, Segovia said, people in the Church are held together by trust, not in the sense of handing over their governance to a ruler, but in the web of mutual confidence created by leaders who are credible to their comrades. Faith for the conciliarist did not mean the submission to authority set forth by Augustine, but the mutual trust of relationships among equals in Christ. Authority arose in the web of trust created by open collegiality grounded in the one Holy Spirit.

Not only was authority created by conciliar action, so was power. The process of congregating together raises the energy level of the individuals as they find resonance with each other through argument and mutual education. The animation of conciliar action binds participants together in the very energy of the Spirit. Power does not arise from the domination of the strong, but from the cooperation of equals.

Thus did the conciliarists seek to bring together Christian convictions with republican patterns in order to propose an alternative government for the Church. While its ultimate practical failure cannot be traced solely to theoretical weaknesses, they can be detected in the fissures of its collapse. Prominent among them were its undeveloped understanding of proper constitution and of representation.

Because of the mystical organicism infusing their perspective, the conciliarists had great difficulty moving beyond a kind of town meeting direct democracy. They still operated within a medieval focus on the virtue of the personages assembled rather than the formal relationships by which they were related to each other. Fraternal charity was more important than systems of constitutions and covenants for delegating authority in a complex way.

With this communal model the council, as Black often points out, could not enable outsiders to participate in any effective way. Democratic governance always must deal with the question of representation, since not everyone can appear at once in a conciliar forum. By trying to create a microcosm of the Church as its approach to representation the council was forced to exclude active participation and therefore collaboration by the wider Church.

The type of democracy it did generate eventually coursed into the veins of Jean-Jacques Rousseau, whose version of solidaristic popular will is still alive today in radical and populist movements. Its muted plea for a more adequate Christian constitutionalism found responses in the Calvinist reformers of Holland and England in the next two centuries. Our story therefore leads to Puritans and revolutionaries of the early modern period.[20]

V.   The Rise of the Modern Republican Ideal, 1650–1800

A.   The Puritan Revolt: James Harrington and *Oceana*

The conciliar memory continued to emerge after the failure of these councils to become the dominant model of Church government in the fifteenth century. We find it in the synods and councils of the Lutheran and Calvinist reformations. In the seventeenth century English revolt against bishop and king it gains full articulation and recovers its classical memory.

To identify the key motifs of this vision we shall turn to James Harrington, whose *Oceana*, hammered out in the turmoil of Cromwell's protectorate, inspired the theorists of the American Constitution.[21] Though surrounded by a host of others, such as Gerard Winstanley, John Milton, and John Goodwin, Harrington presents us with the most systematic expression of the republican ideal in Christian garb.

1. Beyond Monarchy. With Harrington, as with his contemporary John Milton, we see the first revolt against the monarchical principle preserved in the classic Polybian ideal of the mixed polity of king, aristocracy, and people. The true kingdom of Christ is a commonwealth, or republic, of equals.

To drive this point home Harrington constructs a theological and a political argument. Ancient Israel, he argues, experienced God-given republican government under the judges. The era of the confederacy was a genuine theocracy ruled by God through the covenant law. It was only with the rise of a monarchy that Israel fell into sin and alienation from God. The theocratic ideal is confederal Israel, an ideal which can be realized once again by the reign of Christ's law in our hearts and the active citizenship of his elect in the world.

For his political argument he turns to the example of "the most serene republic," Venice. Here the classic ideal of stability is realized through a complex system of election and legislation. Venice was the proof that a system of conciliar government did not have to be unstable. Indeed, its stability lay precisely in the way it arranged republican order.

Rome also provided an example of government by covenant rather than force, to use Harrington's words. Its stability lay in its covenant between senate and people. Here also we see that stability lies not in the presence of a single ruler but in a commonly agreed upon covenant, or law, among the people. The real cause of Rome's instability and decline, Harrington believed, lay not in a fault in its constitution but in its abandonment of the economic base necessary for genuine republic life—an egalitarian agrarian order.

2. The Equal Agrarian. Harrington claimed that republican government demands not the proportionate participation of the elements of the old feudal order (king and nobles), but the equal participation of self-sufficient people. In a pre-industrial era that meant farmers who could control their own means of subsistence. This is the "private property" necessary for participation in republican government. This is the economic basis of the "common-wealth" of justice and stability.[22] Indeed, this emphasis on private property gives "commonwealth" a basically different meaning from republic. The former increasingly lost the common in the competition for personal wealth. The latter, though endangered by nationalistic fevers, preserved the attributes of a special public sphere of participation.

In any event, bound to this view of a commonwealth was a popular army defending the interests of its members rather than the honor of its lords. It was in the experiences of this common army of the realm under Cromwell that a genuine public consciousness arose. The famous Putney debates of 1647, in which ordinary soldiers debated the proper form of governance for their revolutionary enterprise, brought this civic consciousness to full display on the historic stage.

Harrington, and with greater force Milton, then began to drive this equality back into domestic relationships as well. For Harrington agrarian equality meant that marriages would no longer be arranged for the sake of feudal property ties, but for companionship. Milton was even more forceful in lifting up friendship rather than property as the key consideration of marriage.[23] Indeed, in its absence divorce became a justifiable action to honor personal dignity rather than a sacrilege against Christ's rule of the Church.

However, this move to marital equality was only preliminary and partial. Household rule remained essentially patriarchal, even though tempered with the considerations of a kind of friendship between husband and wife. While the governmental sphere had to be republican and democratic, the private sphere, where the emotions of the heart were schooled, remained under Christ's monarchy. As Harrington maintained, "Paternal power is in the right of nature. . . . [The] derivation of power from fathers of families . . . is the natural root of a commonwealth."[24] With the Puritans monarchical models retreat to the household in order to ensure the personal virtue necessary for republican action. Without it democratic action could not be conjoined with traditional wisdom to form a stable republic.

3. Democratic Wisdom. Harrington still operates within the classical understanding of reason as a sense of relationships within a public, or common order binding human beings together in sociality. Unless Christ rules the heart our lesser passions and private interests will override the wisdom necessary to attain the "common reason" underlying public discourse and debate. Without self-control and a contemplation of God's order made possible by Christ's rule we cannot live by this common reason. Public virtue arises from Christ's kingdom in our hearts, a kingdom formed in the little school of the patriarchal household.

Along with many peers, Harrington believed that when Christ is able to exercise his liberty in our hearts and minds, then we can express this liberty in the public sphere. The common reason is the language in which we give voice to the conscience formed by Christ. Public expression and conversation are our "soul responsibility" out of obedience to Christ. Through his rule in our soul we can move from the kingdom of the Father to the commonwealth of the Son.

With this image we can see the emerging antagonism between patriarchal and democratic order. The old monarchies and hierarchies, rather than setting forth the right proportions of reasonable order, are set aside for a direct relationship between individuals and the principle of right order made incarnate in the Son himself, our brother, with whom we are one in baptism.

For some radicals this immediate relation with Christ and his word implied an anarchist vision of government. Indeed, many Anabaptists were earlier hunted down, tortured and killed precisely for this reason. Harrington's vision, however, is firmly welded to the republican heritage. The rule of Christ in our hearts can only be realized through specific structures. For his examples he turns to Rome and Venice.

4. Constitutional Order. For Harrington, in the perfect republican order the law is king, and since the law is known in the people's hearts ruled by Christ, the people are king. With this assertion we know we are still moving in the afterglow of a Christendom illuminated by a single religion. In that homogeneity the separation between Church and government is unknown and irrelevant, since both aim at the creation of a Christ-ruled republic.

Because the law is king, legislation and parliamentary action become the central task of government, as Milton points out even more clearly than Harrington. Here are the religious as well as political roots of the radical parliamentarianism lifted up by the English radicals. However, the elaborate structure of institutional checks and balances was still uncondensed in the vapors of these dreams. To achieve the stability threatened by a parliament that could always redefine fundamental laws, Harrington turned to regular rotation in office to ensure that parliament stay tuned to the reason of ordinary people.

Regular elections are the cure for tyranny. Both Milton and Harrington agreed on this fundamental point, though Harrington went on to demand rotation in office along the old Athenian model. Again, to drive home his argument he uses both a religious and a political example. He points out that the original Church was governed by apostles *elected* by the people. Unfortunately, because the Greek word for "elect" (*cheirotonein*, meaning "holding up of hands") was confused with that for "laying on of hands" (*chirothesia*) the patriarchal Church came to approve of a kind of ecclesiastical inheritance rather than election as the model for transmission of authority.[25] Just as Harrington wanted to replace apostolic succession with congregational election, so also he replaced monarchical succession with regular election and rotation in office, lest a hereditary nobility seize parliamentary power and rule over the people like a collective king.

For this model he turned once again to Venice as well as Athens. In addition he appealed to the understanding of nature emerging with William Harvey's discovery of the circulation of the blood. Just as blood circulates to nourish the whole body, so citizens must circulate through governmental offices in order to overcome political corruption. This is a rhetorical example, but it also vividly indicates a new conception of nature, different from that of the hierarchy of the great chain of being, to undergird his political conception. Christ's rule of the heart and God's orderly rule of the cosmos cooperate to legitimate republican governance. Both nature and politics share a common wisdom.

Rotation through elective office is not enough, however, to give expression to the common reason formed by Christ's kingship in our hearts and our natural experience. Harrington recognized that this common reason is still unformed in many of us and some have greater capacities in this regard than others. Therefore, he drew again from the deep well of mixed polity to order the governmental process into three functions—the debate, the resolve, and the execution.

His senate, like the elders of old, brings together the greatest wisdom where the common reason is most likely to arise in debate and argument. It is the senate which has the authority to propose laws and policies most likely to achieve the common good. It exercises the function of debate.

However, to guard against the senate's own possible captivity to special interest, a popular assembly has to have the authority of the "resolve," that is, of veto. They may not have the capacity to initiate legislation for the common good but they at least have the ability to see when this proposal might harm their own permanent interests. They have the right to defend themselves against unjust senatorial initiatives and ask for a new proposal.

The executive has the power to execute the decisions debated by the senate and resolved by the assembly. Through rotation in elected office and reliance on a popular army of agrarian soldiers the executive can be constrained to its legislated task.

With this machinery of election and decision Harrington felt that Christ's rule could gain a public expression so rooted in the nature of things and God's design that it would be not only stable but also immortal.

5. *The Immortal Commonwealth.* Harrington's *Oceana* was a thinly disguised proposal for the reconstruction of English political order after the death of monarchy. It was written with the millenarian belief that in this historic moment Christ could finally establish his governance on earth, namely in England. In seizing on the republican tradition and giving it a basis in Christian tradition and symbolism, he brought together the two streams which flow, with various cargo, into our own time.

Harrington's vision, though grand, was ephemeral. The monarchy returned to England to provide order before the new immortal order could be established. Harrington's vision rode with pilgrim emigrants to the shores of a new Oceana—New England—where it finally flowered in the imagination of the founders of a new republic.

Moreover, his vision floundered because it was still rooted in classical notions of proportional reason, the economics of an agrarian people, and the homogeneity of a culture innocent of the pluralism that has emerged in a world of refugees, immigrants, and special interest groups. The conception of reason, of nature, and of the institutional relation of the Church to government would all have to be reworked in order to convey these remarkable visions into a new setting. His synthetic effort, however, remains an important landmark in our own struggle to recover and reconstruct the republican partners of biblical faith.

The vision of a perfect republic, rooted in the common wealth of Christian agrarians, would have to go through the refining fire of American revolution and philosophical deism before assuming the form we must engage in the contemporary world. The American experience had to recast Harrington's constitution and transform or ignore his Christian faith in order to found a new nation. John Locke provided the appropriate translation of Harrington's ideas for this task.

In his *Two Treatises on Government*, this secular son of Scotch Calvinism devoted himself to the destruction of patriarchy, and with it monarchy, as the central principle of government.[26] He sought to replace the bonds of biology with the contractual relations constructed by will and reason. The echoes of his attack on patriarchy are still reverberating in the farthest reaches of domestic, political and corporate life.

Locke realized that the republican principle required the severe restriction of the patriarchal foundations of kingship. He sought to replace filial bonds by bringing contract to the fore. The contracts of society and of government could provide the undergirding commonalities necessary for a public life. In his wake, however, the idea of contract gave increasing emphasis to the free wills of individuals and to the whole panoply of personal rights we have come to associate with liberalism. The bonds of sentiment and nature that still ran strong in his own life gave way to the pressures of free market individualism. The struggle for a richer understanding of the web of public relations lies behind the vision of federal republicanism I am developing here. In order to understand the way republicanism took on the clothes of contractual individualism we need to turn to the drama of American constitutionalism at the end of the eighteenth century.

B. The Republic in America

The constitutional debates ignited by the American Revolution propelled republican theorists into an intensification of some themes and a transformation of others. They gave rise to the modern republican views which require our subsequent theological engagement. Gerald Stourzh has provided a synopsis of key republican concepts which can help us identify the central issues demanding our critical attention.[27]

While there was great controversy over what a republic was or should be, Stourzh lifts up seven points of general agreement that brought people together as republicans in the early nineteenth century. Some of these were simply refinements of the ideas developed by radical puritans like Harrington. Others were genuinely new developments.

We shall take up each one in turn before looking at the underlying cultural transformation that locked them as well as their contradictions into place.

1.   The Structural Revolution

(a) From Mixed Government to Separation of Powers. Classical republican thought since Polybius had construed a republic as one in which the virtues of the major estates (king, nobles, people) had been represented in a balanced way. With the parliamentary revolutions of the seventeenth century the monarch's position had gradually eroded in the face of parliament and, more specifically, the commons as representative of the new commercial interests. The problem of republican government shifted from a balancing of representatives of the estates to a balancing of the powers of a governmental apparatus resting on popular will. As we saw with Harrington the old estates of king, nobles, and commons began to take shape as three functions of government. Once they became functions of a single governmental order, attention turned from the task of balancing and mixing them for the sake of stability to that of separating them for the sake of liberty.

Montesquieu had already prepared for this development with the distinction of the functions of government as legislative, executive, and judicial. Each must be institutionally separate from the other in order to preserve constitutional liberty. In this shift from a policy based on organic social orders to one based on governmental functions, he still preserved a role for the monarch in the executive, which he saw primarily in terms of foreign affairs. Here the executive had to manifest the unity of the nation over against other nations. The unifying functions of monarchy were still important in this regard. Within the nation, however, Montesquieu had little notion of a domestic executive. Rather, the people would meet their domestic needs through their own free enterprise and local communities, regulated only by the laws they establish for themselves.

The American constitutionalists refined this idea, ultimately producing the institutional distinction between the legislative, executive and judicial—a pattern subsequently emulated widely. The importance of this power perspective lay in its ability to move beyond dependence on monarchical noblesse oblige or a blind faith in legislative wisdom. Each branch could actually check the other with power rather than an often vaporous appeal to the common good, whether enunciated by monarch or assembly.

However, this was a dangerous development as well, for it dissolved the unity originally made possible by an organic representation of the estates searching for the common good. In its place we have the modern conception of competition among interests which cancel out each other's excesses. This has increasingly become the model for marketplace, politics, and government itself. It yields a common good of the least common denominator. The concept of a republic turns from one that can find the common good through representative assembly to one in which a shifting sea of interest groups can be constrained to observe the minimal rules of procedural justice. This is a deep deficiency necessitating our subsequent retrieval of covenantal concepts.

(b) Anti-monarchism. Through their struggle with King George III and the British parliament the American republicans brought themselves firmly into the anti-monarchical camp. Henceforth, republican government would be non-monarchical government. This was the culmination of a number of developments.

First, the frequent use of the term "commonwealth," which originated with the Puritan parliamentarians, was an explicit rejection of the idea that the crown wealth should define the common good of the people. The people and their property were no longer to be considered the household of the crown, whether or not this was distinguishable from the king's own person.

This was clearly an expression of the rising merchant class whose wealth was not derived from the land, with its time-bound connection to the crown, but from commerce and manufacture. Thus, the crown wealth became one interest among many. A commonwealth existed apart from the crown and could be advanced only through a conciliar structure representing all people of property. This became a defining principle of republican government. It was a commonwealth beyond kingship.

Second, since government rested on an assembly of persons of independent wealth, it had to become democratic in spirit. The principle of reasonableness underlying its discourses could no longer be based on paternal order but on democratic consensus in the marketplace of truth. This meant that public office had to be open to all. It could not be inherited. In short, an hereditary ruling group, rather than stabilizing public discourse, was seen as a special interest cabal which would only subvert the public argument to its own narrow purposes. With the exclusion of aristocracy, kingship was eliminated as well.

Finally, it became a popular belief, occasioned by Montesquieu, that monarchies were inherently belligerent, while republics were inherently pacific.[28] Monarchs had to go to war either to defend some irrational honor or to pay for their costly excesses at home. Republics, however, were limited by the self-interests of the many, who simply

wanted to go about their business. Their commerce abhorred the irra-
tionality of war, just as the aristocratic order needed it to gain the land,
glory and fame garnered in conquest.

The crucial separation of republicanism from kingship and monarchy was thus based on the rise of a whole mercantile class for whom
heredity, social unity, aristocratic honor, and ascribed inequalities
clashed with the virtues of advancement according to merit and achievement, pluralism of interests, and systematic savings.[29] This new class
combined strength with independent farmers to claim republican ideals
linked to democratic participation rather than organic social order. The
republic could only be built on the monarch's aristocratic grave.

(c) Democratization. Alexis de Tocqueville observed in the nineteenth century that "a democratic republic exists in the United
States."[30] By this he meant that government rested on majority rule.
While he saw it as a "tranquil rule," this majoritarianism soon moved
away from a customary consensus created by social homogeneity to the
statistical outcome of the competition among interest groups.

So long, however, as there could be a rough equality of power, at
least no great harm could come from this. Noah Webster claimed that
the equality of land was more important than the cultivation of virtue
for the welfare of a republic. Indeed, "an equality of property, with a
necessity of alienation, constantly operating to destroy combinations of
powerful families, is the very *soul of a republic.*"[31]

Alexander Hamilton, on the other hand, found this faith in an
agrarian equality a weak reed of nostalgia in the face of the hurricane of
commercialization overtaking American life. Democratization of a mercantile economy and the monopoly tendencies of capital would inevitably undermine the social unity necessary for external defense and
internal harmony.

To deal with the demon of private interest democratization had to
depart from a simple expansion of the public sphere to the development
of some structural mechanism to enable people to pursue narrow self-
interest without destroying society. The theory of checks and balances,
along with the bicameral legislature and the electoral college, was designed to this end.

Along with these structural components of a sound republic, democrats turned to the need for mass education in order to inculcate republican virtue among the people. It was not enough for a religious elect
to know the Bible. Every citizen had to prepare for a life of elections
with a childhood of learning. The public school was the finger in the
dike of commercial avarice, a dam against the flood of private self-interest aroused by a rich land waiting to be exploited.

Thus, the role of wisdom once supplied by monarch and elders was dispersed into impersonal mechanisms of checks and balances or inculcated by the schools staffed by professional educators. The public realm, which was once the school of excellence in pursuit of the common good, became an arena for registering votes of groups who did not need to talk with each other. The republic had been infused with democratic ideals, but risked losing its original substance in the process.

(d) From Organic to Voluntarist Representation. Two things happened to this republican ideal when it became more democratic within the context of an expanding nation. First, as we have already noticed, the public sphere was no longer the manifestation of the "orders" of the society. It no longer reflected an established social structure of mutual and often hierarchical rights and duties bound together with a sense of honor and public virtue. The councils of the republic no longer represented the whole society. Rather, the public was composed of individuals who were able to gain the majority vote of their constituents, first of propertied white males, then of all males, and finally of all adults, save felons.

The councils of the republic therefore changed from being forums in which the interests of the whole people could be represented through a process of discussion, debate and discernment. They became neutral arenas governed by precise legal procedures to enable combatants for private interest to play the game of politics—namely, dividing up the common wealth. As Harold Lasswell once put it, politics became the game of who gets what when and how.[32] The councils were representative only in the sense that the elected members gave voice to the interests that the majority of their constituents had decided upon in their private spheres. Thus, the very idea of a representative assembly changed in the process, with all the difficulties and dangers many critics have pointed out.[33]

Second, the American constitutionalists faced the problem of how the individual republics of the wards, counties and states could be involved in the governance of the whole nation. The principle invoked by Montesquieu, out of even longer tradition, was that republics by their very spirit had to be linked in confederation, lest a unifying monarch destroy their liberty. Thus, a confederal or federal principle was at hand for the founder's use. The significance of this concept, of course, forms the inquiry of the next chapter. What is important to note here is that with the selection of a federal principle, people began to apply the new concept of representation to this federal structure.

Thus, the states, like the people, came to be seen as represented in the federal congress. With this new democratic view of representation the congress replicated differences rather than cultivate consensus about the national common good. It was unable to be the great legislator to govern people in liberty. Inevitably, the president moved from being a chief legislative convener and foreign minister to being the administrator of a vast executive branch of government. The president started to become the new monarchical figure in a republic which had not created a place for monarchical functions. The task of representing the whole, which republicans had wanted to assign to the legislative council, began to devolve back onto the president, now in danger of becoming a new monarchical figure.

The principle of representation, which historians like Gordon Wood see to be the crux of the principle of federal government, was actually inadequate to the task because it had been severed from the traditions which had first enabled people to see the way a council could be more representative of a people than even their own king.

(e) The Sovereign Law. The organic theory of representation, by assembling the society in microcosm, had served to curb the radical impulses of the mob or a short-sighted majority. The interest of the whole was mediated through the assembled estates. The king, finally, articulated the unity of that whole through his person.

With the rise of interest group representation a new principle emerged to replace the king and the organic representation of the estates. Rooted in ancient tradition, appeal to God's higher law finally found expression in the sovereignty of the law in political order.[34] Law itself became the representative of the people's unity. How did this happen?

First, the law, as enunciated by parliament through its conciliar process, took precedence over an increasing number of monarchical decrees. James Harrington had already maintained that "as in the commonwealth of Israel, God is said to have been king, so the commonwealth where the law is king is said by Aristotle to be the kingdom of God."[35] The sovereignty of the law was then repeated by David Hume (still in a monarchical context), John Locke, John Adams, and the American constitutionalists.

However, it was not enough to say that the law, as enunciated by the legislature, is sovereign. A higher law had to curb even the excesses of legislatures. Government had to rest in a prior, fundamental law which articulated the underlying compact binding the people together in mutual trust. Where once the king had intervened to protect individuals from the petty tyrannies of the princes, now a legal constitution was needed to enable courts of law to do the same.

A republic emerged as a political order containing institutional and legal curbs against the tyranny of majorities as well as monarchs. The rise of bills of rights in Virginia and then in the constitution solidified this development.

Thus, the ancient Hebrew allegiance to a non-personal Torah as the highest loyalty of collective life was realized in the political forms of the West. An impersonal attachment to principles replaced the personal bonds of fealty which had undergirded social order in all past millennia. Little wonder that John Adams and many others thought its survival could rest only on divine pleasure.

In becoming the new political god, the written constitution risked falling into legalism even as it could become a sacred object of devotion. An oft-amended constitution could become a fallen god, unable to command the allegiance it required to curb the passions of tyranny.

The sovereign constitution exhibited some fundamental weaknesses. It existed primarily to curb excess and tyrannical tendencies, whether of individuals or of groups. It was a structure of restraint. Though it could inspire awe, it did not exist, like the ancient king, to evoke action. It did not call people out into public life, but constrained them from destroying it. God was no longer made present through the personal demands of a king, but through the laws of polity and of nature. The motivation for public life no longer arose from within the bonds of regal and familial loyalty. It had to spring from interests rooted outside the newly christened public sphere.

(f) Pluralism and Liberty. The actual motive power for public life had to arise from the multiplicity of lesser "permanent interests" which impinge upon the common welfare. The motivation for public life took refuge in the desire for the liberty to pursue private interests. The desire for liberty, first emblazoned on the shield of English republican tradition by the radicals of Cromwell's time, gained expression in three forms.

Liberty rested first on some independent economic base outside the grasp of monarch or government. This private property, whether it was agrarian or mercantile, was the indispensable basis for exercising public power without fear or favor. Only with independent economic security could people be free to speak their conscience in the public debates.

This private property made possible a public personality. One could have a "persona" only if one had a prior "proprium"—properties under one's own control. Some people have had a rigidly deterministic view of how our personality is created by these material circumstances. They have seen that one's class position and material interests can create typical personalities which move out into the public sphere. Others have seen how the public sphere itself creates or reshapes personality in the intercourse of public education and debate.[36] In any case the widening

of the public sphere through a guaranteeing of personal liberty has created new issues for human psychology. The formulation of a psychology which can resonate with the highest aspirations of our commitment
to a public realm is a task we face in Chapter Five.

Second, this personal liberty had to be guaranteed not only through
private property but through the functions of republican order. Thomas
Jefferson saw a republic as a vehicle for the expression of democracy.
Hamilton saw it more as a means for guaranteeing collective security,
especially against foreign antagonists. In either case, they wanted the
public to be a sphere of liberty rather than fealty. While this liberty had
become a secular notion it was rooted in the original Reformation and
Puritan demand for Christ's liberty to be manifested by the consciences
of individual Christians. If Christ lived within each Christian's soul, and
not merely in the Church, then this liberty could be expressed only
through the liberty of these individuals to give voice to their conscience.
Liberty was a means for Christ's sovereignty.

Over the years this liberty has detached itself completely from this
wider ordering principle. It became a freedom from any obligation to
give witness to a common ordering principle such as the mind of Christ.
It became a legitimation of privacy rather than an obligation to publicity. This fundamental distortion of the principle of liberty undermines
rather than undergirds the preservation of a genuine public sphere
where people can search together for the common good.

In its original expressions liberty did have institutional meanings.
In the independent cities of Renaissance Italy it had meant the liberty
of the city itself. With the consolidation of an American republic it came
to mean the liberty of certain institutions that could create a public life
superior to government. These were the churches, the press, voluntary
associations, and the spontaneous assemblies of the people. Government
was to be a special kind of association within the public life of the
people—a compact among compacts, as Locke's forebears would have
said.

This carried to a constitutional conclusion the demands of more
radical church groups like the Baptists, who held out for a free church
in a free republic.[37] Christian faith could not be free without republican
government. Republican government could not exist without a privileged sphere of faith to nurture the independent consciences of citizens.

Unfortunately, there has always been a tendency for this freedom
to go the way of personal liberty—namely to be interpreted as a freedom
from governmental interference and from participation in the political
process. It has ossified in a doctrine of "separation of Church and state"

repeated in ironic form by despotic governments as well.[38] Separation has subverted publicity as the symbol of the Church's relation to public life. Critical engagement with public policy has given way to the privations of a purely individualistic religion. Religion became privatized in the same way as did personal liberty. It became the freedom of private consumers selecting among a marketplace of religious alternatives rather than the freedom to engage in public debate about a common faith undergirding their relationships.

As we shall see in the next part, the underlying purpose of liberty and freedom was to enable a public sphere to exist and individuals to participate in it. The goal of freedom was public action. Only with a recovery of this point can we begin to move out of our present impasse in which freedom is seen as the capacity to escape public life.

(g) Public Virtue. Both the classical and the Augustinian notions of virtue had been used to form the kind of personality necessary for public life. In the Augustinian tradition, which we still find in Harrington and Milton, virtue lay in Christ's rule in our hearts over the wayward passions of our lesser loves. The monarchy of the Christian soul made possible the republic of Christian liberty. Here the fatal sin was still pride—disobedience to Christ's rule—although this pride was an arrogance against the Christ within rather than the virtuous public resistance to tyrants, kings, or unjust governors.

The problem with this understanding of virtue was that it could easily fall back into the old quietism which beckoned the self away from the allurements of public power into the sacred haven of the home. It was suspicious of public power and became overly concerned with limiting it rather than encouraging people to participate in it. Its ascetic roots ultimately created a disaffection with the public realm, especially as the persistent presence of Christ faded in the mind.

The classical notion of virtue, which we find in startling clarity in John Adams and many of the American constitutionalists, was that virtue was a "passion for the public good."[39] Virtue lay not so much in self-control as in self-expression. But this was not simply an expression of interests formed outside the company of others. It was an expression which arose in the deep desire to emulate others who had received the ultimate honor—the loving memory of a people. The desire for public fame and glory—the glory of being remembered, not merely by "history" but by one's people—was the driving force resulting in public virtue.

From the ascetic standpoint this could only result in vainglory and tyranny, but within the classicism of Adams and others it was precisely this craving for public approval which provided the most important safeguard against the tyranny of ambition. Adams summed it up with these words:

> There must be a positive Passion for the public good, the public Interest, Honour, Power, and Glory, established in the Minds of the People, or there can be no Republican Government, nor any real Liberty; and this public Passion must be Superior to all private Passions. . . . The only reputable principle and doctrine must be that all things must give way to the public.[40]

Thus, the desire for expression in public life found its suitable limit in people's deep desire for confirmation from their peers. This was the dynamic of public virtue.

These two themes have deeply intertwined in American life. Both, however, have been distorted into a third, composite form created in the milieu of the capitalist revolutions of the nineteenth century. The Christian emphasis on internal, private self-control merged with the classical concern for reputation to create the concept of virtue as private credit-worthiness. Virtue became the capacity to sustain contracts, whether in the marital or the mercantile spheres.[41]

To the degree that the republic was construed as a commonwealth, and, in Adam Smith's terms, the power of the nation derived from its industry, then virtue had to lie in the capacity to create wealth through commercial activity. The backbone of commercial relations lay in relationships of trust built on honesty and promise-keeping. Without honesty in sales, purchasing, loan commitments, and investment offerings, the elaborate framework of commercial empire would collapse. In the world of commerce, as Daniel Defoe pointed out, credit replaced honor as the virtue necessary in human relationships.

Virtue as credit-worthiness was still relational and reputational, as the classicists held. It still lay in self-control, as the Christians maintained. However, its focus was no longer the public sphere but the labyrinth of contracts supporting the lofty monuments of public glory.

As we seek to move beyond the limits of these concepts it is clear that our notion of virtue has to be recast if we are to claim key elements of our republican and biblical heritage.[42] Just as the world of corporate commerce as well as government is being dragged into greater public visibility, so the internal asceticism of Christian virtue needs to be seen in the light of public action if we are to move toward a new and vital symbol to occupy the center of our faith.

Let us pause to summarize our findings before examining the cultural revolution fostered by modern republicanism. We can see that these seven themes in republican thought in the formative years of the American constitution demonstrated innovation as well as the capacity for distortion and decline.

The famous republic of a mixed polity was transformed into a separation of powers. While this institutionalized the desire for balance, it tended to substitute the competition of narrow interests for the collaborative search for the common good.

While democratization expanded the original republican impulse and removed public life from the subtle tyrannies of the king's household, it also tended to reduce the public discourse of a council to opinion polls of isolated individuals. The wisdom that was once sought in debate was reified in institutional mechanisms to guard against the tyranny of majorities. The democratic child of the republic has threatened to overturn the house of its birth.

The kind of representation necessary to include a variegated citizenry tended in turn to lose the capacity to represent the interests of the whole rather than simply the sum total of partial interests. Procedures have replaced criteria for the common welfare, and the federal structure soon tended to lose its coherence as an expression of the complex integration of limited and general polities.

To fill the vacuum of representation the president has assumed more and more of the old monarchical functions of representing the unity of the people, even apart from their rich web of relationships. The principle of unity begins to approach once again the forms of ancient monarchy.

The sovereignty of law and constitution still prevail in this picture, both in public mind and in actual fact, as the Watergate and the Iran/Contra scandals have shown. The victory of law, however, has never had a Marshall plan for the broken bonds of personal fealty that motivated self-sacrifice for the common good in the past. The public springs of action go untended in the underbrush of self-service.

Republican life brought personal and group liberties to the center of civic consciousness. Personal expression and confirmation found an open space in which to thrive. At the same time the purpose of liberty was lost in the freedom to pursue immediate gain. Even churches were tempted to fall away from public witness to pursue their denominational interests separated from the political world.

Finally, the virtue necessary for public life has always been precariously divided between the lofty panegyrics of the Periclean authors of the constitution and the ascetic suspicions of the Augustinian tradition. Even the credit-worthiness of the commercial era is threatened by the loss of connection between personal good and public interest. Credit becomes fixated on quarterly dividends rather than community contributions. People on many sides see the need for an account of personal character that leads us to the public sources of common life.

Thus, the modern version of republicanism so close to us today reveals its double-sided character of promise and portent. Its institutional lines are sharper just as its wider cultural context becomes blurred. The task of critical theological engagement becomes more complex. To lay the final groundwork for summing up the challenge and potential of the republican heritage, we need to examine this wider cultural base as it emerged in the eighteenth and nineteenth century.

2. The Cultural Revolution. Changes in the structural form of a republic could only be sustained through profound transformations of the cultural bed in which it flourished. In this cultural metamorphosis classical categories of thought had to be articulated in a different way. This cultural shift crystallized in a new understanding of *reason*, a new view of *nature*, and a new conception of *time*. We need to grasp at least the chief elements in these changes so we can see some important issues and implications arising in a religious engagement with our republican heritage.

(a) Reason: From Proportion to Interest. The world of James Harrington still believed that human reason inexorably tended to reflect a cosmic harmony. It was drawn toward the proportions and relationships grounded in a universal natural order ordained by God.[43] This view of reason still tied mental action to the emotional bonds of a social order, first of all that of the family and secondly that of "nature." It was the thinking of a body which had been projected onto the family, the body of Christ, the crown body, body politic and the body of the cosmos.

Reason was thus the mental activity of expressing an essential pattern of sociality and relatedness. Reason was social in its conception. It was the tool of sociality, though still within a wider unalterable cosmic order. While Harrington knew of a "private reason," and even a limited reason of a single state, it was the "reason of mankind" which was truly right reason—the reason of the most extended social world.[44]

However, by the end of the eighteenth century more and more supporters of republicanism had elevated private reason to the highest rank. This was the reason of calculative self-interest. It was reason as "means-ends" thinking, reason as the tool for achieving specific ends of an individual or of a corporation. This is the reason Max Weber was later to identify with "modernization" itself, though with enough misgiving for him to see it as the bondage of an iron cage rather than the social bonds of a cosmic commonwealth.[45]

If classical reason had been the child of the city or the manor, interested reason was the offspring of the marketplace. It was the reason of buyers and sellers locked in negotiation for the best price. It was mental power in the service of personal advancement rather than social bonding. It was a reason which broke the bonds of the old bodies, freeing the persons to explore their own potentialities in a new world, still uncharted, waiting for a pristine renovation.

Both of these forms of reason fall ultimately short of satisfying the needs of a perfected public. The classical forms were caught in the unyielding foundations of a patriarchal world. However, the reason of the marketplace could not connect the minds of individuals to wider bonds, except through blind appeals to the social Darwinism of the marketplace. It yielded only a pre-political concept of reason.

Yet each one bore seeds of a possibility both old and new—an understanding of consensual reason. This was the reasonable truth pursued by the Council of Basle. It was the governance by reason rather than will.[46] It was a sense of truth that emerges in the argument of equals who must persuade each other of the implications of their fundamental mutual commitments—whether they be to place, to community, or nation.

This public reason partakes of "private reason" as well, because each participant is grounded not in some preconceived natural harmony or cosmic will, but in the partial vision of his or her interest. There is a genuine debate amidst real conflict in the search for the common way. People do have some "private property" from which they can advance into the public light and hold their own, but this is a reason and a property which knows that its light is but one candle in the dark. It is a means for entering public discourse, not for building a wall against it. It is a social reason that makes possible the wider relationships of public life.

It is this kind of reason, partially emergent, partially distorted, that represents the center of the republican tradition and which still seeks a maturation in our own time. It is the reason grounded in public discourse.

(b) Nature: From Forms to Motions. Our understanding of reason is embedded in our view of nature as well as of personal agency and relationship. A shift in our understanding of reason necessarily implies a change in our view of nature. This was manifested no more clearly than in the cultural transformations of the eighteenth century.

Classical reason had rested in a nature which was simply an extension of the lord's manor. Nature was a feudal domain writ large as the empire of the Lord. The order of the agrarian household was a microcosm of a divine and cosmic economy. That was the inherited vision of Christendom, still alive in Harrington's traditional view of family authority as a little kingdom preserving the personal basis for a commonwealth.

Modern republicanism rode in on horses of a different color and hoofbeats with a different rhythm. The body of an earlier nature had been stripped of social context and become a "body in motion," to use Thomas Hobbes' prescient phrase.[47] This celestial mechanics served a number of republican masters, because it could justify a political order that was in constant motion due to the cycle of elections (Harrington), the collision of forces (Madison), or the creation of harmony out of divergent vectors (Adam Smith). This mechanical body could be disassembled, reconstructed, and replaced without violating the integrity of the parts. There was no common spirit to escape the nostrils of this Leviathan. For Hobbes the motor of government was the fear of death rather than the hope of glory. Governmental mechanics did not obey the loyalties of emotional bonds but rather the indifferent laws of a universe in ceaseless motion.

Again, the gap between two conceptions of nature reveals a deficiency deep within the structure of modern republicanism. Republican theories tend to lack a vision for holding separate parties in a common argument, bringing separated persons onto common ground, and understanding the underlying relationships among the powerful forces in a state of conflict. In this stark contrast between the views of a formal and a motile nature, however, we can also identify some common strains which lift up a nature fit for genuine public life. These strains are reunited by new models flowing from the contemporary sciences.

Both the social and the mechanical understandings of nature had a conception of how things could hold together—the first by the attraction of an underlying frame, the second by the impact of forces. However, just as the social frame of classical nature was burst asunder by the immense migrations of people and by new modes of communication, so the mechanical view of nature has been transformed by the explosion of the atom and our insights into the invisible electromagnetic web which holds each atom of the universe together, both internally and externally.

This electromagnetic principle picks up both the mechanical conceptions of Newtonian physics as well as the organic frame of the stoic views of nature which accompanied early republicanism. We find a singular expression of it in the conciliarists' insight into the way a council produces a new level of energy among the participants that they lack when confined to their own separate orbits. It is in this experience of resonance among participants in a public that we find the hinge between human relationships and a coherent approach to how the universe hangs together. This is the clue to a theory of nature which can undergird a renovated theory of the republic.

Our purpose here cannot be to spell out the kind of metaphysics this notion of resonance implies. It is clear that the direction first set forth by Alfred North Whitehead and then followed up by students of process thought is the most productive path to pursue in this respect.[48] Unfortunately the implications of this philosophical conversation for political thought have found only fitful expression.

What we do need to highlight, however, is the general conception of resonance within the theory of a federal republic. At the symbolic level, it enables the symbol of "republic" (as well as covenant) to find alliance with those images of a physics and chemistry that have reconceived the motions of matter in terms of electromagnetic dynamics.

By providing a model for approaching life, they open us up to the way that reality, whether political or material, arises from the presence of resonance—a field of force created by the coincidence of even smaller, yet compatible energy fields. The universe is a system of systems of resonance, as "general systems" theorists would say.[49] It is a public of publics, a field of fields, each one given power and presence by an invisible web of attraction.

This is the kernel of a theory of nature which draws on important aspects of our cultural tradition and lifts them up in a new form. Reality, whether "human" or "material," is not composed of discrete blocks colliding randomly and arranged in happenstance combination, neither is it a preconceived form, but a systematic process of powerful attractions.

(c) Political Time: Republican Eschatology. As J. G. A. Pocock, Harrington's most recent editor, has pointed out, classical republicanism had always been besieged by a cyclical theory of history, summed up in the recurrent image of *fortuna*.[50] Republics were caught capriciously in an inexorable revolution through monarchy, aristocracy, and democracy. Polybius' conception of the stable republic had been an effort to halt the wheel of political fortune by incorporating the three principles into a single polity. He envisioned a republic that might transcend the cycles of nature.

This vision was buried with the collapse of republican Rome and nearly extinguished by an Augustinian contempt for the fortunes of the human city. Resurrected by Machiavelli, Polybius' vision of an immortal republic was soon welded to the Christian belief in Providence to produce the messianic republicanism that swept over England to the New World in the seventeenth century.

For these Christian republicans Christ's republic was no longer a city at the end of and above history, but an emerging accomplishment in the course of time.[51] Revolution was no longer a cycle of fortune but the creation of a new order. This "new order for the ages," as the American constitutionalists put it, had roots in the primitive past—Israel's confederation, the Athens of Pericles, and the Rome of Cicero.

Some people were caught up in the urge simply to re-create these ancient forms, hoping to secure the memory of their experience in a new and different world. The architecture of public buildings, the language of republican statesmanship, and the Protestant appeal to models of the early Church all bespoke this eager "restitutionism" of the early, oft corrupted forms.

However, this new version of history's culmination was not merely an eschatology of return to some Edenic past. Too many changes had occurred in technology, social order, and culture to envision a simple reactionary movement. The republican vision of the future embraced a new unfolding, a progressive realization of old ideals in new materials. The emerging republic was an ancient goal but also a pristine realization of something almost unimaginable. Orestes Brownson, the Transcendentalist convert to the Roman Catholic Church, condensed the progressive vision in these bold words: "Christianity in the secular order is republican, and continues and completes the work of Greece and Rome."[52]

While the horrors of two world wars, the corruptions of our public world, and the darkness of the tortures all around us make us timid of enthusiastic hope, this explosion in our world a century ago can still yield light for us today. Our republican intimations have been firmly wrested from a time immune to divine action or human response. In escaping a too-zealous belief that our own republics are God's perfected public, or that our own histories are God's greatest story, we need not give up the search for institutions that enable us to give witness to that culmination of our hopes.

The heritage of this republican eschatology can still invigorate our efforts to form and maintain public worlds in which we can emerge from darkness into a common life of public recognition. However, we are not simply on a train moving away from our origin into our future. We are surrounded always by a host of witnesses who sent us on our way and will welcome us at our final perfection. There is also a public constituted by our history that can infuse the timely efforts of our present deeds. Time is not so much a one-way track as it is an arena in which the incandescence of the most energized publicity is at the center (regardless of the deeds' position on a chronological track) and the lesser lights of deprivation, secrecy and tyranny recede beyond the seats into the night of isolation and amnesia. This is the kind of transformed sense of time that can nurture our present actions and visions with the witness of resonant events spread out across our history.

These three cultural revolutions in our sense of reason, nature, and time undergird our modern and emerging sense of republic. They have implications for how we organize our publics and also for how we think about God and the Church.

Obviously, neither the structures of modern republicanism nor the cultural views undergirding them are a single system. A central symbol like "republic" affords a number of distinct models and theories. However, out of this historic argument we can distill some themes with which to put together a vision in our own time. The republican tradition offers us a vision that is coherent but incomplete. It strains toward a partner to complement its weaknesses and contain its contradictions. To understand the significance of this partner we need to survey briefly the current state of this republican image.

VI.   Republic: Principle and Practice

A.   The Dominant and Ambiguous Symbol

Most of the world's countries, with allowance for linguistic differences, now use republican language in their title. Others, such as Great Britain and the Netherlands, are monarchical republics in the classic Polybian sense. While the native meaning of this term may vary widely in a particular country's history, the symbol has become firmly entrenched in political consciousness, from the Islamic Republic of Iran and the Union of Soviet Socialist Republics to the Federal Republic of Germany. Ironically, the oldest republican states, Switzerland, the Netherlands and the United States of America, do not employ the term in their title, yet have given the symbol some of its most precise meaning.

As a political symbol it is dominant in our vocabulary and imagery. As a particular structure of government it is highly ambiguous. The practices legitimated by this potent symbol vary widely. There are constitutional monarchies, democratic republics, federal republics, communist republics and confederations, not to mention the nations of the British commonwealth.

On a global basis we occupy a great divide between an epoch of personal rule and one of republican governance. The ancient bonds of kin and clan, epitomized in monarchy, are giving way amidst enormous conflicts to some form of republican polity. The symbol has taken root.

It is its flower that is yet unknown. The practices this symbol will legitimate still stand in question and dispute.

The initial cultural task has been accomplished. Nations are struggling to be known as republics. Such a deep symbolic shift is religious in nature, for it redefines the basic orientation of our life. It is the nub of faith. It is the flag of our fidelity. Because of its centrality in our lives it should also be central to our religious vision. The symbol of a republic should have a central place in a biblically rooted faith.

But just as a theology must consist of more than a few symbols and slogans, so must a political theory. As we grope toward more authentic republics we need to forge some central principles to guide us. We need some midwives for the incarnation of our faith. The concept which may help pull together the many strands of republican tradition is that of publicity itself. Though it occupies a lowly place in our vocabulary, it can bear some burdens necessary for our journey. We conclude this survey of our republican heritage with a brief examination of the way the principle of publicity can illuminate some fundamental ambiguities in republican practice and open the way to its religious partner, covenant.

B. Publicity

The full meaning of publicity will arise only as we turn this crystal at many angles to refract its colors on the screen of our concerns. At its root, however, we shall use it to mean the dynamic by which people enter into and preserve a public realm. Publicity involves the capacity to express ourselves in this common world, to persuade and be persuaded in the furtherance of a common life. It is the dynamic of public action. To grasp some of the contours of this dynamic we need to see how it relates to coercive forces, to its internal form and content, and to the structure of participation.

1. The Force Field. From its inception, republican advocates have recognized the antagonism between government by persuasion and the coercive forces of economics and militarism. Economic necessity, as Aristotle, Locke and Marx all knew, controls the degree of people's participation in public life. If nothing else, poor people are simply too exhausted by the sheer struggle for survival to engage in a public life that goes beyond the satisfaction of their immediate needs. Moreover, economic position shapes the way people participate by forming the private interests which they then seek to advance as public goods.

These are unalterable facts of life, but they say little about whether we should struggle to establish and maintain a sphere in which people can be drawn forth from isolation and where their private pretensions can be refined in the fire of open debate. This is finally an ethical and religious question about the vision which shapes our purpose and evokes our energies. What is important is not that we fold our flag in the face of resistance but that we not confuse our hopes with contrary realities. Private interests posing as the public good are still a hoax. A public robbed of full participation is not yet a complete republic. These are simply facts which an ethical vision must address, not surrender to.

Once we legitimate the integrity of our ethical vision aside from observations about its distortion and misuse we still have to face perplexing problems about what kind of economic order is best suited for republican life. It is quite clear we cannot return to Harrington's "equal agrarian" or Jefferson's yeoman farmer. Nor can we find refuge in Hamilton's entrepreneurial capitalism. Indeed, the requisite structure cannot be defined in detail. All we can do is draw on the central idea of publicity and say that people must have some property by which to enter into the publics around them.

Publicity as a principle would lead us to accentuate patterns of housing, income, household and family maintenance, communication, and information gathering which would enhance people's capacity to participate in public discourse with reasonable independence and security from arbitrary deprivations. Each republic has to try out patterns designed to achieve this end, and each will have to struggle against entrenched interests who want to dominate the public spheres as if they were their own households. The struggle is ceaseless.

The constraints of economic order may be more extensive than those of militarism but never more pronounced. Military force can silence the public arena by violence and terror. While a republic can be poor, it cannot be violent. Classical republicans held that the only solution to this problem was to avoid a standing army at all costs. Moreover, they held that any military force should be composed of the citizenry rather than mercenaries, who would not have the public good at heart. While this ideal may have been possible in the simple technology of past warfare, it seems unattainable in our own time.

Two alternatives in dealing with military power face us. The ancient ideal of a citizen army still exists, though perhaps in a distorted form, in the guerrilla warfare of countries poised between autocracy and republicanism. However, the intermingling of factions within the population and the lack of a coherent consensus among the people leads to a terrorism which annihilates the basis for any subsequent public life. Guerrilla soldiers, while grounded in the people, often lack a wider public covenant to form their purpose and their strategy.

On the other side we have the standing professional army of the established nations. The professionalization of military life has been the compromise solution to the dilemma of a standing army in a republic. As a professional the soldier operates with self-restraint within a clearly defined sphere of authority under citizen control. Military life is a profession of its own, not an estate with automatic governmental power. Without this differentiation of military order from public power, even the autonomy of public authority we see today would not be imaginable.

Under present conditions we must continue to support this pro-fessionalization of military order, but without isolating it into a blind expertise. The principle of publicity demands that the professional be aware of his or her role in preserving the public accountability of all professions, because they are intrinsically public trusts, whether they be medicine, law, ministry, or military service.

This does not mean that the military as such should occupy a large public space. This would only aggravate the potential pollution of vio-lence in the public sphere. It does mean that military people be com-mitted to the precarious joys and responsibilities of a republic. It requires a greater percolation of people back and forth between the two spheres, so that military people treasure the public action which they are authorized to defend. That is the difficult path a republic must pur-sue in the face of the dangers of militarism.

When economic necessity and military force combine they produce the primary distortion of republicanism in our world—nationalism. If republicanism is ever a Trojan horse, then nationalism is the band of Hellenistic warriors hidden in its dark interior. This is the force that penetrates and shatters the relative autonomy of community, city and our limited publics.

Nationalism, however, is even more ambiguous than this, for it is also the vehicle by which tribalism and parochialism have been over-come in most countries. Unfortunately, it does not necessarily nourish the republican heir to our monarchical ancestors. It may arise with wider patterns of communication, as Karl Deutsch has pointed out, but it can also centralize this media power in an effort to crush debate and popular self-governance.[53] With centralized planning it can not only di-rect people's economic destiny but silence them in turn. The principle of publicity, while indebted to the power of national movements, must always subject them to its wary criticism. Without this, the bulldozer of nationalism can obliterate the public square rather than clear a road for the people to come together.

Publicity, however, is not a breeze without considerable power. It can become a gale that flattens out the military sails. Where public com-munication can galvanize many sectors of a population, it can constrain the use of force—whether it be the use of torture on particular prisoners, or genocidal warfare. The victories of human rights groups like Amnesty International or the role played by publicity in limiting and ending United States involvement in Vietnam should not be ignored if we are to see the way toward a world where publicity has finally overcome force.

Publicity is a principle which can help us deal with the nearly overwhelming forces of economics and militarism. It may be able to help us steer these forces to some degree in order to advance greater publicity. There still remain, however, other dilemmas in the movement toward a greater republic. The first of these is the balancing of "substantive" and "procedural" publicity.

2. Publicity: The Substance and the Procedures. From one angle the republican ethos looks for certain kinds of behavior and performance: that people engage in public debate, elections, information gathering, education, policy initiatives, and public conversations of all kinds. Moreover, the public spaces and media they use for this purpose must be adequately maintained. These are substantive marks of the public process. A republic exists when people actually exercise a public life.

Others focus on the procedures by which the debate goes on—especially its legal and constitutional frame. Regardless of how many people participate or what the outcomes are, they want to know if the proper procedures have been followed to provide fair debate or electoral competition. They search for the procedural marks of public life.

People concerned about the first point often turn in a socialist direction. Like Michael Harrington they seek to constrain economic life so that the maximum number of people are freed for public action.[54] While not all socialists are republicans, a good case can be made for a socialist republicanism which focuses on the substance of publicity— people freed from necessity in order to engage in public affairs. Without this prior substructure of economic equality, they argue, republican forms are simply a veil for rule by a small elite.

Defenders of procedure usually stand in the camp of liberal democracy. While they are often assailed for their legalistic preoccupations within a burning city, they also lift up important claims. Full publicity requires conventions of discourse and debate. It requires commonly known procedures for reaching conclusions. Without them argument dissolves in cacaphony. Procedures can be a dike against arbitrary action and a guide for ordering our thoughts for public inspection. Publicity demands more than liberation from necessity. It requires training in articulation and participation. These are the values of procedure.

Both of these claims have their distortion. The substantive socialists can create a potemkin village of coerced publicity. The procedural liberals can create a labyrinth eliminating all but the dogged and the privileged from public power. Yet each has a legitimate claim. While it is too facile to harmonize them here in any simple manner, both must be accommodated in the movement toward a more authentic republic which embraces as well as orders our participation.

3. Participation and Polity. The embrace and the ordering that arise in the debate between substance and procedure also find expression in the final argument of republican theorists. That is the tension between a polity favoring widespread involvement of individuals and that devoted to maintaining a complex structure of publics and countervailing powers.

On the side of individual involvement we have the long-standing desire for "direct democracy" in which each individual has one voice and one vote. Concern focuses on the rights of each individual to freedom and public expression. Democracy represents the extension of the principle of publicity to every individual. It leads to support for direct elections of all officials as well as procedures for recall and referendum during term of office.

When pushed too far this democratic thrust begins to contradict its own principle of participation. It can eventuate in an individualism which defends personal freedom apart from its proper realization in the relationships of public life. Freedom can become the act of choosing goods to consume in private rather than the public conversation which demands our courage and self-sacrifice. Moreover, the call to direct participation overlooks the limits of public engagement, which must occur in many smaller republics woven together with the threads of constitutional agreement.

It is at this point that the voices calling for structures can enter with their plea for the maintenance of numerous spheres of public life, some divided by function, as with the legislative and judicial publics, others divided by spheres of authority, as with the state legislatures and the national congress. Genuine participation, they point out, can occur only within this mansion of many rooms. Only in this way can the aedifice of republican life be erected and maintained.

Of course, this thrust too has its excess. The call for a complex republic can reintroduce the tight control of the senate which guaranteed Venice's notorious collective dictatorship as well as its serene stability. Complexity, like proceduralism, can choke off the wider publics and the populace deprived of public voice.

As with the struggle between socialist and liberal visions we need to hold both claims together, for both are intrinsic to authentic publicity. Every person has legitimate rights to public life, but public life has its own dynamics which demand the discipline of numerous special, limited, and interwoven publics. The argument of republican life must always hear both voices and seek to bring them both under the principle of publicity.

4. Toward a Federal Republic. Republican theorists have always had to realize that true publicity demands a limited population and scope. Otherwise it is impossible to build up a pattern of trust, mutual recognition, and commonality necessary for the expression and response intrinsic to republican life. Because of the limited size of any particular republic, any adequate republican theory has always had to turn to some principle for relating these smaller republics into a more encompassing order of governance. From the time of the Greeks and Hebrews down through the leagues of Italian and German cities and the confederations of Switzerland and the United States, republicans have turned to the ancient concept of federation. In Montesquieu's words, a "confederate republic" is an "assemblage of societies" that "prevents all manner of inconveniences."[55]

There are two resources which republican advocates seek in the federalist tradition—one legal, the other cultural. Together they comprise what is necessary for the "constitution" of a republic. Both aspects are necessary to build up a context and a common world of mutual trust essential to the dynamics of publicity.

Most of us know federalism as a legal and constitutional means for relating individual states to a central government. This is what it means in the United States of America, the Federal Republic of Germany, or India. It is a framework for distributing power and authority in a complex governmental order. This is what is meant by a federalist constitution—an interweaving of publics in order to balance the claims for participation, stability, and liberty. In this light Thomas Jefferson could say, "We are all republicans, we are all federalists."[56]

There is a second, more biblical meaning which accompanies this. Here, covenant is not only a compact among people, but a relationship between them and their ultimate source. It is a covenant between God and God's people. Through this special sense of common loyalty a people develops the common points of reference by which public discourse can be guided. It provides the basis for a common cultural world that is necessary for a life of persuasion. Behind federalism stands its ancient root—covenant. Only by understanding this original concept can we unpack the meaning and importance of the federalist tradition for republican thought and life. To that task we devote the next chapter.

Federalism: The Covenantal Heritage

4

The kingdom tradition has left us with an awareness of some deep underlying needs and aspirations in our life. However, over the centuries it has had to yield to patterns of governance summed up in the symbol of republic. This powerful republican vision itself has been a flawed and incomplete vessel which yearns for a partner to correct its main weaknesses. The covenantal tradition can help supply that need. By bringing together these biblical and republican traditions we form the composite symbol of federal republic.

This chapter rehearses the development of covenantal conceptions through our history. We examine this history in order to identify the central themes in covenantal thinking so that we can proceed to our constructive task. Since its biblical origins covenant has moved from being a term of international diplomacy to being a major way of understanding creation itself, both political and personal. By looking at its origins we can see a full conception of covenant which needs to be recovered in the midst of the partial forms underlying our present constitutionalism. This historical and theological perspective enables us to use covenant as a critical tool for advancing a theory of the public appropriate to our own time. In turn, our contemporary understanding of publicity helps correct covenant's tendency to foster a closed community of the elect.

I. Kingdom, Republic and Covenant

A. Kingdom and Covenant

Covenant can help us meet certain challenges presented by the kingship tradition. As we saw in Chapter Two, kingship provided an answer to the questions of group and personal survival, social stability, appeal to transcendent justice, and the socialization of people into the wider bonds of group life. Kingship arose in the *oikos* which fused together family, religion, and household. As protector of the whole economy of life, the king provided a model of effective leadership which could press for a wider scope of justice beyond the arbitrary tyrannies of lesser households and local princes. The king could claim to represent the whole people. He was elected by God to be a steward of the whole realm. Kingship was a way of providing the cultural ground necessary for common life.

Kingship's weaknesses lay in its extension of biological principles into the social life of free agents and in the restricted applicability of household models to the governance of a larger population of diverse people. Kingship could not accommodate adult intimations of equality and the desire for a liberty to profess one's own convictions. It extended the patriarchal dominance over the home to the whole of human relationships. In our own time kingship has become practically equated with sexism—that is, the exclusion of women from public life. The characteristics that enabled it to provide stability and socialization also limited it as a model for a genuinely political structure.

Covenant provides an alternative way of approaching these tasks. It appeals to bonds forged in voluntary association, structured in law, and extended to many spheres of life. This chapter will spell out its ability to accomplish the purposes once pursued through kingship.

B. Republic and Covenant

With the republican ideal we saw the rise of the principle of mutual consensus among equals as the basis for common life. This consensus was reached through a process of persuasion and argument. Over many centuries public life extended to increasing numbers of people—first elders, then propertied males, then all males and then all adults. The public principle once limited to a senate of the virtuous now seeks to live within the corporations, associations and even households throughout the world. Models of publicity are being generalized to every area of human life.

Republican thought over the centuries developed increasingly sophisticated ways to carry on this persuasive public process. While in the beginning it focused on mixing the orders of society in order to create a stable context for public life, in recent centuries it has turned to institutional means for balancing power against power in order to limit the exercise of arbitrary decisions apart from legal processes.

As an independent strand of thought and practice, however, republicanism has often become a constricted emphasis on personal liberty apart from the public bonds which make participation and publicity possible. It has oscillated between theories of direct and representative democracy apart from the actual bonds of association that sustain us over the long haul. It has emphasized legal procedure rather than substantive commitments to human needs. It has been corrupted in simple nationalisms that overwhelm the constituent polities of a people. Its legal constitutions have not been able to evoke the kind of public-spiritedness that saves professionalism from commercial self-interest and patriotism from jingoistic excess.

The republican body cannot run on one leg. It seeks out a partner to lead it from the stumbling byways of a simple individualism or an arrogant nationalism. It needs better contact with the ground of its existence and advancement. For that task we turn to the ancient Hebraic symbol of covenant.

II. Biblical Covenant

God's covenant with Abraham was a relationship with a whole household—family, tents, livestock, possessions. It was a covenant with a whole *bayith* ("house")—the Hebrew equivalent of the ancient Greek *oikos*. Covenanting did not exist apart from this wholistic view. All the components of their economy were taken up in the covenant.

It is crucial for us to see that the original meaning of covenant embraced this entire ensemble of life. In the subsequent differentiation of these components from each other covenant often became fastened on only the individuals, leading to a distorted interpretation of its proper focus. This differentiation appears most dramatically in the history of the Greek *oikos*. The household concept originally bound up in this word found its way into Church life (ecumenics), production and distribution (economics) and the science of natural relationships (ecology). It was also used by theologians to speak of the way God acted to save the world through a divine "economy."[1] The history of these words reveals their original integration in the ancient household. While we cannot and ought not recover this primordial fused structure we do need to attend to the process of integration it fostered.

The biblical idea of covenant drew on treaty formulas between the heads of clan households. While they usually occurred between a superior chief and a dependent one (as in God's covenants with Abraham and Moses), they also found their use in relations between equals (Jacob and Laban, Abimelech and Abraham, Jonathan and David). They were pacts that knit two houses together beyond the bonds of simple kinship. They were the earliest form of social relationship that transcended familial patterns, though they often drew on kinship terms in a metaphorical way. They replaced procreation with promises in order to create mutuality and symbiosis between people. They are the primordial alternative to the family as a principle for political order.

Once transplanted from this inter-ethnic world the covenant principle could be applied not only to God's relation to Israel but to the relations among the twelve tribes. Their presumed common ancestry in Abraham was transmuted into a covenantal bond. Their common covenant with God joined them in obedience to the Torah revealed through Moses. Confederation and law rose above tribalism and paternal decree. Covenant became a principle for the internal order of a society.[2]

It is to this confederal order among equals that James Harrington later pointed when he held that ancient Israel was a republic. Covenant life and republican polity reflected and reinforced each other. Kingship, when it arose, was always seen within covenantal order. First the covenant was exercised through a council of the elders, who appointed Saul king. David and Solomon, in abandoning this tradition, still appealed to a hierarchical covenant between them and God. They replaced the stability found through confederation with the security of monarchical military leadership. Nevertheless, the Hebrews lifted up the norm that the king was only king within covenant, a principle carried on in the medieval claim that kings were only kings within council.

III. Greco-Roman Loss of Covenant

When the early followers of Jesus tried to understand his significance for their lives, covenant had already become interpreted not only in terms of a particular non-familial pattern of relationships, but as an historic promise of divine salvation. Covenant meant primarily God's eternal promise to the Hebrew people to lead them into a promised land. With the failure of the Maccabean revolt in the century before Jesus' ministry this promissory covenant became oriented increasingly toward a future, radically different order. Covenant came to point to an historic and even future-worldly hope rather than a living polity.[3]

Christians seized on the Davidic covenant, therefore, to understand Jesus as God's promise to us for all the ages. The monarchical principle of the Davidic covenant triumphed over the confederal form of the Mosaic. The distaste for law and the preference for paternalism exemplified in St. Paul further distanced Christians from the confederal heritage, replacing it with God's special covenant with Christ, the redeemer who will come again.

The only real attention given to covenant in the Christian testimony occurs in the Letter to the Hebrews. Here we find the combination of priesthood and covenant redolent of the themes from Israel's origins and the Maccabean vision. Christ appears as the new high priest in a new temple erected through God's special covenant with him. This picture of a covenanted royal priesthood in Christ, however, simply leapfrogged over the heads of the early Church, carrying this ancient covenantal view into the Middle Ages. The covenantal order rooted in the symbols of the ancient cult was largely lost on an early Church that returned to household patterns of patrimonial descent to erect a Church order and a political attitude more compatible with Roman imperial models.[4]

St. Augustine typified and crystallized this reduction of covenantal thinking. Certainly the political and structural implications of covenantal thinking were as irrelevant to him as were those of the republicans. Just as the idea of the two cities was recast into an anticipation of personal salvation, so the promissory notion of covenant was the sole remnant of this heritage in his thought. Even here, however, the history of God's promises was retrieved through the eyes of genealogy rather than through the struggle for a covenantal social order.[5] The model of the patriarchal household informed not only his monarchical orientation but also his historiography. Covenant at best was restricted to the Davidic promise which was to be realized in Christ's second coming.

At the same time that Augustine turned away from the search for political justice, the wider Church in the West was seeking an appropriate accommodation to the Roman heritage. As Ernst Troeltsch pointed out years ago, it accomplished this engagement by adopting the Stoic conception of natural law, though adapting it to take account of the difference between the pristine human state in creation and its fallen state after Adam.[6] This embrace of a Roman legal orientation which focused on an analysis of individual human desires further distanced Christians from the political understandings flowing from obedience to a Torah revealed through God's process of covenanting with a people.

While covenantal and natural law traditions are not mutually exclusive and both offer a variety of strands, they do work from different starting points. In taking up the natural law tradition the Latin Church had to attenuate its covenantal heritage. Law through covenant always contains the element of voluntarism—both divine and human. The law emerges from divine intention and becomes a covenant in human acceptance. It is attuned to the surprises of history rather than the developmental regularities of science. Thus, covenant always tends to overflow predetermined orders and patterns in order to extend the divine will into every facet of life. All of life becomes a divine-human encounter in search of a trustworthy relationship in the face of chaos.

Natural law theories, however, begin with an analysis of human life, usually adopting the ways of thinking associated with the sciences. They search for the regularities, tendencies, and patterns of mature fulfillment observable in human life. They have therefore thought more in terms of accommodating to the regular orders and patterns of life, rather than being anchored in a divine-human encounter that transcends the ordinary experience of existence. In this respect a natural law approach enabled the Church to accommodate to the dominant patterns of normalcy in late classical life—to its patriarchy, monarchy, householding models and concern for individual development of virtues within a stable social order.

In embracing the natural order of paternal rule the Church suppressed the energetic covenantal process of encounter, negotiation, and agreement. All that was left of the covenantal tradition in Christian discourse was God's paternal covenant with Jesus, Lord and King.

Some elements of biblical covenant remained within the camp of its republican ally. That was the republican emphasis on leagues, federations, and treaties to bind together otherwise weak republics into a stable defensive unity. The inter-ethnic and international notions of covenant still remained alive in the republican visions of Polybius and his successors, but without their wider biblical meanings.

IV.   Medieval Resurgence of Federal Relations

A.   Feudum and Foedus

With the gradual collapse of the urban centers of Roman civilization, common life retreated to the paternalistic patterns of the manor. Bonds of personal fealty rose up in the disintegration of the Roman law. Life retreated from the mercantile bustle of the Roman transportation system to the agrarian isolation of a multitude of lords.

Among the manors and demesnes people could recover some semblance of the ancient *oikos*. Life became more tightly integrated, even fused, around the household, land, kin, and a domestic faith. The elements of ancient covenant found resurgence in the feudal world.

From the ninth to the fourteenth century European society was held together by a dense and shifting network of personal loyalties between serfs and lords, vassals and princes, princes and kings. It was the very pattern of reciprocal loyalties that had characterized the early covenants. In this sense it was a covenantal society, a veritable forest of covenants. Through these covenants people were bound in faith to each other. They exercised, as the Latin word for faith, *fides*, would tell us, fidelity toward each other. Drawn from the same root was the Latin word for covenant—*foedus*.

Here once again God, the people, the land and even their livestock were tied together in a web of mutual obligation. Indeed, the very word "feudal" seems to have come from an old French or Germanic word meaning cattle.[7] The "feud" between lord and vassal centered on the possession and use of the valuable means of sustenance on the land. The *foedus* lived within the *feudum*. Feudal society was also federal (*foederalis*).

While this covenantal network was theoretically coherent and stable, in fact medieval life was constantly overturned by competition and warfare among the lords, whose bonds were only personal and rarely survived two generations. Wider relationships were always at the mercy of the fluctuations of personal favor. It was in this turmoil that the Church and dominant kings turned to each other to create a more stable peace. With the Carolingian empire inaugurated in 800 the crown of Constantine passed to his medieval successor.

B. The Covenant of Election

It is in fact with the coronation of Charlemagne that we see the actual focus of the biblical covenant in the popular mind. Constantine, in taking on Christian robes, had understood himself to be exercising a stewardship given to him by Christ. He was the elected and anointed servant to bring peace to the world. Charlemagne saw himself mirrored in the face of Constantine. As representative of the Franks he led an elect nation whose historic mission was to pacify the European world. As one recognized by the Pope he became the elect one with a special covenantal relation with God—namely, to be God's servant.[8]

This covenantal remnant preserved by Constantinian imperialism began to reopen the door to covenantal understandings of political life. It began with the servanthood covenant between a king and God. This itself was a mirror of the covenantal relation between God and Christ, between YHWH and his suffering servant. Over the centuries, as more and more Christians became self-consciously grafted into Christ through baptism, the qualities of kingship passed on to them as well, as we shall see in the Puritan revolution. The royal covenant was later to become a personal covenant of citizenship. In Charlemagne we see this development in germ.[9] With Milton and Harrington we see it in flower.

The covenantal heritage comes to us through the lens of election. Charlemagne was elected by God through the Pope and acknowledged by the people. The concept of election was originally tied to God's initiation of a covenant. Election meant the assumption of a special kind of covenant to serve God and receive God's blessings of peace and justice for the realm.

Among the Germans election was mediated not through the Church but through the princes. Election, in this respect, gained a more popular footing as a covenant, or *Bund*, among the nobility. With this concept of election the medieval notion of king in council also attached to the emperor. The emperor, like any king, was robed in covenant as well as glory. The king could only exercise authority within the election and covenant of a council. Here again, the threads of covenant and republic were woven into the governmental vestments of medieval society.

These developments still left the major questions of stability and tyranny unanswered. Covenantal theory, like feudal practice, tried to limit lords through appeal to their covenant with God. Covenantalism was a theory undergirding the arts of moral suasion and education for limiting kings through their conscience as public mirrors of Christ. Public justice was welded to their soul's destiny. Many a mirror was held before the young prince to form him in a mold of moderation, courage for the right, and justice.

This, however, was not an institutional expression of covenant. It was personal, even as the feudal order was personal. To the degree it gained a constitutional form it was in the ancient constitution of the mixture of estates, whose composite virtue would guarantee the justice of the whole. Restraint of power finally rested more on defense of personal honor than on the legal formulation of the promises contained in covenants. This mixed polity, though linked to covenants of kings, was still far from the countervailing powers of a pluralistic republic. In fact, the pluralism known in their time was simply the condition for wars of honor, not the pre-condition of republican stability.

The medieval era saw the resurgence of covenantal ideas through the emperor's resumption of the ancient Davidic covenant, now mediated through Christ and Constantine. This covenant began working its way through Christian consciences—first of princes and then of lesser nobility. It took many centuries, however, before this covenantal notion could flower in the ferment of the Renaissance and Reformation.

V. From Renaissance to Reformation: The Rhine Flows to England

A. Federal Society

While covenant was reunited in its monarchical and hierarchical form with medieval government, the republican tradition of leagues was not forgotten. It was rekindled in the revolts of the northern Italian cities against imperial and papal rule. Florence, Milan, Verona, Venice and other cities sought to safeguard their emerging civic liberty in a succession of leagues—the covenants of republican defense.

To the north Germanic trading cities banded together to secure their own autonomy against the narrow concerns of the land-based nobility. Most famous was the Hanseatic league, which enabled many cities to maintain their liberty even down into the nineteenth century. In both these developments patterns of covenant were woven into the fabric of the early modern costume. People became used to life in leagues and covenants to secure their civic liberty.

Within the emerging towns and cities the covenant of kingship began to merge with the leagues of republican liberty. One way to understand the Reformation is to see it as the extension of Christ's kingship to every Christian. While this intensified the anti-Jewish bigotry of Christians it also laid the basis for a new understanding of covenantal political order. It was a covenant among Christian citizens as equals, rather than a hierarchical covenant within the feudal ladder of being.

To grasp this sixteenth century development we turn to Johannes Althusius, the German Calvinist. Althusius conceived of our life together as a "con-sociatio" of mutual symbiosis.[10] What we now call society is a covenant of covenants, a pact of pacts, among various individuals and groups to secure their well-being. The organic, naturalistic images of the body which had legitimated the rule of the head (read emperor or Pope) over the members gave way to a functional organism created through the covenants of its members.

Althusius thus helped build a bridge from the organic notions of the Middle Ages to the voluntaristic perspectives of the later centuries. He set forth a social theory in which covenantal bonds provided the framework for a whole theory of politics that was both scientific and normative. Covenant created the symbiosis through which people could live interdependent lives and find fulfillment. The kind of covenantal theory expounded by Althusius to a whole generation of Dutch ministers soon burst forth in the upheaval of the English revolution of the seventeenth century.

B. Puritan Principles

In the cauldron of Puritan debate several covenantal themes were recast into a form which has endured into our own time. The Puritans wove together covenantal theories of citizenship, political structure and history to lay the foundation for modern federalism. Moreover, this theory was not a detached speculation but a reflection of their activity in establishing covenanted churches and public associations to secure the common good.

1. Baptismal Citizenship. First, as we saw with James Harrington, they took the monarchical covenant and bound each individual believer into it through baptism. Indeed, this connection of kingship and baptism was so strong that some of them took over the Anabaptist belief in adult baptism in order to tie baptism to people's mature entry into public life. Baptism was no longer entrance into the ascribed roles of familial and paternalistic society. It was the badge of citizenship in Church and polity. Baptism made one a public person.[11]

Once Christ could exercise rule within the conscience people had to express this fundamental covenant with God in the form of covenants with one another. The first form of this was the church covenant developed by early congregationalists such as Robert Browne.[12] In the wake of the emergence of these church covenants, which bound the members together in the mind of Christ, the Puritans proceeded to make political covenants, not only the "Solemn League and Covenant" of the Presbyterians in 1643, but the various "agreements of the people" among the more radical soldiers in Cromwell's army.[13]

Thus, the monarchical covenant mediated through David, Christ, Constantine, and Charlemagne settled in the hearts of individuals who committed themselves to covenants among equals as the basis for ecclesial and political order. Covenant gained a structural and political form.

2. Covenantal Association. This notion of covenant as the internal structure of a people could then find an echo in the old republican commitment to leagues among the cities and nations. Not only were people to govern themselves through covenant, but they were then to extend this pattern to the relations among nations, thus creating a world order of federations. The world as a federation of republics began to replace the world of imperial designs. A new pattern of government that could be extended from the town to the globe had reached articulation. It reached its explicitly Christian form among the Puritans and its philosophical expression in Immanuel Kant, who envisioned a world order of constitutional republics creating eternal peace.[14]

The covenantal theory of citizenship and association could then be placed within the ancient covenant of historic promise to galvanize the people's hopes for a new creation in which God's governance would be supreme. The millennium of Christ's rule would be a republican covenant of the baptized. It is this millenial hope that lies behind Harrington's vision, a vision that emigrated to the New World.

Covenantalism, in associational if not republican colors, could then be strung out on history's loom. To be a covenanted people meant not only to stand individually in covenant with Christ and collectively with one another, but to be standing in a temporal warp where God's shuttle dispensed a rainbow of divine mercy. Covenant became a way of understanding the epochs of history leading to Christ's ultimate victory over injustice and death.

3. The Puritan Achievement. This "federal theology," as it came to be called, defined the way Puritans understood their role in history.[15] New England gave them a stage on which to play it out. Covenant was a master theme binding together self-understanding, political and ecclesial participation, and history—all in relation to God. The land, however, which had been inextricably tied to Israel's covenants, was reduced here to a stage to be cleared for the historic drama. The American covenant thus began with one partner already disabled and waiting to be completely subdued by the individuals who came to exercise dominion over it.[16]

In spite of these limitations the Puritans successfully brought together central elements of biblical covenant and republican order that have then played their roles in masks pruned of Christian symbols in the modern era. As Max Stackhouse has recently pointed out, it was within the social matrix created by covenantal thinking that our modern notions of human rights found their original germination.[17] These very ideas of personal rights, however, played a not unambiguous role in the subsequent development of federal polity.

VI.   The American Covenant and Its Vicissitudes

At the same time as the American constitutionalists refined covenant into political federalism, they fired off as dross essential parties to the ancient covenant; namely, God and the land. They reduced history to hope and society to an activity apart from government. To understand this crucial development we must unpack these pithy observations.

A.   The Partial Covenant

Israel's ancient covenant had included relations among God, the people, and the land. Christians had augmented this in the classical period by distinguishing between the corporate covenants of the people and the covenant of individuals with God through Christ. It was this individual covenant that wound through the monarchical theology of the Middle Ages to the personal monarchy of each saint emphasized by the Puritans. With the American constitution this individual stripped off his Christian garments and emerged as the individual citizen—at least as male citizens. Women have had to wait two centuries before emerging into full publicity.

Simultaneously the role of God and the land in the full covenant receded to make way for the expression of the individual. The monarchical God operated to curb the passions of the heart in order to enable people to exercise self-control in public debate and industry, but played a declining role in legitimating the structures of public life or ordering the relationships of the full covenant. God came to play a vestigial though not non-existent role in currency, oaths, and electioneering rhetoric.

The land which had formerly bound God and the people together in sustenance and sacrifice was no longer a party to the covenant but a space in which to exercise individual dominion. While many people oscillated between indifferent exploitation and romantic wonder, there was little place in law to secure the land from exclusive control by individuals and later giant corporations parading as persons before the law. It is only recently, as American history has faltered in its achievements and its hopes, that the land has re-emerged as a party with rights in a fuller covenant of life.[18]

One of the reasons that land became an open space rather than a party to the covenant was the peculiar way Americans came to view the course of time. In American mythology the trip across the Atlantic was an exodus from bondage and the forging of a covenant of hope. Americans rejected their past and were obsessed with their future. Destiny, promise and progress obliterated ancestors, tradition, and origins. The land was neither monumental nor defined but bare and limitless, a space in which to expand and express one's sovereignty. It is only with the closing of expansion that our land has begun to fill with historic sites, sacred shrines, and inviolate wilderness areas. The land is beginning to re-enter the American covenant as America re-enters a history that ties it to the rest of the world's time.

B. The Contractual Republic

In focusing the old covenant on the individual the constitutionalists reduced covenant to contract, just as John Locke had translated the covenant idea into his notion of the two contracts forming society and government.[19] The difference between covenant and contract is not merely one between intimate commitment and detached legalism. It is only partially the difference between fundamental commitment and specific promises. It is most importantly a difference between a full covenant that recognizes the claims of God, the land, and the historic people and a partial or fragmented covenant consisting in a series of isolated contracts among individuals. In the American development covenant was practically replaced by contract. The American covenant, in Robert Bellah's terms, was not only broken, but incomplete.[20]

We can see this for instance in the way election changed its practical and theoretical meaning. The election that originated in God's covenant with the Hebrew people had become, with medieval kingship, a divine election of a king. From there it devolved to being the appointment of any individual for public office by the saints who lived under Christ's monarchy in their hearts. With the American constitution elections became a regular pattern of appointing officers by majority vote of the citizens. God no longer elected either a people or individuals.

What fell out here, to the subsequent frustration of all rational democrats, was the acknowledgement that the election of an individual to office is much more than a tally of individual desires.[21] In an election the decisive questions emerge once again: What kind of people are we? Who can best personify us as a people? Who best represents not our rational, contractual interests but our very persona on the stage of history? Who is most likely, not to honor some implicit contract (or mandate) between us and the candidate but to give honor to us as a people of this land?

All of these questions, blown up in the drama of an election campaign, are the "irrational" issues that lead us back to the fact that election is the process of establishing and reaffirming a full covenant, not simply a contract to exercise an office with a legal job description.

Because of their desire to protect the liberty and property of individuals, the constitutionalists began the process whereby the goal of full publicity was lost in the erection of walls to create privacy by protecting property from tyranny.[22] The constitution became a bulwark for privacy rather than a grammar of publicity. Nevertheless, it did clear the ground for a new way to put together the elements of the ancient full covenant. It has forced even the religious traditions of our culture to transform themselves in order to help establish a new covenant of publicity to overcome the privation of the old.

The institutional form of this privation occurred in the separation of society from government. Society was founded on the first of Locke's contracts, government on the second. The initial purpose for making the distinction was to limit governmental tyranny over people's voluntary covenants. In order for free individuals to respond to the call of God and conscience, the powers of government had to be limited to a constitutional form.

There have been two problems with this distinction. First, the human need to act within a full covenant was ignored. "Society" dissolved into a marketplace that could not sustain a full covenant. Instead people were caught between two spheres—one that sought to secure their personal rights to make contracts and the other that cloaked economic relations in a blanket of privacy.

The second problem arose in this new meaning of privacy, which was extended to large corporations. The private sphere, rather than being the repository of the full covenant, became immune to it. In the public effort to solve the abuses of racial and sexual discrimination and economic injustice the governmental sphere has expanded to the point of seeking to claim to be the exclusive bearer of the full covenant.

In short, reality has exploded the Lockeian distinction of society and government. Instead we have the mantle of the full covenant in the wardrobe of the welfare state without the independent seedbeds for the voluntary covenant with God. The contractual republic suffers from the contradiction between the original fullness of covenant and its actual tendency to separate into enclaves of privilege and exploitation.

C.   The Covenant of Freedom

What was lifted up in the American covenant was the people as a collectivity of persons expressing their freedom. Providing a governmental structure to perfect and expand the public world was the signal accomplishment of the founders' legislation. A process was set in motion that eventually drew slave and immigrant, male and female, aborigine and newcomer into fuller publicity. The constitution established a republic of republics federated into a unity in foreign affairs and a plurality in domestic life.

We can understand the American constitution as an incomplete effort to guarantee a series of public spaces where citizens could argue out their common life without arbitrary interference from monarchs, generals, and the mob. What they were very good at, as Hannah Arendt has observed, was clearing away the hindrances to this public life—

kingship and its deity, arbitrary arrest, petty tyrannies, and democratic excess. What they were not so good at was creating structures that would maximize participation—such as parties (non-existent in the constitution), popular councils, and, for Arendt, a structure of wards and federated assemblies.[23]

However, it is not clear that these purposes could even be achieved legislatively or through a legal constitution. These are really, from the covenantal perspective, products of the full covenant—how people live out the *oikos* constituted with God, the land, and their primary groups. It is a task that demands more than a conception of free individuals and legal processes.

The American covenant gained constitutional expression with some costs but with some victories as well. It offered a structure for federal republicanism which has been imitated and emulated around the world in various ways—in South America, Vietnam, India, and Germany, not to mention the Soviet Union.[24] The costs we are increasingly aware of—individualistic privacy, personal isolation and the loss of little publics, destruction of the land, and a failure of cultural coherence. However, the achievement needs to be remembered lest its shadows engulf it in a barbaric oblivion.

In order to bring us to the present engagement of covenantal and republican traditions we need to understand more exactly the shape of modern federalism's defects and the character of its expansion to a global symbol of right order.

D. Covenantal Crises

The American covenant has developed along two primary fault lines. Irreducible tensions along these two lines have created the earthquakes that have threatened American society at its foundations. The first is the relation of the little and the larger covenants, between the specific constituent and the inclusive general publics. The second is the expansion of original covenants to include wider groups. The first is over scale, the second over participation. The thrust toward expansive inclusion found an imperial face in the notion of American "manifest destiny" and a republican face in the extension of the vote to the unpropertied, former slaves, and women. Today it reaches a new challenge in the citizenship of the refugee.

These are not peculiarly American problems. An examination of them may well be useful in understanding the dilemmas of the federal hope in other societies as well. Let us first look at the shape of the covenantal challenge in the American Civil War, one echoed in many other societies.

The question of the relation of the little and the larger covenants in American history reached its most poignant intellectual expression in the work of John C. Calhoun of South Carolina. Calhoun was one of the most eminent statesmen of the ante-bellum years.[25] He was the son of sturdy Scotch Presbyterian settlers in upland farm country. Reared in the republican perspectives of the Revolution, he thought the patterns of covenant instilled by his forebears without necessarily speaking the language. His was the secularized language of federalism, yet he lifted up most sharply the clash between limited and larger covenants.

Calhoun understood that any political order is embedded in a wider social and economic matrix. Legal structures are only a partial expression of the full covenant of people's lives. For Calhoun this meant that local conditions (that is, people's lived *oikos*) should dictate the shape of the wider covenant. True federalism required the primacy of local constitutions. The states of the federal union should retain their sovereignty. They should have the authority to nullify the acts of the central government. At that point *con*federation became inextricably bound to a theory of local sovereignty, federalism with the idea of indissoluble union and ultimate sovereignty of the central government. One became the wisdom of "states rights," the other of nationalism. The Civil War was a bloody effort to settle this argument through violence.

Abraham Lincoln emerged as the prophet of the wider covenant's permanence, pitted against Calhoun's belief in the voluntary confederation serving the smaller covenants. The Civil War was first of all a controversy over the indissolubility of the wider union but soon became an argument over the fullness of its covenant and the rights of all people to public life within it.

At this point we can see how the second fault line intersects the first, for the pressure behind the federal controversy was whether or not slaves were to participate in the full covenant of publicity set forth by the republican experiment. The clash between the two federal notions was forced by the question of slavery. Who is called to full covenantal publicity?

This is the penetrating issue raised by Robert Bellah in *The Broken Covenant*. The brokenness of the American covenant lay in its inability to accommodate the aboriginal Americans and African slaves into its fold. The promise of the covenant has been its gradual effort to bind these people, as well as women, in public covenant. Its distortion has lain in the imperial effort to force other nations into the little covenant of the American people. The promise has been easier to comprehend, since it has required that American practice conform to republican principles. The arguments of Martin Luther King, Jr. epitomize the struggle to bind all Americans in a republican covenant—that is, a fully partic-ipatory one grounded in our history.

The distortion has been more difficult to resolve, because it de-mands a new engagement with the land and with the God of history within the covenantal process. It is not a question of the covenant's pop-ulation, but of its founding partners. Dealing with imperialistic and na-tionalistic expansion, Americans, like everyone else, have to come to terms with God's demands within the full covenant.

Divine commands, as Joseph Allen pointed out in *Love and Conflict*, lead us to the full panoply of fundamental human rights as well as an attention to the basic needs of people, especially their economic needs.[26] God's covenantal claims involve more than this, but these claims are fundamental to limiting any imperial effort to force a particular, limited covenant on any people. Within the vision we are exploring here, God's covenant proceeds by building up publics through persuasion.

The claims of the land set limits for resource exploitation in the nationalistic search for military and economic power. As we saw ear-lier, republican theory always has had trouble on this point. The dis-position to coercion ultimately subverts the struggle for publicity. The use of coercion is always a rape of the land. It is only as we help the land re-enter the covenant with its own claims that we can form a wider covenant capable of sustaining not only human life but publicity as well. People's increasing ability to see the globe as one ecology is the first step in building an *oikos* which can sustain a wider republic of persuasion.

E.   Publicity: The Dynamic of Expanding Covenant

The American experience of the tension between little and larger covenants is not unique. Covenant's weakness arises when a people make their covenant into a tool of fear and domination rather than as a means for entering God's wider purposes for all people. This was the Hebrew prophets' continual witness in the face of Israel's pretensions. It was Roger Williams' cry against the arrogance of Massachusetts Bay. It is the World Council of Churches' critique of the covenantal theology of apartheid that has been widespread in South Africa. In all these cases the power of covenant to raise a people into more intense publicity is turned against the struggle of others to come into a public world. Cov-enant becomes an idol in the service of group aggrandizement.

Here the dynamic of expanding publicity challenges the introver-sion of rigid covenants. The God who covenants with people is also the God who confirms them in expanding circles of publicity. Just as a full understanding of publicity demands covenant, so covenant also demands publicity lest it fall into the defile of idolatry. Republican and covenantal traditions can correct each other and draw each other into a fuller expression of God's purposes for human life. Both of them need a God that leads them to more universal covenants with other people and creation. Both of them need to sense their place within the history of their promises.

American crises of federalism and republican expansion have brought to a focus perils confronted in other nations as well—India, Nigeria, the Soviet Union, the Philippines, and South Africa, to name only some prominent examples. These are enduring dilemmas of federal republics. They are also the seedbed where we can see the cross-fertilization between covenantal and republican traditions which can help correct their individual deficiencies and lead us to a fuller life.

F.   The Spread of Federal Republics

It is always difficult to appraise the war from within the smoke of battle. Our times have experienced so much wrenching violence that it is difficult to believe that any divine purpose is at work in them or that any elements of our heritage will survive. However, it is possible to gain some perspective on the conflicts of our time as we seek to trace some responses to God's covenant call to fuller publicity.

The most important fact this book seeks to draw to our attention is that the making of constitutions and the design of federal republics have continued as the major way people try to build peace in the obliteration of old orders. Some see the symbols of this effort as only a thin veneer on the cabinetry of oppression. However, it can also be laying down, like patient sedimentation, the foundation for a culture of republican life. These constitutions and political symbols can become the points of crystallization for a new public order.

The wars of our time are no longer those of imperial expansion, though cold warriors in the superpowers may seek to construe them as such. They are wars for publicity by local peoples. These "wars of liberation," as they are often called, arise when little networks of communication enable isolated groups to taste the intimations of a public life apart from the old patriarchies and hierarchies of clan-based life. They are, in various ways, republican revolutions.[27] Warfare has not ceased, but its reasons have shifted. In this shift we see fresh evidence of people's aspirations for a fuller covenant of public action.

This is all a very contorted process. Inasmuch as we seek to act or respond at all, we must forge some tool to hack through the jungle of confusion. The tool we have chosen is the vision of a federal republic in which many small publics are bound together in a network of covenants embracing both the *oikos* of our landed household and the perfect public where we all are known by God. It is the vision of a global federal republic.

VII.   Toward God's Federal Republic

We have traced the pilgrimage of covenantal understanding and practice through our history, examining its deep engagement with the promises and dilemmas of the republican heritage. Our history and the events of our time evince a longing for a fuller covenant and a more perfect publicity. Binding these two themes together is the purpose of the symbol, God's Federal Republic. American history has been one important stage for the drama of its development. We now pull together our themes with reference to American dilemmas as we look toward the global struggles which have emerged in our generation.

A.   Recovering the Full Covenant
The development of federal theory needs to recover the fullness of the ancient covenant, in which the claims of God, the land, social groups and individuals were recognized within a complex web of mutual obligation. This is not to say that the exact terms of these covenants would be replicated. That would be the death grip of reaction, which frequently occurs under the impact of "modernity." We are witnessing it now in Iran as well as in the resurgence of American fundamentalism.[28]

What we have to do is provide for these original parties in the construction of our current covenants. The original Hebraic covenant contained the people, God, and the land. It is not enough to have a purely secular state if the claims of transcendent loyalty are not mediated to it at least in some indirect way. This is the valid element in traditional religion's criticism of secular constitutionalism. The resources we turn to for meeting these claims are provided by the principle of publicity itself, which provides for free public space in which the claims of God can be exercised through persuasion and argument rather than rack and rule. Where once we turned to kings for this cultural base, now we turn to publics. Here the principles of persuasion supplant those of paternal admonition to forge the tools of public conversation.

The claims of the land, however, need more explicit constitutional articulation. They need direct expression in our political covenants if we are to preserve a world where we can fit and one that is fit to live in. Developing these constitutional covenants is one of the great challenges of our time.

We need to move the arguments over federalism beyond the shell game of political and fiscal power. The clashes over federalism in America in the last century have deteriorated into fights over whose budget will pay for which governmental programs. Shall it be a responsibility of the states, or of the central (miscalled "federal") government? Is this or that civil matter properly within the jurisdiction of a state legislature or the national congress?

Deciding which shell these peas shall hide in is not the central problem of federalism, though it is one facet of it.[29] The full covenant asks about reciprocities among the partners, about the impact of economic activity on people's capacities for publicity, about the welfare of the land, the memories and hopes present in this chapter of history, and governmental openness to wider publics. Questions of the shell game need to consider the shape of our economy and culture as well as of our laws and fiscal policies. That way lies the path to fuller covenant and a more adequate federal vision.

The second aspect of finding a fuller covenant demands that we evaluate our attention to legal procedures from the standpoint of their effects. As Joseph Allen maintains, human rights cannot be simply a matter of due process but of meeting the real need of the neighbor. Publicity is one of these essential needs and purposes of human life. We have to ask, therefore, whether the legal process enhances people's capacity for publicity. Filling in some of the details of this criterion will be the task of the next chapter.

B.   From Separatism to Covenanted Publicity

Republicanism has moved from a theory of "mixed estates" to guarantee stability to one of a "separation of powers" to prevent tyranny. The victory of the mixed polity was a civil peace in which people could anchor a civic consciousness in their hearts.[30] The triumph of the separated polity was the establishment of personal liberty. A full covenant now demands a framework for covenanted publicity. Personal liberty is not enough to maintain a republic. A mixture of estates or classes is not enough to secure economic justice. The principles of publicity and covenant have to be extended into what we call the economic sphere as well.

We see these efforts in the struggle for economic democracy, co-operatives, and participatory management.[31] Even as covenant directs us back to the interrelationships within the whole *oikos* of work, family, land and faith, so the drive for a fuller federal republic requires extension of public principles into the basic structures of our lives.

In the political sphere proper it means the ongoing efforts to lift up expressions of covenant which expand the public and include its essential parties. Rev. Jesse Jackson has sought to do this explicitly in his idea of the rainbow coalition as expression of a fuller American covenant. The New Abolitionist Covenant has sought to do it with regard to nuclear armaments. Covenants for racial justice, ecological conservancy, labor-management relations, and community relations demand continual argument and rearticulation in order to fill out the otherwise sclerotic strictures of the law.[32]

The social separatism pointed out by Michael Walzer resulted from the defense of personal liberty. However, personal liberty has often degenerated into a privatistic isolation which subverts the very publicity it sought to advance. We need to move beyond simply the defense of individuals to a nurture of the relationships people develop as they struggle for fuller public expression and confirmation. The right to privacy has been recognized as a constitutional right. Now we need to see that the right to public participation is not only a constitutional right but a constitutional principle as well.

Finally, in the search for a more profound federalism we need to examine the voluntary associations, corporations, professional and occupational groups, unions, clubs, and societies to see the crucial role they play in preserving publics and constructing covenants. This web of "mediating structures," as Peter Berger and Richard Neuhaus claim, exists not only to defend individuals from the state but to enable people to achieve public life and participate in wider covenants than simply those of the family.[33] In the last chapter I shall turn to the Church as a peculiar kind of association. It has a crucial role to play in the creating of a truly federal republic.

Federalism is not merely a matter of law and constitution but of the vital activity of these associations. In them people cultivate the capacity to covenant and act in public. Without them the glue of persuasion cracks under the force of military and economic coercion. Each one of them, especially the professions and unions, needs to be criticized from the standpoint of whether they contribute to the establishment of wider publics and fuller covenants.[34]

C. Toward a Covenant Culture

These efforts to draw our political and economic institutions into line with our covenantal and republican convictions must have a cultural ground of powerful symbols, loyalties, and a world view. We must articulate a general orientation to life that yields the echoes found in federal republican orders. Drawing on our survey of the rise of these two symbols we can point to some of this culture's key components.

1. From a Commercial to a Media Public. We can see two previous eras of republican thought that rested on two different cultural orders. The first, classical model rested on a world of graded hierarchies—kings, nobles, aristocrats, and bonded people. This yielded the famous mixed polity based on the character common to each class.

The second, mercantile era found republican roots in a different culture, one based on the relationships rising out of market relations. Honor was replaced with honesty, crown was replaced with credit, covenant was reduced to contract. This culture of individualistic contractualism has permeated every aspect of our life from marriage to psychotherapy, yet even as it reaches its culmination we enter a third era in which to anchor republican visions—the media era.

To focus on media and electronic communications is not to ignore the grinding coercion of much economic and military life. It is to add a crucial new dimension. We are increasingly tied together with other peoples through instant communication. Their wars are our wars, their torture chambers are ours, their beauty is our beauty, their heritage feeds our own. It is a world of refugees and of expanding recognition.

The media revolution is changing the shape of warfare and diplomacy. It is diluting provincialism and nationalism in the face of global sensibilities. It provides a new base for a vision of covenanted republicanism. The media culture has to be treated as a fact of human relationships at least as decisive as was the marketplace in the industrial revolution and feudal bonds in earlier times.

Media relationships not only bring the value of publicity to the fore, they also reshape it. In many ways the possibility of publicity is closer to more people than ever before. A personal incident of injustice once left to oblivion's mortuary can now become a global picture, whether it is a starving baby in Ethiopia or a political prisoner in South Africa. Even relatively closed societies begin to be cracked by the public eye of television. What was once hidden in darkness begins to grope for the light. A fully public world begins to enter our imagination.

There are, of course, distortions which the current state of our media create, not only in what it is to be a public person, but also in our vision of a truly federal republic. Our media can create centralization of power in charismatic leaders. They can undo the covenantal bonds of small and middle-sized communities. They can throw people into passive projections rather than active communication, dialogue and debate. The commercial slogan can replace the congressional argument.

Indeed, it is the hand of commerce which has stained the very symbol of publicity. In our context here publicity means our striving for expression and confirmation within a covenanted public. For much of the popular mind it means a form of deception in which we trade appearance for integrity. But such a conception of public interaction is ultimately privatistic in its assumptions. It assumes that we are really known only in our private lives where, supposedly, pretense is set aside. The next chapter will flesh out a position quite different from this misconception.

The struggle over the meaning of publicity in a media culture lies at the heart of the transformation we are experiencing. It is a development rich in possibilities as well as perils. This is only to say, however, that the shape of media becomes the terms in which we work out the dynamics of publicity and covenant in our time. The media of communication form a cultural ethos and set of practices which compose the raw materials we must work with in our time.

2. From Instrumental to Covenantal Reason. A culture includes an awareness of how we think. The dependable relationships of a common life rest on a trustworthy notion of how other people are thinking. Public discourse is especially concerned with developing common ideas about the thought processes of participants. Thus, our view of reason is an important component of our public culture.

In reviewing the development of republican thought we saw that the reason of the classical era was concerned with conformity to a well-proportioned harmony. The most important regulative form was the body itself—its head, hands, feet, and heart. Reason was imbued with the images of body thinking. To be a reasonable being was to be governed by thinking that conformed to the proportions of the human body.

In the explosion of science in the seventeenth and eighteenth century a mechanistic and instrumental view of reason emerged to undergird the new politics. Reason was the capacity to put together means and ends. Rationality meant the conformity of means to whatever ends had been chosen by a free and independent self. This reason exploded the conformities of the old order and made possible the advance of human liberty.

In our own time we are aware of the limits of this instrumental reason and are beginning to recover a covenantal theory of reason. Here reason arises in the generation of resonance and trust among beings. This resonance theory, so closely allied with the focus on atomic physics and electromagnetic theory, finds a more social expression in the concept of covenant. Covenantal reason is that form of rationality in which beings seek to ally themselves along the lines of resonance with the other beings in their world. Reason is an effort to bring relationships to awareness and formulate them as conscious commitments over time. Reason is the articulation of covenants that undergird us. It is the capacity to construct new covenants and projects to guide us into the future.

This is the direction a theory of reason can take in our own time. It is congruent with our scientific as well as our political understandings. "Come, let us reason together" is not merely a biblical aphorism endorsed by a wily politician, but an insight into the very nature of reason itself.

Reason, then, is to be understood in relational rather than individualistic terms. It is not merely the architectonic plans of a builder but the dialogue and logic of an argument within a wider covenant. It is mental activity oriented toward some kind of conformity to patterns that transcend the actors, but these are not patterns given in biology. They are patterns flowing from the historic relationships of a people. Reason, like language, is historic and social. This is the kind of approach to reason that can undergird movement toward a fuller federal republic.

3. Nature as a Resonant Covenant of Being. This concept of reason, as I pointed out earlier, is knit within a wider concept of nature—the given being that cradles our life. Nature itself is a covenant of being. This is a term found not only among theologians like Karl Barth or Thomas Oden, but psychologists and philosophers as well. On the republican side we find the pluralist philosopher William James speaking of the federal republic of being. This was the only way James could hold together his perception of real pluralism and the undeniable connectedness of life. His Harvard compatriot, Alfred North Whitehead, echoed this thrust with his vision of a world in which even the relationships among stones had a dynamic quality of resonance which he called prehension.[35]

For all of these people life itself exhibits a kind of voluntary, pluralistic quality, yet is held together by affinities and resonances which point to the argument of a republic or the mutualities of covenant. With conceptions like these we can direct our thought, ethics, and faith to a world which is historical and a history which is bound to nature. With this view of nature we can begin to reintroduce the land to our covenants and our compacts to the divine source of all being.

4. Time as Promise. We in the North Atlantic countries have passed through a time of shattered dreams. However, dreams are built more on hope than success, and hopes spring from awareness of our deepest needs and longings. We need to move from private dreams to public visions, much as Martin Luther King, Jr. did in his famous "I Have a Dream" speech at the Lincoln Memorial. Visions spring from experiences of that which energizes and elevates our lives to new levels of power and worth. Events of loving acceptance, friendship, liberation from oppression, and victory over our fears arouse in us the hope for a future in which the hidden secrets of our dreams become a public confession of our vision.

Time is thus the struggle of our hopes, it is the journey toward promises embedded in our visions. It is the matrix of promises from which we launch our search for more resonant being. It is anticipation of as well as a trust in a public bound in covenantal trust. Understanding time within the context of a struggle for more resonant life points to what people usually call the "felt quality of time," as if time were an object totally outside us. The notion of time I am pointing to here is more closely bound to the activity of our history and of the divine struggle to complete a fully public covenant of being.

It is not possible to develop a philosophy of time here, but, as with the other components of a covenantal culture, to point out a direction for us to take as we seek to orient our lives toward each other and our common public world. This notion of time as the working out of a promise and a hope is a "political" conception of time. It is also a covenantal one, for it binds us to generations past and present who struggle toward the light of full recognition. Like covenantal reason, it is a view of our passage that envelops the ticking of our clocks within the echoes of our relationships. It moves time from being a track of mechanistic incrementalism to being the dimension of promise in a magnetic field created by profound experiences of life in public covenant. This is the direction we could take to unfold a covenantal understanding of time.

D. The Promise of God's Federal Republic

These cultural components of media relations and conceptions of reason, nature and time take us to the general ideas and values which orient us in our action and relationships. They ground our efforts at covenant and publicity in the very nature of things. They provide a perspective through which we can see our lives as a struggle toward a fuller covenant and a more perfect public. They draw us to a certain awareness of our possible future. On the basis of all we have surveyed, it is a future of full presence within God's Federal Republic.

It has been the burden of these past three chapters to lift up the historic functions of kingship in our lives and the way republic and covenant take up these functions of stability and cultural grounding within a wider and more satisfying framework. The symbol of God's Federal Republic serves to bring together in a vivid way these two strands of our heritage which we share increasingly with other peoples.

By speaking of *God's* Federal Republic we point to the future wider public to which we are drawn by hope and promise. This visionary ideal is rooted in our own most precious experience, but it also has been refined by our thought and conversation. It sloughs off some of the blood and dirt of our sufferings in order to become a mirror for our judgment and our hopes. It can serve as a critical lever against our present pretensions at publicity and covenant. It can help us criticize those of us who call our nations federal republics and God's only hope for humanity.

It can also serve to guide our actions toward paths congruent with the divine promises embedded in an historic faith expressed in Abraham and Sarah's journey, Jeremiah's judgment and Jesus' community. Yet we also see some things unique in our own time. Our hope has a slightly different content now. St. Augustine had seen in all our struggles the craving for peace—a peace of contemplative order. It was this kind of hope of peace that coursed through Christian veins for many centuries. However, it was a conception of peace which was often privatized into the life of the single individual. It easily was turned against the covenantal hope of full publicity. It could rest with a kingship of Christ over a City of God that was reduced to being a quiet and orderly household.

The symbol of God's Federal Republic fills out the hope for the City of God in a different way. By it we are moved by the promise of full covenantal publicity, in which we shall know as we are known in the conversation that finds the ultimate God presiding over our controverted arguments. By it we can find a Christ who persuades us in the midst of our covenanting and leads us to a more perfect republic whose founder is God. This is the symbol and the vision arising in our history. It is the task of the next part to fill in the vision so that it can guide our lives.

5 | The Covenanted Public: A Contemporary Theory

Federalist and republican traditions have a mutual affinity for each other. They need one another to mend their weaknesses and to confirm their strengths. A covenantal approach to life needs a commitment to publicity lest it be reduced to a narrow enclave of the elect. Republican concepts need covenantal visions to secure them from the temptations of libertarianism on the one hand or statism and nationalistic arrogance on the other. Both are needed in concert to draw us out of the deprivation of our individual isolation.

Many elements of our vision of a federal republic as the center of our governing symbol are now in place. Now we need to refine this central symbol in contemporary terms, giving it greater clarity so that it can become a model for action and aspiration. First, I want to establish the main features of an approach to public life within a covenantal framework. Then we must look at the direction an appropriate theory of personality would take within this framework. In the next chapter I shall turn to the expicitly theological dimensions of our engagement.

I. The Meaning of Public

Our contemporary notion of the classical idea of public is mediated to us through the Anglo-American thought of people like John Dewey, Walter Lippmann and John C. Murray, and the European reflections of Hannah Arendt and Jürgen Habermas.[1] Both strands agree that the public is a kind of discourse to which everyone has potentially equal access, whose content is people's common concerns, and whose outcomes are governed by reason and persuasion rather than by force or deception. Moreover, as I noted in Chapter Two, this public demands some common world of basic cultural reference points as well as material bases and geographical space in order to exist. A public is a peculiar pattern of relationships among people inhabiting this world together. What then are the meanings of these themes of participation, commonality, persuasion and worldliness?

A. Participation

People differ in their extrapolation of these four central components. With regard to participation some may stress the equality of access to the public realm. People should have equal opportunity to publish their lives and engage in public discourse, whether they decide to do so or not. Others emphasise an equality of power within the public realm. Certainly equality of access is important. Moreover, we face real contradictions when we start forcing people to participate in public life, as Michael Walzer has pointed out. However, with a broader sense of what publicity means, we need to stress the importance of actual participation in some kind of public or a variety of publics. Without this actual participation, the publics die and we ourselves never experience the risky entry into the presence of wider judgment and wider power. Ultimately, in religious terms, we shrink from encounter with the power of the living God. A theory of the public needs to emphasize actual participation in the acts of publicity.

We can also affirm that some kind of rough equality of power is necessary in order to preserve the persuasive quality of the relationships. Moreover, this must be an equality of access to information. This information, these basic facts of the argument, must be available for examination and testing by all. In this respect the requirements of science are the same as for a public. Habermas, Lippmann and Dewey all argue this point rigorously and persuasively, though with differing approaches.

Equality of power, however, cannot exist apart from actual participation. Power is not a substance that can exist apart from relationships. It emerges in the actual activity of participation in decision-making, forming of coalitions, the conflict of opposition and argument. It too must be seen as a dimension of participation. Rather than treat equality as a separate mark of a public realm, I include it under the category of participation in order to stress the entry into engagements and the building of relationships that really characterize public life itself. Too great a stress on some mathematical equality can too easily fall back into a focus on characteristics of participants rather than of their common life.

Participation contains another important implication which decisively distinguishes a public from a family or an association based on a familial model. Here the natural and intrinsic inequality between parent and child is set aside. A public is inherently a realm for adults, who at least have the potential for equal participation.

The public's peculiar demand for publicity can be extended beyond the family to the economic realm in general. Here is where republicans could take up the socialist flag as easily as the liberal capitalist one. Both approaches assume that one must have some secure, roughly equal economic base in order to participate in a genuine public sphere. Socialists have sought to establish governmental means to control the outcome of public processes, and liberal capitalists have believed that some invisible harmonization would enable a competitive economy to produce the conditions for a public sphere. Here we have the decisive difference between Habermas and Harrington on the one hand, and Milton Friedman on the other.[2]

Participation in the public sphere is so important it emerges as a basic human right. Underlying the rights of property, privacy, individual liberty, and freedom we must see the fundamental right of people to have a public life. The right to privacy is only an instrumental right subordinate to the right to publicity. This basic right must be given sharper clarity in order to regulate how we approach appeals to these other rights. Claims to exclusive use of property have to be seen in terms of their impact on the need to preserve spheres of public action. Claims to unlimited autonomy have to be regulated by the need to enable people to engage in the arguments of public life. This misplaced emphasis on the right to privacy in American life today only aggravates our individualistic isolation and ultimately expands bureaucratic control, rather than open up new arenas of public participation. The formulation of a right to publicity would help redress this imbalance.

This right to publicity is not to be seen only in terms of some individual characteristics possessed by individuals as human beings. From the standpoint of God's covenantal engagement with us, the call into the full light of publicity also evinces the divine purpose. Our right to publicity flows from God's covenant with us in this divine intention as much as it flows from any intrinsic qualities we have as human beings. Public participation is a divine demand that flows from the characteristics of divine covenant itself, a theme we will explore in the next chapter.[3]

B. Commonality

The second point of agreement is that a public concerns common things. Commonality has a different meaning for a public than it does for a community. In a public these are not matters that pertain to each individual, such as the need for necessities. They are matters that arise out of the fact of living together. They are the results of what Dewey calls the "consequences" of our interaction.[4] The "common man" who acts in the public, as Carl Friedrich has maintained, is one who is concerned with matters common to many other people.[5] Public discourse focuses on what we have in common because of our desire to live together and to meet the demands of our life, which may include in some way our necessities, together. A public, therefore, does not naturally arise out of our economic or biological necessity. It has a gratuitous, unnatural quality. It is a cultural creation. It is a kind of creaturely grace.

Because the public focuses on the commonalities of our life together, it excludes many aspects of our life that we have as creatures or as unique personalities. It excludes both the animal and the angelic. This is how it differs from community, in which everything is equally exposed.[6] The public, by its very nature as a realm of structured appearances, creates a realm of excluded concerns—the private sphere. The distinction, not found in community, is crucial to the viability of a public.

In order for this more restricted category of concerns to be common they have to be objective and visible. Feelings and thoughts cannot directly enter the public realm. This is what Lippmann and Arendt mean when they call the public a realm of appearance, of objective disclosure.[7] It is a dramatic sphere, a theater of effect and consequence. Without this capacity for objectification and appearance there can be no public. At the same time, as Lippmann pointed out, our incapacity for bringing the invisible world into this visible arena is one of the great frustrations of public life. It is also the point from which we will depart to develop our understanding of sin in the next chapter.

The tension inherent in the dynamic of appearance is summed up in the contentious character of the word *publicity*. The degeneration of publicity into chicanery impoverishes our language. Publicity, quite properly, is the activity of making something public. Publicity is simply the process of becoming public. As one early publicist put it, publicity "is the entire gamut of an idea or of an institution."[8] Without publicity, in this sense, there can be no public. Publicity is the action of exposing some claim to public inspection, debate, and refinement.

The problem, as we have found out, is that unrestrained hucksters have violated the canons of truth and sincerity in order to make quick private gains. Because of our inadequate publication of the invisible facts surrounding the published ones, the act of publicity itself has become suspect. But the answer to this is not to extinguish the public and remand these concerns to a few experts. It is to have more publicity, a greater sense of public responsibility among professions, and more imaginative ways of revealing the inevitable duplicity in our midst.[9] From the standpoint of the general theory I am advancing, publicity is the heart of human existence as it strives toward a more perfect public. Without it we stumble in the darkness of the wild imaginings of our own hearts, the sheol of amnesia and insanity.

C. Persuasion

Because the public is a realm of rough equality, actions and responses must arise from the persuasion, consent and compromise of the participants. To the degree that equality of strength and power characterizes the participants, they must resort to argument in order to change each other and forge a common course of action. This is the meaning of treating other people as ends rather than as means. Persuasion is intrinsic to the nature of public life.

The persuasive character of a public depends on its being a product of culture. Persuasion is a certain kind of communication pattern in which the behavior of others is affected by appeals to the implications of commonly held convictions about their history, their life together, their hopes, the facts at hand, and the nature of reality in general. Habermas has spelled out in detail how the very logic of discourse itself provides a common frame of reference underlying the persuasion process. Dewey, like Lippmann, appealed to the process of scientific inquiry as forming the world of assumptions making possible genuine public discourse, persuasion and decision.[10]

This appeal is by no means limited to strictly intellectual, rational, and cognitive claims. It embraces the whole arena of symbolic action. Habermas has diligently refined the way in which the very structure of language and "speech acts" constructs the basis of public life. Publicity is above all an activity of self-presentation. The eye and the ear are our primary instruments for public life. Speech and clothing are their media. Habermas has filled in the intellectual side of this publicity. Dewey, Lippmann and Richard Sennett have fleshed out its more symbolic features.

Awareness of symbolic depth is central to Lippmann's and Dewey's understanding of publicity. The power of symbolic action may threaten to overturn the ordered public, but without it we lack the motivation to participate.[11] The impact of immediate artifacts, clothing, and the whole panoply of artistic production can overwhelm our search for enduring covenants with the gratifications of our narrower and more intense desires. However, we cannot abandon either the symbolic or the rational components of this engagement in public covenant. Our only alternative is to entertain these social gods with a reasoned devotion and cultivate those with the most potential for preserving our fullest publicity and our widest covenants. The role of symbols must revolve around the creation and continued vitalization of a world of common commitments and understandings. Finally, the public arises around the search for a truth by which people can live together.

With Habermas we see a fulsome theory of the way language functions to enable us to come to a consensual kind of truth through public discourse. It is a philosophical development of the theory of reason we already lifted up in the earlier chapters. Theologically it is a theory of *covenantal reason*, in which "truth" emerges out of the public argumentation within a covenantal framework. It arises not merely as a consensus among participants, but also stands in continual judgment and revision through God's insistence on leading us to ever larger covenants with the whole creation.

D. Worldliness

Everyone agrees that a public finds existence in the context of some kind of "world" of common reference, be it stories, facts, agreements, or laws. That is, the reality of a public takes form as a *re*public—a particular constellation of "public things." This array of public things is known to all. It has publicity. It is not hidden, but is open to everyone.

Arendt focused on the way in which stories house our potent symbols and form a common world of reference that makes persuasion possible. With stories we have drama, the arts, and all kinds of symbolic action. They provide scripts by which we can move into action with some sense of security, detecting our entrances and exits, our antagonists and friends. The symbolic world of narrative and devotion creates a frame of meaning, a world of reference enabling us to engage in a common drama of action. It is a world, like that of Genesis' creation, made possible by speech. Word, world, and truth are linked together in the dynamics of public action.

The conservation of this public world makes possible the stability of the republic. Its creation lies at the root of the ancient search for republican stability. In our own time we have moved from a worldly stability founded on patriarchy and kingship to one resting on election and covenant. Its most pronounced political form is in presidential election and constitutionalism. This is the cultural world making possible a federal republic.

This world is not only a cultural one, however. It is also a physical and geographical reality involving our architecture and land use. How we arrange our areas for work, rest, recreation, and worship articulates our sensibilities about the nature of our public order. This worldly stage for publicity in one era lives on to shape the next. Care of this world is crucial to a vital public life.

This life upon the land shapes the way we engage in work, family, and religious life. The Greeks called this dense triangle of activity the "oikos." The shape of this *oikos* deeply conditions the kind of public life we can have. Role assignments in the family and at work decide who can enter wider publics. The way we live on the land shapes whether we shall sit alone in our separate suburban homes, or meet each other in many intersecting concerns in the public square. Our *oikos* can be a cradle of our publicity or a tomb of isolation.

Marxists and socialists have focused on the way the *oikos* must be transformed in order to create a public life, but have often lost sight of the very publicity it needs to sustain. Feminists and liberation movements have also demanded change in our worldly base in order to find a wider public life. The importance of this kind of transformation for creating a world for covenant and publicity must not be overlooked.

This thumbnail sketch of four central characteristics of a public—participation, commonality, persuasion, and worldliness—open up many avenues of inquiry we cannot pursue here. In order to develop this contemporary theory of the public as the frame for reshaping our theological view we need first to attend to the central dynamics of the public realm and then to the theory of personality which accompanies it.

II. The Dynamics of Publicity

The struggle for publicity leads us to search for a more adequate public. In the give and take of demands, discussion, argument and persuasion, we set in motion the dynamics of emancipation and legitimation. The public drama that emerges is sustained by a variety of actors and scripts. To fill out a contemporary conception of public life we turn to a consideration of the dynamics of emancipation, legitimation, and plurality.

A. Publicity as Emancipation

The transition from domestic privacy to civil publicity demands not only a broader sphere of participation, but also particular powers, abilities, and strengths in the participants. Emancipation symbolizes our entry into this world and the acquisition of the powers necessary to publicize ourselves in it. To find a confirming public we must be able to *profess* our convictions, needs, interests, hopes, and understandings. We must express our claims on others in the public argument. The act of emancipation must begin with the act of profession. Profession is the public dynamic by which we express our lives in the search for resonance and confirmation.[12]

Groups also experience the dynamic of profession as they seek to sustain and enhance their own internal patterns of mutual confirmation and affirmation. In professing their own vision they seek a wider confirmation, a wider world, and a deeper resonance among their members.

In this resonance of the professing group we find the generation of power. Here is the enthusiasm of the movement, the sect, the battalion. The kind of confirmation that arises in a shared anticipation of change is crucial to emancipation. Power, as Arendt held, resides in the mutuality of promising made possible by this fundamental resonance.[13]

Habermas seems to be getting at the same motif through the concept of communicative competence—that is, the capacity to participate in rational discourse that advances in the direction of an ideal speech situation characterized by equality of participation, freedom from coercion, sincerity of participants and the exercise of critical dialogue. This ideal reflects the components of a public we have already examined. Even in Habermas' work it is a vision offering judgment as well as hope in our struggle toward a more perfect public.[14]

The weakness in many theories of emancipation is that they overlook the peculiar importance of this speech world and the human relations it orders. The emancipation of the weak and oppressed demands the development of a public conversation in which their reasonable claims can be registered and honored. Their emancipation does not lie merely in the exercise of coercion but in the augmentation of a public in which they can participate. Emancipation is as much a cultural matter of forming a common world of confirmation as it is an economic matter of securing physical resources. It is the form of God's call to a reasonable life within a perfected and universal covenant. In political terms, it is a rational discourse only possible within a federal system which preserves publics of a size and character appropriate for sustained argument.

Having said this I want to point out that the concept of property also arises directly from a theory of the public and of emancipation. The act of profession at the heart of emancipation means making the properties of the self and of the group a basis for communication, whether these be land, goods, personal attributes, or other gifts and achievements. That is, in order to profess ourselves we have to have some basis from which to act—our *properties*, that which is proper to us.

Both Marxists and liberals tried to get at this point but failed to hit it squarely enough. Property is not merely some possession, but the medium for our entering into a public realm and finding confirmation in it. Socialization, from the Marxist vantage point, would be a process of returning properties from their state as alienable things to their rightful role as media of expression and communication. From the standpoint of liberal theory, property "interests" would no longer be looked on as directed back on the narrow household of the private "owner" but on their capacity as avenues into the public life.

From the standpoint of a theory of the public, we must seek ways to transform property relations into being once again matters which are "proper" to a self as a being seeking public action. Thus, everyone must not only have some property, but this property must be oriented to its function of being a medium of publicity. A job, for example, is not enough if it is merely a source of monetary power. Jobs, in reality, are much more in people's lives—a source of general meaning, confirmation, and psychological support. They are a primary stage for public action. People's attitude toward their work reveals the desire for a greater publicity.[15]

Emancipation, then, is grounded in the dynamics of publicity, of creating a confirming public. Within the dynamics of profession we already see the genesis of power. Within those same dynamics we also see the source of authority—a cultural process which is often pitted against the freedom implied in emancipation. However, emancipation and authority share a common root in the generation of a public. The creation of a confirming public makes possible that rational order implied in the idea of legitimation.

B. Publicity as Legitimation

The very possibility of a persuasive order hinges on the presence of legitimate authorization. The dynamic of legitimation entails agreement about the essential character of right social order and of the purposes of social life. Legitimacy demands a mutual belief, a "faithing together," or *con-fidence*. It is the public form of mutual confirmation experienced even in intimate relationships. It is a public confirmation of the common existence of a people. Legitimation rests, then, on a *confession*, just as emancipation rested on a *pro*-fession.

Legitimation exists to the degree that practices, policies, roles, and commands can be tested in public discourse. In this sense, it depends on the capacity to present a rationale based in the common world of the people affected. This is what gives legitimation its rational character.[16]

The very act of publication intrinsic to emancipation always lies at the heart of the preservation of a social order in which people can gain the publicity they need for their lives.

When emancipation and legitimation are cast within the framework of the public we are able to see more clearly the relationship of freedom and authority. Freedom is the capacity for publicity. Authority rests on the confessions publicity makes possible. Freedom and authority have a common ground in the dynamics of publicity.

Inasmuch as legitimacy finally rests on this common public confession and mutual confidence, it appeals to the root dynamics of covenant. Without the process and products of covenanting there can be no public realm of persuasion and argument. There can be no peaceful adjudication of disputes without the benchmarks of judgment provided in an underlying covenant. It is this covenant beneath the constitution that must be lifted up in a theory of covenant publicity. This is the expanded notion of federalism that needs to enter our common vision.

Covenant points not only to the ground of legitimacy but also to the bonds among publics. Covenant forms the tissues of a pluralistic world. What has always been a problem in republican tradition is the historic need for publics to be rather small. Smallness was necessary in order to achieve the high level of mutual recognition, communication, and common faith needed for publicity. The dynamic of publicity inherently creates a plurality of publics rather than a single, uniformly expanding organization. The dynamics of publicity contained in the processes of emancipation and legitimation therefore lead us directly to the structural question of pluralism in the public order.

C. Publicity and Pluralism

Publicity demands and creates a plurality of groups, organizations, and institutions because of three interlocking dynamics. First, our process of emerging into fuller and fuller publicity occurs in groups of varying size and intimacy—families, friends, school, associations and institutions of increasing size. Second, because power resides in groups, the demand for rough equality of power requires the existence of counterbalancing power groups. Third, because the public is essentially a pattern of discourse, it is continually going beyond formal social arrangements and creating new ones. This is particularly true of the distinction between the public and government. Each of these aspects of pluralism flows into the other.

1. Plurality of Scale. By seeing the dynamic of publicity at the center of human activity, we have bridged the usual distinction between public and private. Publicity is a dynamic. The distinction between private and public is structural. What we have is a variety of arenas for publicity differing according to scale. We can see a spectrum of publics from the small association to the great conventions. The dynamics of profession and confession extend from the small mediating group to the large mediated public of the airwaves. They appear in our constituent publics as well as in the inclusive publics of the nations and international confederations.

The style of our profession and the method of confirmation vary whether we are in a marriage, a friendship, family, club, or church. Each of these groups has a certain integrity because of its size and the kind of rewards we find there. They establish our initial confirmation in this world. Since we are largely involuntary members of these groups, we become confirmed simply by our existence rather than our achievement. There is therefore often a deep kind of resonant acceptance in them. This is one reason why they have frequently been confused with the proper arena of salvation and grace.

As important as they may be, their very exclusivity keeps them from offering patterns of confirmation that can be expanded to include the greater and greater variety of life that human beings experience. Even though these smaller arenas are constantly being broken open by the dynamic of publicity itself, they each retain a peculiar power because of the kind of affirmation, confirmation, and publicity they offer us.[17]

No one of these can or should have an exclusive claim to our loyalty. Neither, however, should the larger institutions deny their integrity. For instance, there are many forces in our own society that would bring into marriage, family, and friendship the patterns usually found in government, law, and business. We start trying to make them just, rational, contractual, or cool.

Certainly intimacy itself, so characteristic of marital values today, demands the kind of self-exposure and mutual confirmation characteristic of publicity. The kind of equality of personal power that makes this process possible and necessary is similar to the equality of power necessary for actual justice. But these expectations of fairness and justice begin to override the spontaneity of mutual self-giving. Desires for equality obliterate the hard fact of inequality between parents and children. We try to make our intimate life into a church or state. An inappropriate public form begins to dissolve the tender nuance of love.

This confusion of spheres also occurs in the opposite tendency to romanticize politics and nationality—cultivating intimate relationships between governors and people, and feeding an expectation that officials ought to be parental to the people. The inescapable fact that publicity emerges in different forms within differently sized groups creates and demands a plurality of groups.

The differences of scale among groups occurs not only because of the developmental demands of the growing and changing person. They also arise from the fact that we pursue differing purposes in life. We have varying interests. Some can be served by small groups, some by those of medium scale, and others only through institutions that embrace a whole territory. Just as we don't need a state to organize softball games, so we find family charity inadequate to organizing an industrial economy. There is an intractable pluralism that arises from the differing ways we seek to publicize our lives in intimacy, play, education, work, scientific research or war.

2. *Plurality of Power.* Plurality is not merely a natural expression of our peculiarities in development and interests. It is also a demand that the value of public life places on our organization of power. The need for power to constrain power has long ago become a simplistic slogan— so much so that it can even be used against the values of publicity itself, as when Richard Nixon appealed to it to block congressional inquiry into his executive actions. Here the doctrine of separation of powers undermined the very republic it was supposed to stabilize. The point of plurality, we must remember, is to make publicity possible, not contravene it.

Obviously, this cannot be the only value in a theory of the public. Yet in some way it is indispensable. Classical liberalism assumed that a competitive market economy would create the plurality of power which would give people the private base they needed in order to make their professions fearlessly in the public order. We often overlook the way some socialist theories also seek to disperse power among communes, cooperatives, and small groups.

Both of these strands of thought knew that power had to be dispersed. Unfortunately, both cultivated in indirect ways a centralization of power, whether in corporate monopolies or in state bureaucracies. Nevertheless, the value itself in a theory of the public must be maintained. What needs to be developed is a fresh perspective on the practical problem, one that keeps the values of publicity clearly to the forefront even as we seek to achieve them through various strategies.

3. *Critical Pluralism.* The public discourse is always a *pro*fession and a *con*fession. Professions usually arise in great profusion because of the inherent variety of personal experience. Confessions, while being a coalescence of past and present professions, usually exist in some variety because of the plurality of interests and bases for commonality. The

struggle for greater commonality and more intense confession inevitably creates critique—a comparison demanding judgment.

Without pluralism a public cannot receive all the peculiar professions of persons and groups, each needing its own language and conventions for its task of confirmation. In the clash of argument each of us is drawn out of the more comfortable confirmations of smaller publics to enter into or create larger ones whose language may be a more reliable guide to thought and action. While we ought to avoid reducing this debate to the metaphor of the marketplace of ideas, it seems unavoidable that truth is more likely to emerge in broader than in narrower publics. Publicity not only gives rise to power, authority, and plurality. It also provides the context for truth-seeking.[18]

The crucial practical import of this plurality can be found in the need to reaffirm the distinction between the public (or the publics) and the state, or governments. That is to say, the power of publicity must always have leverage over the settled institutions of power, and the public must never be reduced to government. The authority of the coercive sectors of life derives from the confession and legitimation of the public. It is finally rooted in the covenants which are created and honored in this public argument.

The older form of this prescription—"society precedes the state"—is not adequate. "Society" meant in fact the collectivity of property holders. It meant that the relationships arising out of economic life and its class structure would determine political life. To say that it is the public which precedes the state affirms that relationships arising out of the dynamics of publicity must take priority over the state. The shift from "possessive individualism" to "public personality" as the basis for the political order is a profound one. It is one of the main colors in the garment I am weaving here.[19]

4. The Limits of Plurality. A plurality of groups and organizations arises because we are people seeking to profess our lives and find confirmation for them. Plurality arises from the dynamic of publicity and is also a value to be sought in order to preserve it. Plurality becomes an ethical ideal within a theory of the public. Pluralism soon becomes a prescription for our tendencies to monopoly and tyranny. By dividing power among many publics, we can curb our tendency to domination. But this pluralistic antidote for our political woes soon reveals its pressing weakness.[20] It is not evident how our energies can be directed to common tasks beyond our immediate self-interest, nor how to ground the resolution of disputes among the groups in a common world. Pluralism undermines the wider public realm.

The main solution to this anarchic fragmentation is some theory of contract, but its strength is limited. In seeking to bring people together for wider aims, it misses the emotional and motivational depth of historic memory, the ordered affections of communal life, or the visionary calls that give a people hope. In trying to present a basis for governmental restraints against tyrannical concentrations of power, it either resurrects a Lockeian social contract myth or buries us in legislation arising from the contracts reached among legislators and narrow interest groups.

In short, the contractarian solution to pluralism's weaknesses founders on a truncated vision of the self as an individual seeking rational self-interest, rather than as a person seeking publicity. The contractarian position does evidence a desire to avoid the sheer imposition of force that has often crushed pluralism, but it misses the wider meanings that can be garnered from the concept of covenanting contained in our religious tradition. We need the voluntarist pulse of contract within the wider body of covenantal bonds.

The limitations within pluralism lead us back to the question of limits within the idea of public and republic itself. I have just mentioned the distortion of republicanism into some statist order of nationhood. The idea of nationalism, in which all the confessions of a people are frozen in a legal order backed up by armed force, fundamentally deranges the processes of publicity. Moreover, the only global vision of human life that nationalism can yield is some contract among "sovereign states." The notion of national sovereignty is a hollow stone for the foundation of a global republic.

The idea of federalism offers a more salubrious way. The federalist theory of a covenant of publics pushes us to develop a better approach to the way an ultimate public order might be represented. Unfortunately, when federalist theories rest on a contractualist understanding of human affairs they easily lead to a legalistic statism rather than a genuine covenant of publics. A federal conception revitalized by its biblical roots can guide us to a way of relating publics that takes into account the underlying importance of covenants with the land, with God, and with the ultimate inclusive public to which we are called. Covenant helps us see that the public realm is not constituted by individuals pursuing private interests but by the web of relationships grounded in a people's history and confession on the land.

D.   The Problem of Representation

A plurality of publics inevitably raises the problem of representation in public life. As Madison and others saw, a democratic republic would have to be a representative one, since only a few can debate the common issues of the many. However, representation in a pluralistic republic involves not merely the way many persons can be represented in one, but how the many publics in turn can be represented in the federation. Publicity in large publics inevitably drives us to some procedure for representation.

By placing this republican problem within a covenantal context we can draw attention to a different view of representation. If the unity of the federation lies in the kinds of relations developed among the many publics, then it is represented not so much in elected delegates as in its underlying covenant. God, that is, the underlying preserver of our life, is present not so much through the king figure, such as the president, but through the sustaining covenants themselves. The question of our relation to a representative takes back seat to the shape and content of the covenants by which power and authority is distributed.

What is important is not so much that a delegate speak our interests to others, but that this delegate speak out of a covenant we share as participants in a complex plurality of publics. When the quandary of democratic representation focuses only on the relation of voters to officials it is reduced to an individualistic calculus. A covenantal theory presses us beyond that to consider the actual web of relationships that bind a whole people together so that all the historic parties to a full covenant can be represented among them—God, the people, and the land. It presses to a theory of representation which asks about the land, future generations, and other people as they are present to the arguments and decisions of public life. By reshaping the question, this covenantal revitalization of federal theory might open up new ways of approaching the relationship of constituent and inclusive publics.

The need to articulate a proper relationship between larger organizations and smaller groups drives us back to the concepts of commonality and worldliness. Every pluralistic theory demands that the plurality of groups have some common consensus for the peaceful adjudication of disputes. This does not mean that we would agree on the important issues, leaving the trivial matters to the plurality of the public. It means that there must be a public world in which the important and divisive issues can be addressed, leaving the less expansive ones to the smaller publics.

A public is marked by participation, persuasion, commonality, and a world of shared symbols and space. The dynamics of publicity unfold through acts of profession and confession which emancipates people from their isolation and legitimates a public order. The trust and promises of covenantal bonds constitute the sinews of public life. They hold people in argument as they search for consensus in the midst of historic change.

The preservation and cultivation of this changing world demands something stronger than consensus. It demands themes that can be introduced with the idea of covenant and its child—federalism. Behind this theory of covenant stands the notion of a God who creates a world through speech and promise—the God of perfect publicity.

The many covenants of public life create a pluralism of arenas which demand federal forms for respecting their integrity and drawing them beyond their weaknesses and limitations. Our little covenants always exist within the wider covenant of God's intentions for the whole creation. These intentions focus on God's desire that we all come out of the darkness of our isolation, fears, and wild imaginings to find the light of mutual expression and confirmation in a world upheld by a persuasive God.

When we see the covenantal context for a federal republic, we can see that these covenants pertain not only to the relations among and within publics, but to the divine ground for each person's life—the covenant with God. Our theory of publicity requires a fuller development of this personal entry into covenant. We need a federal theory of the self as well as of the republic if we are to engage the religious depths of our key symbol.

III.   The Performer Self

Vitalization of public life is not merely a matter of institutional transformation. It demands an appropriate understanding of human personality as well. How are we to understand our individual energies and the way we struggle for publicity and confirmation? How can our deeply interior energies lead us into public life? How do these dynamics engage the institutional life of the public sphere? What psychological tendencies dispose people to public action? What hinders us from a wider existence?

From a societal standpoint we desire not only to find ways that individuals can mobilize the strengths and visions to engage in public life but also to recover those private spheres where these motivations and characters can be cultivated. Moreover, we look to private spheres for additional institutional arenas with which to countervail the pressures of enormous bureaucracies, whether they be governmental or corporate.

Our interest is twofold. First, what psychology is most appropriate for public life in our time? Second, what is the shape and significance of private spheres, both for sustaining personality and for critiquing or offsetting the power of the large organizations that dominate our lives?

This section will focus the psychological question around the possibility of seeing the self as a performer. It will secondarily articulate an understanding of the private sphere in which this performer self is cultivated and in terms of which critical stands can be taken to sustain public life in the face of the clandestinism of large bureaucracies. Obviously our attention here is only to point out the direction that inquiries should be taken in response to our commitment to God's Federal Republic as the central symbol of our faith. Other explorers would have to develop a more detailed theory of the self.

A. The Public Person

The previous chapters have shown how most Christian theories of personality saw the self in monarchical terms. The self, whether feudal, regal, or republican, was a psychological monarchy whose throne could be given over to Christ, reason, or the devil. The public self had to be a repressed self, as Freud so dramatically observed at the watershed into our own time. As this stream has flowed into our present life we have moved from a self of monarchical repression to performative expression, from filial submission to mutual confirmation.

The discovery of an expressive self in the Renaissance and again in the ferment of early revolutions broke the dominance of this view, but it has taken many centuries to begin to move to a self more in line with a federal and republican vision. It is this kind of personality that we need to articulate here. In the language of process philosophers it is a "presidential" self, in which a center of identity within us responds to various feelings, memories, perceptions in an effort to organize them for the activity of expression to others. It is a self constantly reconstructing its identity in the process of self-expression and confirmation.

Another way to speak of this kind of personality is to compare it to the earlier titles of *homo sapiens* (rational self), *homo faber* (self as maker), *homo laborans* (laboring self), and *homo symbolicus* (self as symbol user). Each term lifted up a central dynamic of human life in order to create a coherent philosophy. The governing symbol of Federal Republic leads us to the self as *homo publicans*—the self as seeking publication in the midst of others in a public world. It is also a picture of the self as *homo foedans*—the self as a covenant maker in a public world.

In this approach to personality we see the self as driving toward public disclosure. The self is led by a longing for publicity. Its energies are not merely inchoate instincts, neither are they directly longing for sociable companionship. We do long for gratification of our basic needs, but it is a gratification that proceeds from bodily survival to worldly confirmation. We do long for sociableness but it is a sociality that presses beyond the intimate to a more public realm of profession and wider confirmation. The two dynamics of profession and confirmation are nodal points in the development of a performing and public self.

1. Profession. In order to enter a wider public we must be able to publicize our existence. We must make a profession of ourselves. We see here a self intrinsically ordered toward publicity. Publicity denotes all those activities by which people make themselves visible to others in order to establish some confirmation. This effort may drive us to submit completely to the world as we think others perceive it. We will do anything to be recognized on their terms. However, we may also diligently seek to reshape the world we have in common in order to gain confirmation within it, whether through the overt demands of the child or the subtle manipulations of the diplomat. When neither of these approaches works we often turn within our minds and remake them so as to gain some sense of confirmation. Our efforts at publicity and confirmation may take many convoluted forms, some of which we think of as normal and others as deviant and sick, even evil. The drive for publicity underlies our myriad manifestations of the human.

In the act of profession we use our properties as a basis for communication, whether these be land, goods, personal talents and attributes, or other gifts and achievements. That is, in order to profess ourselves we have to have some basis from which to act in a confirming world—our properties, as we observed earlier. These properties, however, do not spring merely from our own labors or individual natures, but are media of our relationships with others in a common world.

Our first efforts at publicity take place in very small circles—with our family and a few friends. Some never pass beyond this world of confirmation. However, most of us have to construct a more complex pattern of confirmation in the midst of a great plurality of ideas, customs, events, and appearances. Not only does reality force this upon us, we also actively seek a wider and wider circle in order to gain leverage on the inconsistencies in our narrow world. When mother doesn't agree with us we turn to father. When neither agrees we turn to friends. When they do not agree we turn to teachers, ministers, and movie stars to find a more cogent confirmation. In the process we also create new and increasing opportunities for conflicts which may disconfirm us in other ways and at other times.

In short, the search for wider and wider arenas of publicity is a natural if not inevitable dynamic in life. Intimate companions may give great intensity but they lack the confirming adequacy of a more comprehensive public. What we seek in the smaller world demands that we go beyond that world.

However, each widening public exhibits its own inadequacy, even as it resolves problems raised in more intimate settings. This drive to a wider public arises not merely from unresolved earlier emotional engagements, as in Erikson's developmental scheme, or from our inadequate conceptualizations, as presumed by cognitive developmental theories. It also emerges from the structural limitations under which these publics and their participants exist. As Habermas would say, it arises not merely from the limits of the communicative competence of participants. It also arises from the inadequacies of the public situation itself. Rather than abandoning the struggle for a more adequate public we should see it as an object of hope and aspiration. The personal dynamic of publicity presses us to seek and secure more adequate structures to satisfy our thirst for confirmation.

2. Confirmation. People seek publicity in ever-widening circles of confirmation. We generally have an intense desire to confirm our lives, to establish an "OK world" which confirms our existence within a trustworthy pattern of human relationships. This drive arises from the general conditions of our existence. As we grow up we realize our uniqueness—some cultures creating this realization more intensely than others. In this individuation we experience an alienation from things and people, a distancing whose ultimate form is insanity and death. Narcissism is one form of this alienation. Here we confront the problem of establishing relationship and communication in a world that seems to be an arbitrary arrangement.

Gerd Theissen calls this the search for "resonance." Freud would probably have turned to the idea of gratification to express the emotional depth of this relationship, where the mother's breast confirms the infant's feelings of hunger, and obedience confirms the father's command. Cognitivists like Leon Festinger would direct us to the idea of cognitive consonance, where expectations based on previous perceptions are reinforced by present ones. Ronald Laing has combined these perspectives in his analysis of schizophrenia as an elaborate conflict of symbolic worlds that preys on our basic insecurity.[21] The concept of confirmation seeks to bring together these various insights into a common human dynamic and order them toward the perspective introduced by the concept of the self as a performer seeking a more adequate public.

Confirmation is not in itself a pleasant experience. The criminal can find confirmation in the courtroom and prison, the mother in childbirth, or the child in school. Though painful, at least a world exists with a place for that person. There is a commonly agreed-upon reality which serves as a common reference point for all the participants.

An intensified form of confirmation appears in the idea of affirmation. Here we pass from Festinger and the cognitivists to Carl Rogers.[22] The process of affirmation ("unconditional positive regard" in Rogers' terms) is a complex activity of decreasing people's adaptation to the existing world of confirmation and enhancing their trust in their own emotional and intellectual judgments. It is a process of preparing people for more authentic publicity and a genuine give and take in shaping a mutually confirming world with others. The power of affirmation enables people to seek to expand their public world beyond the limits of the present patterns of confirmation.

On its painful side the process of confirmation may release us from infantile worlds into isolation and loneliness, where even our bodily senses may not find any object and our expectations may never be met. This is the pain of disconfirmation. On the positive side this process contains the search for ever deeper and more complex patterns of resonance, mutuality, and communion. This is the joy of establishing a common world in which we can perform before others.

3. The Covenantal Self. Public life does not spring simply from our personal efforts at profession. The life of publicity rests on the common stage of reciprocity, where we hear and are heard, where we act and react, receive and give. The process of confirmation demands a common world of reference which makes discourse and argument possible. Publicity always demands covenant. The performer self must be *homo foedans* as well as *homo publicans*.

Previously we have attended to covenant as a key to understanding the grounding of a public order or to covenant as the bridge among limited republics. Covenant has been a decisive structural principle. Now we need to see its personal dimensions. Covenant opens up a certain vista on the self. It helps us see our selves as beings in covenant. Once again I can only sketch the directions such a vista opens up. Others would have to develop this orientation with greater sophistication and depth. We already see some of this work in the tradition from George Herbert Mead, H. R. Niebuhr, Thomas Oden and James W. Fowler. In this tradition the self is always seen in relationships. Mead saw us as "social selves," Niebuhr as "responsible selves," while Oden has spoken of the self as embedded in a matrix of covenantal being. More recently, Fowler, drawing on the Niebuhrean tradition, is seeking to articulate the work of faith as the construction of ever wider covenants.[23]

Drawing on the motifs of biblical covenant, we need to see that a theory of the covenantal self would lift up the way we are constituted by our bonds to history, to the land, to an expanding circle of publics, and to God, who presides over all these dimensions of our lives. Moreover, a covenantal perspective directs us to the process of negotiation by which we take up and transform the bonds of covenant in the course of our lives. A covenantal self is bonded in history but also is called out by promises. It lives in memory and in hope.

It may seem strange to many ears for a psychology to take seriously our relationship with the land. While the Bible may intone that we are dust to dust, the sirens of urbanity have long ago deafened us to the tugging of the land. How we relate to the land makes a powerful difference in our innermost being. Those who are rooted first of all in the cycles and contours of the land are very different people from those governed by the twenty-four hour day, the ever-lit work year and the rule of the technological dominus. These are, perhaps, the polarities of the psychological spectrum. They dramatize, however, how central to our motivation and outlook is our assumption of cycles in our bodies, of rest and activity, of domination and adaptation, tilling and taking. Our relation to the land, and by implication to all of nature, is a fundamental determinant of our psychology.

A covenantal understanding of this bond sees in it both confirmation and argument. Our covenants with the land are both binding and pliable. We are received into the conditions set by the land. We also seek to make a place for ourselves in it. We seek to be received even as we seek to change the land we depend on. We seek to give at least a living. We seek to leave at least a gravestone. Our lives play themselves out in a covenantal argument with the land on which we live. It is a covenant that seeks at least to make the land a stage as well as a partner in existence.

The land as a covenant partner also shapes the theater of history. A covenantal self always emerges within the covenant formed between ancestors and descendants. As so many people are fond of saying today, our little story is a part of a bigger story. Our melody is a line within a vaster symphony. Here we focus, as so many family theorists have, on the self as a nodal point among generations. We experience these intergenerational covenants as parents and children.

It is in these hierarchies of care and descent that we have usually come to understand God. God has been construed as the parental partner in covenant. In much of our tradition this parental God has been seen more as an unchanging rock to which we must adapt. As a parental actor God has been seen as an absolute will dictating the conditions of life for us. However, a covenantal model of relationship sees a constant process of conversation, argument and negotiation. The trust and care we associate with faith in God becomes a covenantal bond of speech and action. Just as the covenantal bonds between parents and children change as we get older, so our relation with the ultimate powers and everlasting partners of our life covenant changes. We move from being dependent children, to protectors and nurturers, and then back to a new and different dependency if we reach old age.

If we move out beyond the covenant among generations to the history of a broader public, we can see that a performer self is living between the givens of the past and the promise of possible futures. Without both of these reaches of historical covenant the self cannot exist. Here we pick up the themes of hope issuing from the work of Viktor Frankl in psychology and Jürgen Moltmann in theology. Both hoping and remembering are constitutive of the self.

Here again, a covenantal perspective understands this thread of past givenness and future possibility as informing a complex process of covenanting and recovenanting. We are actors who are also seeking to recompose, if only in some slight way, the script we have received. How we do it and the extent to which we do it are major contours of our own psychologies.

A covenantal perspective is probably most obvious within the domain formed by our circles of relationships, from friends and spouses to associations and governments. Here the dynamic of covenanting appears as a promise of finding whom we can trust and who will trust us. Who gives us life and to whom shall we pass it on? Whose promises open up our future and for whom are we ourselves a promise fulfilled? Here the covenantal matrix of our personalities is threaded in particular relationships.

Covenanting with others is also a process of building associations. These usually begin with families, as family systems therapists and theorists have shown, and then may move out into wider systems. The groups which demand covenant response from us etch out the main tracks on which we move. Our associations are the vectors of people's lives. As James Luther Adams has said, "By their groups shall ye know them." Not only are we known by these associations, but we also know ourselves through them. They are not only our windows on the world but a lens to our innermost motivations. They are not only a wider stage of performance, they also cast the players in our dreams.

Finally, we see the self in covenantal relationship to the ultimate partner of our existence, God. This has been a widespread theme in theological literature, especially the work of Karl Barth. Here we focus only on the way a covenantal approach shapes our psychological perspective. The divine partner in the covenantal structure of the self both pulls together the covenantal bonds with land, history and people and then redirects them toward their fulfillment.

Put very briefly here, the divine actor brings into being all that we call nature and then becomes the chief protagonist of human history. God is a parent with a special care for each being. God is a governor constantly striving to bring all being together in mutuality. God presides over the argument of being. This picture of God, which I will develop more in the next chapter, draws us to attend to the ways that we are clothed and led by longer threads than those we normally perceive.

Sometimes God appears in our deepest recesses as a hound that chases us from familiar and secure stages, urging us to wider and more risky audiences. Sometimes we experience God as the source of our most resonant affirmation, from which we derive an energy and trust that enables us to show ourselves before others at all. God is our ultimately trustworthy covenant partner. This not only is a source of affirmation, but also of a judgment on the narrower, more comfortable arenas where we seek to hide from the challenges of wider covenants.

The self in covenant before God is therefore shaped by the ambiguity implied by God as ultimate covenant partner. For from this ultimate covenantal argument springs both our most secure affirmation and also the demand to enter into the widest possible, indeed universal covenant laid out by the land, by history, and by peoples of all generations.

This covenantal perspective on the self can be worked out along many theoretical lines. I have mentioned only a few of them here. It is in general a picture of a self in ever changing bonds of promise. I have presented it more in terms of its "ideal" side, that is, the way the self might naturally be led toward wider and wider covenants. There is also a way these drives for confirmation and profession can lead us in another direction—toward a self in isolation. Before moving on to the way the performer self can develop in wider and wider publics, we need to examine a contemporary way this isolated self can be understood.

B. The Isolated Person

The personal dynamics of profession and confirmation revolve around deep interior axes. Just as covenantal publicity fulfills the self, so its absence causes deep derangements within us. The pathology of the performer self is the subject of contemporary discussions of narcissism in the works of Richard Sennett and Christopher Lasch.[24] They also express major concerns of Parker Palmer's effort to set forth a spirituality of public life. All of them are concerned about ways people draw away from social life into self-absorption, whether psychologically or religiously conceived. An inquiry into the problem of narcissism can help sharpen our theory of the performer self. That is the step we undertake now.

1. The Problem of Narcissism. As a psychological *condition*, narcissism is self-absorption—the failure to cathect basic energies onto persons, objects, and institutions outside the self. As such it constitutes a problem for anyone concerned with public life. As a *dimension* of our personal life it points to the primordial processes of becoming a self, what Freud called the primary narcissism of the self. As a dimension, narcissism is the very precondition for a person who can enter into public life. Narcissism is therefore not merely the weakness which Sennett and Lasch see but also the strength which Paul Zweig and Peter Homans detect.[25]

From most psychoanalytic perspectives narcissism is a problem because the self finds its proper purposes in love and work, that is, object cathexis and sublimation. Behind this assumption about people's proper goals stands the view that some kind of social control through psychological repression is necessary to save them from their own self-destructive tendencies. Unless our energies can be hooked onto parental figures such as mother churches and father lands, not to mention our own artistic creations and progeny, we will turn them against ourselves. Thus, the alternative to the repression of instincts we first experience in the oedipal struggle is not freedom, but the torture of a phantasmal interior life. The narcissistic personality oscillates wildly between feverish playing to the grandstand and enormous self-doubt.

From the standpoint of the self's covenantal process, the narcissist is caught in the gap between God as covenant affirmation and God as partner in life's most universal covenant. The narcissistic personality seems to be self-affirming but has no real trust, seems to be a universal actor but forms no covenantal bonds.

In *The Fall of Public Man* Richard Sennett sets forth some connections between the rise of narcissistic disorders and the collapse of a public sphere. Narcissistic personalities lack the inner integrity to make clear profession before others. Moreover, the world of common conventions that makes resonance possible between performer and audience has also dissolved. We therefore oscillate between absorption in the whirlwind of charismatic celebrities and collapse before the deadening demands of bureaucratic conformity.

In the process we lose not only a public realm which can support a genuine human drama, we also lose a private realm. The inability to maintain the theatre of public life also leaves us bereft of means for preserving the little studio of the private realm. We become absorbed in each other's feelings rather than in the complex argument of common life.

The traditional psychoanalytic response to this is to call on social institutions and deep symbolic rituals to rescue the self from its own imagination. This seems to be the course chosen by Lasch and implied by Sennett. It is a contemporary version of the monarchical psychology we examined earlier, in which an adequate republic demands the monarchy of Christ in the soul. Because this monarchy governs primarily the process of people's childhood socialization it establishes its realm primarily in the domestic sphere. The control of schools and families becomes the major social issue.

However, it is not the only way, as we know from the classical public psychologies of the Renaissance. In our own time the humanistic psychologies of Abraham Maslow and Carl Rogers have not assumed that the self is self-destructive. Social environment is as much a madhouse of distorting mirrors as it is the clear optic of reality. Rather than living inside a few great institutions of state, religion, and business, we experience a vast plurality of groups, voluntary associations, corporations, and governments. Rather than offering up the interior life of the self in sacrificial obedience to a single hierarchy we can seek to nurture an autonomous self which creates its own life within the rich complexity of choices before it. The kind of public sphere these psychologies envision is a plurality of groups rather than an integrated system. In this fulfillment approach the interior energies and self-structuration which Freud called primary narcissism can achieve an integrity (Rogers' congruence) which then can address matters of public life.

The two approaches differ in the way they understand the self's interior energies at work in its acts of profession and in the self's relation to the process of public confirmation. A theory of the performer self, with its focus on publics and covenantal bonds, can bring them together and lead us to a federal and republican theory of private life. An adequate theory in line with this approach must show how the inner life has structure as well as energy, relationship as well as individuation. In short, we need a better psychological paradigm, or model, for framing our inquiry.

In the psychoanalytic theory emerging in the collapse of monarchical ideology we see hydraulic and electrical models at work. The hydraulic model illuminates the way we experience immense flows of undifferentiated force. The electrical gives us an image of the way our inner energies cathect on objects, enabling our energy to flow to them.

However, these models present us with undifferentiated energy, a power for good or for evil dwelling forever beyond the discriminations of our eyes.

The fulfillment approach, using a growth model, directs us to the way these energies can have an ordered thrust toward some coherent structure. The self is a thrust toward actualizing potential. However, it too stops short of offering us a clear understanding of the structure of this growth. Instead we are generally redirected toward the life of inner energy for our orientation. This time, however, the whirlwind of libido is confronted as organic feeling struggling for actualization.

The two approaches also differ in their view of the dynamics we are calling confirmation. The difference focuses on the problem of self-esteem. Freudian analysts of narcissism see the self as needing repression and sublimation lest it fall into the phantasmal darkness of its own interior processes. To use Christian terminology from St. Paul, the self needs the law in order not to fall back into bestiality. The deadening impact of moral obligation cannot be overcome by rejecting the law but by incorporating it into the "higher law of Christ," thus entering into a transcendent life of grace.

Fulfillment psychologists, analyzing the deadening effect of the law for self-esteem, would try to strengthen the self so it could change the laws. They would try to focus the energies of the self on its deeply interior integrity so that it could then transform the world through participation in small groups. To draw on the Christian analogy again, they would seek openness to a spirit that would enable them to discover their true self. Whereas narcissism, for the Freudians, entails lack of self-esteem, for the Rogerians it points to the recovery of a self liberated from oppressive conditions of worth.

The limitations in these two approaches show us the need for a model of personality in which we can see the structural dynamics of our inner feelings. It is a model that seeks to relate the psychology of private life to the character of public performers. The discussion about narcissism points not only to the need to see the inner energies more positively, but to identify the characteristic way they are structured. The energies of the self are more a kind of structure than a fluid darkness. This is the kind of relational model that covenantal perspectives would seek to find.

This structuring has to occur through some kind of developmental process. For psychoanalysis it lies in the transfer of our basic energies onto natural parents and then onto the social parents of institutional authority. For fulfillment approaches it involves the gradual expansion of the self's capacity for expression and self-esteem. Our task is to discern the developmental process by which we move from the essential confirmation or disconfirmation we receive in parental nurture to the wider performances of negotiation in public life. The relation of nurture and public authority has to be seen on a developmental continuum lest we confuse the infantile processes of dependent confirmation with adult performance—a perennial problem in psychoanalytic interpretations of public life.

This developmental perspective, whether psychoanalytical or humanistic, needs to be seen as progression through a series of increasingly public worlds of confirmation. Psychological development is not merely a sequence of biologically necessary stages. It is also the product of certain kinds of worlds—private and public—in which the self must seek its confirmation.

The model of the self as a performer offers a promising synthesis of psychoanalytic and fulfillment concerns within the dynamics of the self's social environment. In this approach the self appears as an actor situated in a story performed before various audiences in some worldly scene. Approaches to personality and theology in terms of story tend to presuppose this model of the self. Promising entrees into this view have been offered by Kenneth Burke, his student Hugh Duncan, Eric Berne, ethnomethodologists like Erving Goffman, and psychodramatists like Jacob Moreno.[26]

To pursue this kind of inquiry demands a theory of the private sphere as a series of little theaters. Rather than a stark distinction between the public and the private we have a more pluralistic sense for the spectrum of increasingly public worlds. The dynamics of covenantal publicity permeate all these spheres.

C.   Private Performances

Families, friendships, clubs—these are the traditional organizations of the private sphere. A concern for public life sees them as means for cultivating the kind of people who can act in public as well as for constraining governments and corporations from dominating life and extinguishing the public sphere. A model of the self as performer focuses on the way they serve these two functions by being little theaters, forms of property, and public institutions.

As a little theater the private sphere rehearses our performances as public personalities. As property it is both a means for public profession and also a constituent part of the pluralism necessary for public life. As a set of institutions it constrains others from extinguishing the public sphere.

1. Theaterola. Private spheres are the little stages of our lives. To draw on the old distinction between the ecclesia and the ecclesiola (the big church and the little church within), they are the "theaterolas" of our life. They are arenas of presentation, as Erving Goffman has so richly pointed out. They are studios relatively detached from the larger, more public arenas. These theaterolas occur not only in family settings but in all intimate relationships.

Family worlds are basically involuntary, at least for the children. They can yield a high degree of confirmation and resonance. They may even be able to be highly affirmative in their response to our initial performances. Indeed, some people never move beyond this theaterola to test their professions before bigger audiences. Others, of course, are led out from these theaterolas to find confirmation with friends, associates, or strangers who share a common world of public concerns.

A focus on private worlds as little theaters would lead us to seek out the ways they function as dramatic spaces. What are their patterns of profession and confirmation? How do they provide resources of affirmation for more public performances? How do they press or push their members to find wider realms in which to seek more adequate confirmation? In the words of popular therapy, what scripts do they offer? What family stories form the plot of people's lives?

The performer model yields questions for grasping the relation of private and public life so that we might understand how to revitalize them both. By focusing on our capacity to perform in a covenantal public we are drawn away from an excessive focus on psychological energy as a closed process. Moreover, we are given a structure for construing the relational nature of our energies as well as our patterns of cognitive development.

2. Private Property. Earlier we saw how property needs to be seen as the medium by which people act out their roles in public life. The performative model sees property as the means for profession of the self. Like any actors we all need properties to perform. Some of these attach to us as persons in the drama. Others attach to the common world inhabited by all the actors.

This conception of property focuses on its capacity to build a public in which people can perform their lives. In light of it we can examine the ways property actually functions this way in our society. We can also critique property arrangements which keep people from adequate publicity—whether they be the "owners" themselves or "renters." Indeed, the perspective of federal publicity asks more about the structure of work than about its ultimate owners. How occupations are organized, how work is organized, become key questions. We are asked to explore ways in which workplaces can enable people to have adequate public life—in the way they structure time, energies, relationships, and our life plans and wider covenants. The question of the distribution of property rights between managers and workers, parents and children, capitalists and laborers, and between governments and independent firms can revolve around the issues of covenantal publicity in much the same way that Smith, Locke, Paine, Marx, and George used labor value to approach property.

To say this much is only to open up a vista on a most complex issue. It is also to say that many existing contests between socialists and liberals might be recast in moving away from the self as producer, manager, or laborer to the self as performer. An adequate rethinking of the problems of personality and public life must engage in this kind of transformation of the terms of the argument.

3. The Little Publics. The so-called private spheres already have a public dynamic which constitutes them—the drive of the self for adequate publicity. They are already diminutive publics to the degree they sustain the processes of profession and confirmation. They are deprived, of course, of the wider pattern of confirmation and disconfirmation possible in a pluralistic public. They are spheres of privation, but nevertheless provide the essential "off Broadway" experimentation, refinement, and education necessary for the big theaters of the wider public.

As little publics they have public demands. They exist as public institutions. They perform indispensable and unique public functions in the public life of each person. Moreover, they are also sources of critique over against the stories, conventions, and confirmations of the official publics. They are necessary participants in the plurality of public discourse.

They are therefore not only bulwarks against statism—a function which highly repressive patriarchies could also perform. They themselves are engaged in a critical contest with other spheres of confirmation. They too fall under the critique of the public process. They too can be judged in terms of their adequacy as theaters of existence. The performer self makes claims on all its spheres even as it is shaped by them.

These three forms of private life—as theaterola, as property, and as public—are avenues of further exploration. The model of the performer yields empirical hypotheses as well as normative directions. It can help us understand and organize much of the discussion about personality, privacy and public life.

IV.   Toward Federal Publicity: The Religious Vision

This vision of covenantal publicity and the performer self captures fundamental yearnings and symbols. Even as it draws on our religious heritage it needs a more explicit engagement with it in order to deal with the hopes and frustrations of these impulses in human affairs. The religious heritage itself, however, must be transformed under the impact of this vision, even as it seeks to supply it with a greater fulness. Such a general reordering of our lives leads us to theological questions.

The image of the performer self is not only one that fills out the personal side of the dynamics of publicity. It also fleshes out the meaning of covenantal relations as activities of profession and confirmation in the drama of history. It is both a republican and a federal conception of the self.

Even in sketching this approach to self and public we unearth new questions and problems. How are we to understand the source for personal esteem and an ultimate federal republic? How are we to deal with the chasm between our intuitions of perfect publicity and our experiences of betrayal, mistrust, violence and isolation? Where are we to find adequate theaterolas for rehearsal of our life? How can we sustain those institutions that advance the publication of our lives and release us from the despair of isolation?

These are first of all theological questions about the ultimate source of our life and our final destiny. They are also ecclesiological questions—that is, questions about the nature of the Church as a little public with the mission of being a peculiar theaterola of our ultimate publicity. Here the federal and republican rivers flow into the larger sea of religious faith. The confluence of our biblical and classical heritages transforms this sea's ecology, creating new waters to sustain our common voyage.

6 | Theological Reverberations of God's Federal Republic

I have tried to show how the dynamics and values embedded in our traditions have led us out of kingship into life in the light of God's Federal Republic. This journey has not been a simple abandonment of kingship's heritage but the cultivation of new ways to conserve its original functions of stability, transcendent judgment, unity and socialization in the service of an order of action for all people. The perennial functions of kingship must be taken from its storied husk to feed its heir—a public bound in covenant.

Both republican and federal traditions have found ways to solve these functions. The republican argument developed grounds for stability first in the mixed polity of king, aristocracy and people and then later in the concept of political pluralism. At the same time it nourished a new personality congruent with the fundamental sense of personal election and vocation enunciated in the Gospels. It initiated the exodus from monarchical conscience to presidential responsibility as the hallmark of personal virtue. Out of the controversies of the republican era we enter into the grammar of covenantal publicity.

The conversations and arguments of covenanted publicity demand an even deeper language of ultimate hope and understanding. That is, they finally rest on a deep awareness of our ultimately trustworthy bonds—to our world, to each other, and to God. This kind of faith finds articulation in a general conversation as well as in particular ones that have nourished this broader movement toward covenant publicity. That is, there are both civil and religious approaches to this ultimate faith that feed into and out of our central governing symbol, God's Federal Republic. This symbol stands at the center of two intertwined faith conversations in our life.

It is a faith and a language that takes shape in the midst of a pluralism required by a republican commitment. It nurtures increasingly transcendent judgment through expansion of the public's arguments. Pluralism seeks stability and public wisdom through the arguments and conversations of the open public. Publics seek unity in the form of consensus through the compromise of limited interests. In order to achieve this people must be organized in many small publics. Unity must be differentiated if public life is to arise and be sustained. A republic of any size, if it is to remain true to the exercise of publicity, must be a federation of publics. Publicity must find recourse to covenant in order to sustain itself.

Similarly, republican socialization occurs as the process of rehearsing ever more effective roles and responses for increasing publics. It is a process of entering ever-wider covenants. The child enters public life through public action and the dynamics of profession, confirmation and disconfirmation. Maturation is the movement from childish expression to a responsible profession. We move from mere adaptation or rebellion to the dynamics of discussion and argument bound up in confirmation. Socialization is not the replication of parental structures but the elaboration of our experience as performers in expanding publics.

The covenantal tradition plays a twofold role in the sustenance of public life. It provides the federal principle for relating publics to each other. It also creates a perspective on the process of consensus which moves us beyond a limited contractualism to our wider relations with God, the land, and other peoples as well as to God's ultimate aim at the creation of the perfect public of our salvation.

I am proposing that we use the symbol of God's *Federal* Republic rather than God's *Covenant* Public for several reasons. Most importantly, "Federal" is redolent of the themes of comprehensive governance advanced earlier in the symbol of kingdom. It points to the structure of relations being brought forth by God in our life. Secondly, covenant has unfortunately too often been reduced to a narrow contractualism in our culture. Federalism turns our attention to the wider political context of life. Finally, federal symbolism arouses images of governance among the nations. It is a fully political symbol. Our theory of covenant helps deepen and broaden popular understandings of federalism. It gives us critical leverage resting in its biblical origins. However, the symbol these biblical themes must permeate is contained more adequately in the complex symbol, God's Federal Republic.

Concepts of covenant and republic have argued out a new language for our religious as well as our civil reflection. Each has challenged, sustained, and corrected the other. Their conversation has driven them back to the basic grounds out of which they can exercise a concerted impact on our faith and life. We have been brought to the need for new theological as well as political and psychological formulations.

Theological reconstruction serves two purposes. First, it helps us to ground this governing symbol at the center of the historic biblical conversation. It provides a coherent frame for relating these concepts together around the central theme.

Second, it helps us respond in hope to the frustration of our vision of a fully public life lived in covenant with God, the land, and other people. It fills out the trajectory of a common life that began with Abraham's call and culminates in the ultimate conversion of creation around the presidency of God. Only this extrapolation of the vision can sustain us in defeat and chasten us in our complacency. The vision of God's Federal Republic is ultimately an intimation of an order of life far beyond our present capacities.

I.   Reconstruction in Theology

The central symbol, God's Federal Republic, rests on and transforms some key theological concepts. The various Jewish, Christian and Moslem traditions approach this task of reconstruction in various ways. At this point I am simply setting out some directions that Christians might take as they seek to spell out their faith in the light of God's Federal Republic. While I think other religious traditions can share a great deal of this perspective, they would also bring to bear particular visions, claims and arguments on the public generated by our common search for a more adequate federal republic. The very arguments among these religious publics can invigorate and sustain the very plurality necessary for genuine covenant publicity.

The pillars we need for a Christian reconstruction are those of theological language itself, salvation, sin, God, Jesus Christ, and the Church. These traditional points of Christian discourse are transformed under the impact of our central symbol even as they nurture and shape its development.

A.   Theological Language

Immersion in a theory of the covenanted public leads us to see theological discourse in a new way. We no longer see theological language as a kind of "scientific" describer of some object which we contemplate.

It is not a collection of Sears and Roebuck catalog pointers to some heavenly pictures. It is the exhortative, dramatic, performative language of symbolic action. It comes from worship and prayer. Religious language is the professing and confessing of people pressing for a more complete publicity.[1]

This gives new meaning to the ancient adage that the language of theology should be the language of prayer. This idea of *lex orandi, lex credendi* (the rule of praying is the rule of believing) means that all our language is involved in dramatic, symbolic action. It is the use of speech in order to act. Our words evoke action more than scientific verification. They are performative rather than coldly descriptive. They arise in participation more than in detached observation.

Our speech acts are thus offerings into a wider public. They are all "liturgical" in this sense.[2] Just as our word liturgy comes from the Greek word for public works, so all our religious speech is infused with our search for a more confirming publicity. We offer up a profession of ourselves with trepidation, trusting that our public will return to us an even greater self. The instruments of speech extend the dialogue of prayer to the risky but redemptive offering of ourselves by which we participate in the public of the Church. The logic of our very words points to the perfection of speech in God's Federal Republic. The logic of our language draws us to the Logos of life, our words to the Word.

This approach to religious language has been developing for some time in the work of Robert Bellah, narrative theologians like John Shea, Stanley Hauerwas and Sallie McFague, and religious anthropologists like Victor Turner.[3] However, theories of covenant and publicity require that we resist the reduction of narrative to personal autobiography. They challenge us not only to relate our little story to the great stories and classics, but also to see them as part of a conversation aimed at our publication and the formation of our covenants of confirmation. Shared narrative is part of the sustenance of public life.

Simultaneously, we understand theology not merely as a profession coming out of a private personal experience, but as the language of a particular public.[4] That is, our professions are always our response to the challenge of taking up a part in the historical drama that is already underway when we emerge in this world. There is no "other world" these symbols come from. They are themselves the conventions, symbols, and commonalities by which we take part in the struggle for greater publicity.

B. Salvation

This struggle for a more perfect publicity is the dynamic content of salvation. From the standpoint of the performer, life is an activity in which we strive for more adequate profession and confirmation. It is a dynamic of performance leading us on to more encompassing and diverse audiences. Within this image we find the dynamics of profession, confirmation, affirmation, and confession.

Salvation is a term which indicates both an ultimate perfection as well as our gradual entry into it. It is the grace extended to us by God's invitation to a perfectly covenanted public. It is also the grace we appropriate as we publicize our lives, trusting that we will finally be sustained in God's public. Salvation points to God's preparation of that public. It also points to the acts of profession by which we come into the light of public reception. We do not first "experience salvation" and then profess it in public. The very act of profession begins the process of our salvation—it is entry into grace. It is the first step in taking us out of the darkness of our own imaginings and the nightmare of disconfirmations and unreality. In taking up the ideas of profession, disclosure and light we return to themes central to the Gospels of Matthew and John, with Matthew 10 being a kind of mini-Gospel.

In that set of passages we see Jesus' call to discipleship and healing, the deprivation his disciples experience from having to live in secret, their realization of the power of the Gospel as the very act of public proclamation, and their capacity for persuasion in the midst of violent resistance. The healing mission to which Jesus sends the disciples liberates people from the bonds that deprive them of participation in the common life. The disciples proceed with persuasive peace rather than threats or coercion. They are encouraged by the trust that even in the midst of enemies they will have the power of speech through the power of God's spirit.

With this faith they are enjoined to courageous action, "for nothing is covered that will not be revealed, or hidden that will not be known. What I tell you in the dark, utter in the light; and what you hear whispered, proclaim upon the housetops" (vv. 26–27). This liberated public life overwhelms the old bonds of kinship as brother and sister, parent and child are caught up in controversy by a loyalty that transcends them. This message by and to the early Church lies at the heart of the proclamation of God's Federal Republic.

From this vantage point we can see that the fulfillment of our lives is found in the perfection of our publicity within the divine covenant. Salvation is life lived without secrets. It is a life of full disclosure in a world we share with others. It is life in which the confirmations of our past are rich enough to carry us through the disconfirmations of the present, even as they are deficient enough to demand what Alfred North Whitehead would call an adventure in novelty. Salvation is fully resonant life in God's perfect public.

No act of profession, however, is possible without some kind of public world in which to act. Through the medium of that world people can come together to reach some degree of confirmation of each other. Confirmation is therefore a central dimension of the salvation process. The creation and perfection of a world is indispensable to a public concept of redemption.

The classic belief in the resurrection of the body underlines the importance of distinct bodies for a genuine public interchange. While this may have been influenced by other beliefs, it seems to have come into biblical faith through the experience of the Maccabees (2 Mac 7; 12:43–45). In their struggle to reclaim and re-establish Israel's covenantal order they tasted a salvation that included even those who had died in the struggle. Belief in the resurrection of the body bridged the chasm between their lives and God's eventual victory.

Without distinct bodies we would have no properties by which to act over against others. There would be no basis for plurality and difference. Judgments could not be addressed to particular persons. Promises and covenants would be meaningless. Resurrection of the body is indispensable to the perfection of a public which transcends the limits of our present order and yet preserves the very basis for a published life shared in covenant.

Not only do persons struggle for salvation, so do publics. The very dynamic of a public is to transform itself in argument even as it seeks to maintain itself in covenants of confirmation. It seeks to unfold the logic of its discourse and find an ultimate world in which to sustain its conversation. This is the way in which the one process of salvation extends to peoples as well as persons.

Not only does salvation symbolize fullness of profession and confirmation. It also indicates the achievement of human truth, that is, the truth that arises out of public discourse.[5] The struggle for confirmation is always a struggle against the phantasmal aberrations of isolation. It is a struggle for a genuine world in terms of which we can engage others in trust. It is this truth, this trustworthy creation, which is achieved in salvation. As Parker Palmer points out, the English words trust and truth are both rooted in "troth," as revealed in the archaic marriage vow, "I plight thee my troth."[6] Trust and truth are rooted in a transformed world of covenanted truth. This is how the salvation of the self is inextricable from the transformation of our world.

When the dynamic of confirmation is peculiarly intense a resonance arises which is often described by the word communion. Here we find the kind of understanding, acceptance, and mutual affirmation which underlies reconciliation. The resonance between two people that we call love can take a more fully public form as alliances, communities, and coalitions. It is an important ingredient of any federal republic. Resonant communion points to the bonds of culture and common memory that the great conservative thinkers like Edmund Burke lauded, even to the detriment of expanding the publicity of their age. God as the author of salvation, however, draws us on to fuller publics even while confirming our more limited ones as theaterolas and mediators of wider performance.

This resonance of confirmation and affirmation lies behind the kind of acceptance contained in the word "grace." Our profession and interaction with others is taken up by this public and returned to us as a reinforcement which excites us to higher levels of energy, self-esteem, well-being and power. It gives us the dignity once restricted to members of the royal family and court. It leads us into more profound dynamics of profession as well as strengthening our capacity to confirm and affirm others. This is the kind of enhancement felt in speaking about the love of God. It is an enhancement known in the dynamic of publication.

Confirmation, of course, is also the name of a sacramental rite in which people confirm the baptismal vows made for them when they were baptized as infants. Within the language we are using here, this rite points further than a bond to one's past. It symbolizes our entry into the wider public of the Church beyond one's family and friends. Confirmation is the act of publication at the heart of baptism and the Lord's Supper.

Baptism was originally the profession of one's desire to enter the perfect world God is bringing into being through the power of the Spirit known through the assembly of the faithful. Speaking sacramentally, it is the primordial sacrament underlying all the others. In the actions of the Lord's Supper, or Eucharist, this salvific process of profession and confirmation is further intensified by the symbolic experience of affirmation and loving resonance at the heart of a meal. These rites revivify our awareness of the affirmation necessary to energize our search for perfect publicity. It is in this sense that it is an agape meal of mutual acceptance. However, even this process of affirmation still needs to be filled out by the other acts of publication in the Church, especially that of preaching. These sacramental actions must never be reduced to the private act of an individual or a club. They must be performed in a way that opens us out to the wider public—to the act of confession.

The act of confession is also contained in the dynamic of salvation, for without it the saving public world is not continually made presentable for us. Being constructed of language, action, memory, and symbol, it can fade away like the morning dew when people do not continually renew it with acts of confession that re-present their experience of confirmation. Without confession there is no publicity. Without publicity there is no salvation.

The dynamic of publicity runs all through the personal and collective dimensions of salvation, overrunning our everyday necessary distinctions between private and public, personal and impersonal, individual and society. These distinctions reflect provisional differentiations in a world where profession often leads to betrayal, trust leads to disappointment, and confession leads to premature ossification. This is what we mean when we say that the grain of salvation is always growing in a field of weeds. We live in a world struggling toward more perfect publicity but still far short of it. The concept of publicity helps us understand sin in a new way.

C. Sin

Sin is exclusion from full publicity. It is life lived in darkness and isolation. Without the presence of a confirming public we live in some degree of madness. We cannot construct an adequate grasp of a mutually confirmed reality. We sink into the wild imaginings of our hearts in which demonic nightmares torture us with their phantasmic worlds. It is the hell of unreality.

Sin is therefore the loss of a proper public for the publication of our lives. It is the loss of a plurality which requires that we covenant in trust with others. The loss of a public sphere takes many forms, aside from the universal experience of the gap between all our publics and God's perfected public. In our time we have known it as totalitarianism, but it lurks wherever public discourse and argument are crushed by appeals to absolutes of race, gender, or rule by experts.

We have here a "privational" theory of sin—deprivation of a public. But this is far from the idea of privation in the neo-Platonic tradition flowing through Augustinian tradition. In that view our drive is toward union with God—the *amor dei*.[7] The burden of this book's argument is that we are ordered to full publicity—participation with other professing persons. We are disposed toward participation with others in a perfect public.

This view of sin as privation helps focus our moral antennae. It moves us away from concentration on obediential or contemplative models of faith to an examination of the complex ways that disconfirmation and isolation occur through the crippling of people's capacity to profess, confirm, and confess their lives as public beings.

Christian theology has always recognized that sin is actually a complex reality. It has many levels and dimensions. Sometimes it may appear to us simply as disconfirmation of our own intended meanings. This in itself, however, is just the pain of having to come to terms with other people. Our thwarted efforts at profession and publicity may point to deeper derangements in the public process itself. Here sin occurs as the lies, confusions, and failed promises of much of public interaction. Many factors may play into this systematically distorted communication, as Habermas calls it. We may be unable to profess our lives in terms explicable to others. We may have gained our self-image and expectations from some other public or from a less-publicized sector of life among family and friends. We may speak the same language but not the same meanings. All of these contradictions, however, can also drive the public argument forward. They can be necessary parts of the dialectic by which a public finally finds the truth.

Sometimes publics can no longer overcome deep contradictions within them. They encounter an intractable sin which is always and ultimately opposed to God's purposes. This is the sin of real deprivation. It is the death of isolation, silence, and alienation from a public world. Sin as a pattern of deprivation arises from disfigurements in our activity of professing, confirming and confessing. We may form a little public which systematically excludes the professions of others affected by it. The public we are appealing to may exclude other publics or prevent them from appearing. This is the pattern found in sexist and racist societies. The idea of publicity casts new light on the dynamics of oppression as exclusion from a confirming public.

Finally, there is sin as evil—the active force opposed to our perfection in publicity. Here sin is known in violence and the darkness and silence with which it works. It is the silence of the torture chamber. Evil is found in the actions of those who seek to clothe their acts in secrecy so as to deny their public character. It is an evil we are all enmeshed in because we fear betrayal by gossip and innuendo. It is an evil in those we authorize to act for the common good because they seek in their actions their own private gain. It is the evil with which we contend unceasingly until God's presidency finally inaugurates a perfectly trustworthy public.

All our publics are shot through and through with these forms of sin. Our life is a strain toward a more perfect public grounded in a covenant with all of life. Since our very notions of reality are so conditioned by the publics in which we find our limited confirmation, it is extremely difficult for us to move beyond them, criticize them, and found more comprehensive and adequate publics.

This sense of a more perfect public stands in judgment over all our republics. Each republic is an effort to institutionalize some public pattern. Some values may be achieved more than others. Some may attain a clear confession at the expense of the possibilities for new professions. Others may enhance the possibilities of profession but fail to create means of mutual confirmation and confession. This awareness of our limitations is crucial if we are to avoid making a religious use of the symbol Federal Republic into an ideology defending various nationalistic versions of it.

"God's Federal Republic" symbolizes the dynamic of publicity and covenant informing our lives but also leads us beyond the particular crystallizations of our achievements in securing a public sphere. The symbol points to a forward thrust of emancipation from inadequate publics and the legitimation of more expansive ones. When this movement occurs we speak of the central symbol of transcendence—God, who binds creation together in covenant. This is the God who is our publisher and president.

D. The Covenanting God

In the biblical pattern covenants brought people together around a common purpose involving mutual self-sacrifice and conscientious fidelity. Covenants were ultimately grounded in a response of thanks and praise for the gracious power that had sustained and liberated the people in the past. Covenants reflected a basic trust that this sustenance would extend into the future through the medium of a life lived according to covenant.

A sustained covenant encompassed more than individuals and their divine partner. It embraced the land as well as the groups and institutions by which human relationships endure over time. Covenant, as a promissory bond, creates fidelity over time as well as over space. How then can these elements, expressed here so succinctly, manifest themselves in terms of our central symbol, God's Federal Republic?

Covenants publish the points of resonance and confirmation that constitute a people as a public. They are not a form of imposed order but of published order arising from the people's historic arguments, agreements, and promises. Through covenant-making the confirmation that takes shape in the common conventions of life finds permanence in directing our lives into the future. Covenants express a public form which has been achieved and also introduce us to a process of covenant-making that can relate our publics to others. Covenants not only undergird the existence of *a* public, but are ways of relating particular publics to each other.

I say "particular," because covenant-making is always eminently historical. When Israel recited its primary covenant with YHWH it always told the story of YHWH's history with them (Ex 20:2; Dt 6–7; Jos 24). Covenants do not apply abstract ideas onto a people but publish their points of historical resonance in profession and confession. Covenants do not rest on the calculation of interests suspended above their historical context but on the common memory and possible hopes of a community. Biblical covenant does not see isolated individuals interacting mechanically but people bound to each other and to their history and their land. They therefore can also draw people on in a liberating way to an historically founded possibility of even greater publicity.

Because covenants emerge in history, they are more a matter of cultivation than coercion. They arise in the common consent underlying legal life rather than the codes that result from it. Covenants are confessions to which our life in common persuades us. They reflect the confirmation which is experienced rather than the obedience which is commanded. Covenants therefore should not be confused with contracts—the main pitfall of our own federal tradition. Contracts are agreements to serve mutual self-advantage. Covenants are not made to be grasped. They are not tools to serve us but mothers to give us birth into a more adequate publicity. They are primarily the bases for our interchange, not merely its calculated outcome.

Finally, biblical covenants always involve the land—the wider realm of nature that supports the public world. In our own amnesia we forget that the very land in which we can articulate our public life and in terms of which we can develop our properties is a necessary part of our fundamental covenant. Without this wider covenant our little human publics become prey of the very interests they are supposed to constrain. We devour the land instead of performing our lives upon it.

Covenanting draws us to the universal conditions of a common life in public. It goes beyond the reference to our selves which accompanies contract, and relates our public activity to the general conditions of life. Perhaps more than anything else, it is this meaning of covenant which now has to be returned to the idea of federalism in order to recover it and make it viable in our own time. To be truly federal, a federal republic must relate people to their land, their history, and the general conditions of life. In short, God as the Creator of a world is also the covenanting God. It is in the cradle of this kind of covenanting that more adequate publics are to be born.

The dynamic of publicity leads us to covenants to undergird our publics as well as relate them to each other. Covenants in turn lead us back to the events of resonance, profession, and confirmation which yield up the confessions of who we are and who we are becoming in the course of our history. The model covenants, those of Israel and the Church, relate a history of being drawn out of darkness into the light, out of isolated servitude into the creation of a public order, a holy city. Covenant, like publicity, points both to the dynamic of emancipation as well as to the process of legitimation. Covenants create a new human world.

The kind of world demanded by and created in the dynamics of performance is therefore a verbal and symbolic world. Intrinsic to this world is the kind of relationship pointed to by the idea of covenant. It is the pattern of primordial confirmation making possible the public performances of our lives.

Within a covenantal framework the discourse of the public realm can become the kind of wisdom which was once relegated to the monarchical vicar of God. It was the wisdom of the lone philosopher who could contemplate the transcendent origin of things. However, a federal republic draws its wisdom from the arguments, criticisms, and reasoning of public conversation. Covenantal reason, that is, wisdom emerging in debate, replaces the insight of the monarch as the source of stability. In its more legal form early republicans claimed that the constitution was their king, to whom all are obligated. This has been a major aspect of the shift from kingdom to federal republic as our guiding religious symbol.

This covenantal reality itself is complex. It is composed of covenants we receive from past generations as well as those composed in our own time. The covenant of subordination between a high God and a people points to these received covenants. It is the covenant of YHWH and Moses. The covenant of this generation is symbolized in the covenant of Jonathan with David. It is fundamentally a covenant of equals. Both of these have a powerful place in the publication of our lives.

The hierarchical covenant between generations conveys to us a sense of our history, our origin and our destiny. It is our covenant in time. It also articulates our relation to the earth which is our physical parent—the very source of our creaturely existence. Within these covenants we experience limits. We touch the boundaries of our generative covenants between parent and child, past and future, earth and health. They are covenants we are called to honor more than to create, though even these participate in the covenantal dynamic of argument and agreement. They are living relationships, not cold chains. They are part of God's covenantal publication of our lives.

The covenant among friends, rather than between masters and servants, points to the relationships among performers. This is the kind of covenant implied in Jesus' address to his disciples as friends who are to proclaim boldly to a hostile world all the truth he has shared with them (Jn 15:12–17). It anticipates the outcome of the drive toward publicity governing their lives. Just as the covenant of friendship helps people move from their families to wider publics, so this covenant of equals is the underlying dynamic of public life.

Covenant points to the wider context of human relationships arising out of the dynamic of publicity. Divine covenant is not limited to the intimate relationships of community but urges us on to the most universal public in which we can find ultimate confirmation. Clearly this thrust of covenant drives us beyond our ordinary publics even while legitimating them. The ultimate forms of God's Federal Republic cannot be realized within our present publics, yet we must keep alive the energy and vision which sustain our final search.

God's promising and persuasion flow from God's covenantal nature. God's covenanting expresses itself through the power of discourse, especially the conversation, argument and negotiation around promises and agreements. Covenant points to the work of publicity in which God not only gives us the power to publish our lives but also forms the ground for the publics we need. As covenanter, God is known as our emancipating publisher as well as our ultimate president.

E. God: Publisher and President

We are frequently torn between the conception of God as some kind of actor or person and God as an impersonal ground for ultimate reality.[8] Similar dynamics are at work with the religious vision articulated here. God as the basis for order and stability was lifted up earlier in the conception of God as King. The monarchical principle of tradition, cultural unity, and primordial loyalty was epitomized in the Divine Author of the human order.

The other dimension of God, God as an actor, has often been symbolized in the image of God as a monarch, with the effect of creating more of a dictatorial God than the king of ancient Roman society. In early biblical records God as an actor was principally seen as a warrior, especially in Israel's early memory of the exodus, but also in the later images of God and Christ in the Book of Revelation, the vision of divine judgment in the requiem Mass, and the more recent hymns of militant missionary Protestantism. Today we can see it in the image of God as liberator.

In the modern republican era the kingly God of order retreated into the domestic monarchy of the patriarchal nuclear family, where God's monarchy legitimated the governance of the passions in the service of a personality, that is, the patriarch's son, that could participate in the conventions of a secular civility. However, this union of Christian regal symbolism and domestic order ultimately subverted both the publication of women's lives and the dynamic of expression and confirmation at the heart of marital communion. The Church's retention of monarchical symbolism as the psychological and domestic basis of republican life became a symptom of its own privatization.

These two themes of ground and actor in our divine imagery echo the twin concerns of republican and federal tradition. The first is a concern for the stable ground for an enduring public order. The second is a concern for the appropriate means for the expansion of a republican order and its defense from violence, both within and without.

In the theological vision I am articulating here, these two concerns can be expressed in the dual conception of God as publisher and president. As actor God is a saving publisher for our lives, leading us to fuller profession—inspiring, encouraging, affirming and disconfirming us as we strive to profess and confirm ourselves among others. As president God is the ground undergirding the confession we achieve with others.

God as publisher directs us to the emancipatory and liberating dynamic in God. As publisher God evokes from us a resonance we may not have experienced in any particular public. God enters into our jumbled discourse and leads us to new speech, new professions, a renewed drive for creating a more adequate public to share this fuller life with others.

God publishes us by giving us a new language won from the cacophony of events and confirmed in our historic experience of God's call through prophets, mystics and martyrs. This call breaks through our emotional bondage to the narrow covenants and contracts we have formed with family, friends, neighborhoods, and nations—opening up a wider covenant and a richer language for preserving it.

The publication of our lives begins in these key conversions, whether they are conveyed through the Bible, biographies, or personal contact. We participate in and take on the language and habits publicized in these historic turning points where God's mysterious action creates a new and wider public in the midst of our myopia and darkness. God as publisher creates the Pentecostal ecstasy of a public that anticipates the final universal conversation of creation.

The agony of emerging into this new public occurs most symbolically in our entry into the Church but is also experienced in other analogous ways as well. It is a painful rebirth whose miraculous occurrence in our lives can only be divine in origin. To make it through to confirmation in a new public calls up resources we never would have imagined otherwise. It is God who enables us to join in the authorship of our own lives.

God as president directs us to the legitimating work of God by which our fuller publicity can be grounded in an active reasonableness. God does not rule human affairs like some causal agent. God persuades us to common action. This conception of presidency conflicts with our popular notion of the executive as one who commands and coerces to bring about compliance from others. That is the vision of the president as chief executive officer, who takes responsibility and independence away from others in order to do his or her will.

In fact, as many students of management have seen, organizational leadership finally must rest on the capacity to elicit loyalty through self-sacrifice, publish guiding values, coordinate and harmonize people's actions, and act as an exemplar of everyone's capacity for presidency. It is these characteristics of presidency which come to perfection in God. As president God brings about the kind of unity experienced when people act according to mutually understood conventions. God works through the very logic of our discourse to sustain more adequate confessions for our life together. God is the Logos of the logic of our public argument.

God energizes the processes by which we can confirm each other even in our disagreements. Our limited and distorted publics rest on imperfect agreements that cannot comprehend all of reality or bring about a truly universal public discourse. "God" is the symbol by which we hope for a more perfect public which can confirm us all and sustain us with an ultimate affirmation.

The concept of publicity gives us new ways of grasping the divine reality and interpreting older notions. However, just as the theory of republic evidenced its limits, so the idea of God informed by it is incomplete. God's activity of publication and presidency depends in turn on God's covenanting, by which the fabric of public discourse is woven together and by which a variety of publics is knitted together. In this role God emerges as a Creator of covenants. Through the power of covenant God creates a world in which the plurality of public worlds can be sustained. Both federalism and its republican partner demand a further completion in God, who presides over the history and the land of all peoples and draws them toward an everlasting and universal covenant.

God and the federal republic toward which we are called does not simply float in the air or wait at the end of history's tunnel. God, in biblical faith, is the prime actor in our own historic drama. People may know this presiding action of God in many ways. In Christian faith this encounter occurs through our covenantal bond with Jesus as the publisher and president of our life in the special assembly known as the Church. Let us first look at Jesus within the perspective of covenanted publicity and then turn to the little public in which people rehearse the story of their salvation—the *ecclesia* of God.

F. Jesus: Ecclesial President

Jesus shares in God's action as publisher and president. He is the dramatic appearance of this dynamic in our history. We cannot explore here all the ways Jesus engages in this divine activity. We can only indicate the key points that a full picture of Jesus would develop.

First, I shall lift up Jesus' action as publisher, leading to his death on the cross. Second I want to show how this picture of Jesus recovers some covenantal images behind the early Church's view of Jesus as Davidic Messiah. Third, I shall unfold the inauguration of his presidency through his resurrection and assembly of the Church through the Holy Spirit. With this evocation of the Church we shall then move to our discussion of the ecclesial public.

1. Jesus as Publisher. Jesus' work of publication emerges in his listening, preaching, and healing. In his listening we see the divine responsiveness to our longing and our need. In his preaching we hear a courageous fullness of expression. In his persuading we observe his capacity to convert people from their narrow covenants to the ultimate public of God's imminent presidency. In his healing we see people drawn out of their deprivation, blindness, and lameness in order to participate in the wider community.

We rarely ascribe the power of listening to God. We do not see it as part of God's power. However, the Bible frequently speaks of God's hearing of Israel's groaning (Ex 2:24; Jgs 2:18; Ps 38:9), of the Church's prayers (Lk 18:7; Rom 8:15), and of the travail of creation (Jer 51:52; Rom 8:22–26). In his own ministry Jesus both acted on the faith that God would hear him and was one who heard the cries of people seeking his attention (Mt 8:25; 9:18, 27). The power of listening is usually overlooked because many Christians are fascinated with the power of the word. They believe power lies solely in utterance of commands and promises. Equally powerful, however, is the capacity to hear, respond, and enter into the give and take of discourse. This creates the resonant bond in which power emerges. As a divine presence Jesus begins his work of publication as a supreme listener—one who enables others to publish their lives.

Jesus responds in many ways, but especially in his teaching and preaching. He plays the role of rabbi and prophet. In the act of preaching Jesus takes up the prophetic office in which one expresses the message whose only confirmation is the sense of God's embracing communion. It is expression in the face of the disconfirmation posed by the world's injustice and the powers that maintain those inequities. Jesus' preaching sets about establishing a new order not conformed to the existing society. His preaching is the publication of a new world.

This preaching, however, is not mere harangue. It is not a stone from Mars. It is costumed in hooks and lures to catch people in their present confirmations and covenants, drawing them like fish into other waters. The parable, the interlocution, the allegory, and the syllogism all play a role in Jesus' work of persuasion. With the logic of his discourse Jesus weaves an argument to draw people out of their old world into a new. By drawing people out of their contradictions Jesus makes them whole. He heals with discourse.

It is not insignificant that most of his healing dealt with the ostracized leper, the blind, the lame dependent, and the deaf. Jesus' healing is not only a public demonstration of his special communion with the Source of life. It is also the means enabling people to publish their own lives more fully. As preacher, persuader, and healer Jesus founds a new public order.

Jesus enables us to publish our lives even as he sets about publishing the coming covenant public where God's presidency will be complete. Because the work of publication demands the patient powers of listening, speaking, and persuading, Jesus is ultimately vulnerable to the coercion that grips our fearful world. This is why Jesus undergoes death. In the body of his resurrection these powers of publication and presidency are revealed in the spirit active in the ecclesia gathered around him. To prepare the way for such a discussion of the Spirit in the Church we need to look at Jesus as the wisdom of God and the liturgy of God.

2. Jesus as the Wisdom of God. In the second chapter I pointed out the fateful turn by which the early Church chose to see Jesus in terms of the hierarchical Davidic covenant rather than the egalitarian covenant of Israel's Mosaic confederation. It came to understand Jesus' accomplishment in terms of the hierarchical covenant spanning the generations in promise rather than the egalitarian covenant grounding the rich inter-relationships in the assembly of God's people. Thus, the symbols for seeing Jesus in light of Moses, Samuel, and Judas Maccabeus were sub-ordinated to his position as king, monarch, and ruler. The ancient view of God as a priestly warrior was submerged in regal dominion and pa-ternal care. The royal household of God overwhelmed the delicate fi-bers of the assembly of the saints.

A theology embedded in the symbol of God's Federal Republic re-deems even as it corrects this minority view of Jesus and recovers the most precious elements of our biblical faith from the ashes of a gutted monarchy. We do this by showing how the qualities of publicity correct the militarism of the Maccabeans while claiming the persuasive char-acter of priestly presidency. In his work of persuasion Jesus exercises a presidency rather than a household dominion. The stable ground of God's new order inaugurated with his life rests not on the mantle of personal rule but on the wisdom of the discourse he sets in motion through his ministry. It is this tradition of wisdom, no longer reduced to the prudence of the king, that undergirds the image of Jesus as Logos and as the very expression of God's reason.

In playing this other side of the record we can recognize the bless-ing in the curse of Roman imperialism, for it required that Jesus and the early Church work exclusively by persuasion, lest the Roman sword ob-literate them. Within the depths of powerlessness God refined and forged the ultimate symbol of persuasive presidency. The wisdom of God was revealed in the work of Jesus as publisher and president. This is the key to our vision of Jesus.

3. The Liturgy of Jesus. Our view of Jesus here focuses on his minis-try—his life of public service. His life reinterprets the tradition of Isa-iah's suffering servant of God. From the standpoint of the Church's later worship, we can see that his whole life was an offering to build up God's perfect public.

The Greek word for liturgy (*leitourgeia*) meant a "public work." It came from the practice of people sponsoring events and expenses for the benefit of the whole community. Thus, at the root of our vision of Jesus as the center of our worship, we have the image of the one who offers up his or her life for the upbuilding of the public. Jesus' whole life was a "liturgy" in this sense. It is an image that calls into question the esoteric introversion infecting Christian worship and directs us back to the cen-tral mission of Jesus' life—the inauguration of a new order of covenanted publicity.

The liturgy of Jesus' life was non-violent because it was first of all persuasive. Jesus' public discourse sought to create a web of mutual resonance energizing people to higher levels of existence. It could not be coercive. This is why Christians are called to non-violence, not because they do not wish to cause pain to sentient beings or because they want to obey Jesus' command, but because violence is the enemy of public discourse and persuasion. The goal of the Christian life is not to escape violence as an end in itself but to build up more perfect publics in federal faithfulness. This is why non-violence must characterize the action of people seeking God's new public. Because this conviction does not completely rule out all use of force, it also requires that we enter the arduous ethical debate over the resort to force by faithful people.

Because Jesus' ministry was oriented toward this goal it had to eschew violent confrontation or escape. His death on the cross was the ultimate expression of the virtues of persuasion required by God's perfect public. The cross is the symbol of a life dedicated to perfect publicity—to the expression of his communion with God even in the face of the world's worst disconfirmation. It was a death not to satisfy a God of honor but to introduce an ultimate principle of public order. As John's Gospel says, even in being killed he was "lifted up" to an even greater publicity and became the central symbol of an emerging outpost of God's new order. This is the way we can understand Jesus' death and resurrection within the perspective of our governing symbol.

4. Jesus as President. The resurrection of Jesus and the eruption of his Spirit among his followers is the vindication and ultimate confirmation of his public work. His presidency over the fledgling public is rooted in the resonant communion of his followers. The Holy Spirit known in the upper room at Pentecost is the energy of this divine-human resonance. We will turn to the work of the Spirit in the Church presently. For the moment let us unfold briefly the nature of Jesus' presidency as the Christ.

Jesus exercises his ongoing presidency among his people through the Spirit arising in his followers' willingness to express themselves and confirm one another in the new world of experiences, memories, and language created by Jesus. In becoming the focal point of this new public Jesus creates the basis for a covenant uniting this new assembly and providing it with the framework for its ongoing discourse. In the linguistic revolution of the Spirit's communion the assembly can begin to join into a covenantal bond under the presidency of God. This is the meaning of Jesus as the Christ. Within the vision formed by faith in

God's Federal Republic the ancient notion of the Messiah is recast in a distinctive way to express the presidency of God.

The idea of the new covenant in Jesus is actually not part of the Gospel vision but of the letters of Paul, including the Letter to the Hebrews. In this covenantal vision we see the elements of both hierarchy and equality. The hierarchical covenant recognizes the way our present covenants are always reconstructions of those which have been handed down to us. The Eucharist of the Church is a reconstruction of Hebrew Passover in which the earlier covenant of Exodus is reinterpreted in terms of the emergent ecclesia. However, this reconstruction respects a certain hierarchy of descent by seeking to renew the central intentions of the earlier form. It also recognizes the universal scope which transcends the narrower limits of the nations' languages and conventions.

The egalitarian dimensions of this covenant are realized in the mutuality and exchange among the members—across the conventions of gender and status, wealth and power. The followers come together as friends, not simply by virtue of their natural similarities but because of their willingness to offer up the properties of their lives to the one who has called them out of darkness and into a common light.

Jesus' presidency in the Christian assembly sets forth a peculiar model which should inform not only the many ways we seek to preside in his name, but also the way we mold the presidency exercised in our many other publics. This kind of presidency empowers rather than dominates, motivates rather than manipulates, publishes new words rather than imposes the last word. Presidency is not only the highest form of public service but one that all people are called to exercise in the many publics of their lives. Just as we conceive God's action among us as a kind of presidency, so we must shape our many relative presidencies after the model of God's action we know in Christ's presidency in the Church.

The persuasive liturgy of Jesus' life as publisher and president culminates in the explosion of the energy which creates the special assembly we call the Church. This is the final theological concern I want to illuminate in light of our governing symbol.

G.   The Spirit of God's Federal Republic

Faith in Jesus as president can only occur within a public where the divine spirit presides. The Church itself draws its name from the original Greek public—the *ekklesia*. The symbol of God as Spirit attunes us to the dynamics of publicity as well as covenant. Spirit is the energy created in the intensification of life created by the process of publicity.

Spirit also emerges in the bonds which seek articulation as covenant. Spirit is a fundamental expression of God's covenanting and presidency. To open up this hidden treasure in light of our governing symbol we will examine the ecclesia as a certain kind of public, as a representative council, and as sacred publisher of our lives.

1. Church as Public. The Church is a peculiar public with a culture vivified by a liturgy anchored in Jesus as its founder. This public culture consists not only in the symbolic actions of its formal worship but in the conventions of interaction among the people who emerge into each other's presence through baptism and participation in the manifold mission of the Church. Through this ecclesial culture the ongoing vision of God's Federal Republic can be transmitted to and through us. We can be renewed in hope of its realization even as we are corrected from our wanderings into the seductive privatisms of fearfulness and isolation.

In this mediating process the Church becomes a school of publicity. Congregations can be schools for public life, seedbeds for other publics. They can do this not only by enhancing the "properties" of people through charitable and economic work, but also in preserving and enhancing the conventions of civility which make public life possible. Not only do churches have a responsibility to help people put a material floor under their feet, they also must provide the means for them to publicize their lives. Their meetings are as important as their worship in inculcating the liturgy of covenantal publicity. They have a critical role to play in transforming the civil confessions around them.

A Church led by a vision of God's ultimate republic will cultivate arenas for the profession of people's faith and wisdom, whether in prayer, personal witness, discussion of Scripture, confession, conciliar debate, or initiation of mission programs. It will also exercise its functions of confirmation through its encouragement of the exploration of alternatives, acceptance of critique, open processes of decision-making, and cultivation of numerous small groups for the sharing of mutual concerns. The Church is a kind of public life lived out in congregations where publicity can find a peculiarly intense expression and where we can be schooled in the manners of ecclesial civility that make that possible. In being a genuine ecclesia the Church becomes a school of wider publicity, a tangible manifestation of the perfect public we strive for. It is in this sense that we can say that the mission of the Church is to be the Church.

As a school the Church is a theaterola, in the sense we used earlier. It is a place of performance and must be understood as such, whether in the drama of worship or of congregational business meetings. Easter morning is a dramatic act of publicity, even as Good Friday remembers the ultimate sacrifice we pay to remain loyal to the perfect public of persuasion confirmed in God's communion. As an arena of symbolic memory and anticipation the Church plays a unique role as a stage where we can rehearse a life lived in trust, equality, and covenantal resonance with the source of our final hope.

The actual churches we may participate in, of course, are only partial realizations of these aims, just as are our other publics. These assemblies, even though intense, are also imperfect publics. Even in their tentative achievements, they are only anticipations, dreams, and hopes. They are anticipatory, or proleptic publics. They anticipate even as they only partially realize the more perfect public in which we will be able to disclose ourselves fully to each other in the strength of our ultimate confirmation and affirmation by God. This is the public God has covenanted to bring us into. God's Federal Republic is both the hope that draws us on and the source of judgment over against our present sin.

The Church as a school and theaterola of publicity is meant to nurture us as well as create and maintain theaters of publicity and the properties they and their actors need in the wider society. Thus, churches must attend not only to the quality of communication they promote but to the adequacy of the properties that participants require for the publication of their lives. Economic and political action to secure these prerequisites of covenantal publicity are integral to the Church's mission. This is the guideline for its mission and its ministry as the public of Jesus' presidency in the energizing resonance of the Spirit.

Churches, along with other religious associations, can be seen as publics in which the narratives of our public confessions are rehearsed, in which we ourselves can find voice for our professions, engage in covenanting, and contribute to enhancing the publics around us. These assemblies are sometimes the only open publics in a society, as they were at one time for most Afro-Americans, and remain so for many Latin Americans. It may well be this public character of their life, more than their "religiosity" as such, which accounts for their repression by despotic or totalitarian regimes. They offer a kind of publicity which stands in judgment over the deprivations of their lives.

Religious associations not only have a role in enhancing people's public properties and their political culture. They also can spawn particular associations to press for greater justice and more adequate public life. They have an appropriate political as well as economic and cultural
¹⁰ The theory of a federal republic offers a framework for creating,
ʒ, and judging these initiatives.

2. Church as Representative Council. The conciliar impulse of ecclesial life stands at the center of the Church's life as a little public of Jesus' presidency. This has been a major burden of this book. The Church is to be conciliar in its own life and cultivate conciliar forms in the wider society. One of the difficulties encountered by conciliarism in any large organization or population is that of representation. Our theological extrapolation of the meaning of God's Federal Republic seeks to approach this problem through a particular conception of the Church as a representative assembly.

Republican theory has always had the problem of handling the two aspects of representation—on the one hand the representation of the interests of groups and persons not participating directly in the public, and on the other hand articulating the way the assembly itself represents the people as a whole republic in history. Monarchists worked out a theory to show how the monarch was the head of the popular body, but they did so by extinguishing the public. Modern republicans worked out an interest theory linking individuals to the governing assembly but stumbled in the effort to show how the assembly represents the common good of the people.

This is not an easy problem to solve, because the interweaving of the little and large publics with each other and with the professions of persons is a vision of life in God's Federal Republic which has only a flickering intimation in our own. However, within the dynamic of the Church we may be able to lay hold of the lines which culminate in that ultimate covenant binding these publics together within God's covenantal presidency.

It may help to use the word "vicarage" to understand the Church as a representative council. Vicarage comes from the Latin word for representative. It is usually attached to the pastor as a vicar of the bishop, who in turn is a vicar of Christ. This usage reflects a hierarchical order of feudal bonds—the old wineskin of our faith. If we place it within the framework of a federal republic, we can see that the presiding minister is to represent Christ within that public. Vicarage is vice-presidency of the Church bound in covenant to Christ. The pastor of sheep is transformed into the vice-president of a Christian public whose president is Christ.

This is a peculiar vice-presidency, however, for it has its legitimation only in the re-presentation of Jesus' own work of publication. It is a presidency which must draw people out of their hiddenness, cultivate bonds of trust, establish and clarify covenants, and cultivate a Church public which is genuinely an anticipation of God's own. In this kind of representation it is not enough that the published interests of the most powerful are heard. The president must lift up the covenant binding that assembly to the deprived members hiding at the boundaries of its life.

The assembly, like a civil public, may not need the direct participation of all, but it needs the presidency of those who have a firm grasp of the covenant binding all into a common historic drama of mutual accountability. In this sense the Church public is representative, not only of its living members but of the Spirit working to publish the lives of all before God. The assembly represents above all Christ as the founder of our common covenant and the center of the spiritual energy extending publicity to all. This is why the conciliar life of the Church cannot occur without its constant effort to represent the work of Jesus drawing all people into the publicity made possible by the confirming presence of God.

3. Church as Publication. The Church is a rehearsal for greater publicity through its own self-governance, mission and symbolic action. The worship life of the Church is the wider publication of the covenantal publicity possible in the presence of God. Our governing symbol leads us to reconceive the meaning of the sacramental life of the Church.

Sacraments are the symbolic actions by which God's presidency and covenant promises are made real for us. The sacraments are ways we already claim that publicity even as we anticipate it. They are forms of and for publicity. This focus on sacrament places public proclamation, preaching, and prayer at the center of our worship. The dynamic of profession and confirmation is most explicit in the symbolic enactment of our publication and covenanting. Both baptism and Eucharist are professions of our liberation—whether it is our personal emergence from the family and home, as in baptism, or our corporate emergence in exodus and Passover. These acts of personal and historic publication are rehearsed again in confirmations and reaffirmations of faith, with response from the assembly.

The entry into ecclesial covenants can be varied indeed—whether we are joining a particular congregation, articulating a congregational covenant, joining a marriage and family to the Church, or commissioning people to a particular work within the Church's wider vocation. The covenantal acts of the Church bring to a focus not only the actions of publicity but the bonds of covenant that bind our publics together, even out to the global Church.

Ordination is another form of covenanting which brings the dy-
; of representation and presidency to the fore. With ordinations the

assembly authorizes particular members to carry out its work in special ways. Here a particular covenant is made, vows are entered, and the act of representation takes a specified form within one member's profession. This ordination is therefore not to any individual career, spiritual niche, or immunity from the public process. It is designation to a particular role within the covenantal drama of the Church.

These are some of the ways the Church publishes its life through symbolic acts. Many people would identify these as sacraments and formalize them more than others. Some would attribute a greater degree of ultimate publicity to them. Others would stress the faintness of their realization. In any event the Church as Jesus' federal republic must publish this reality of God's purpose in our lives.

The Church's mission of publication centers in its symbolic acts. The theater of these actions is the sanctuary—the sacred space of persuasion and non-violence. Our treatment of the Church concludes with attention to the meaning of the Church's sanctuary.

Because of the persuasive necessity of publicity, its perfection demands the inviolate sphere of sanctuary. The symbolic anticipations of our salvation and the rehearsal of our brief historical realizations of its blessings must be protected in the perimeter of sacredness. This is the basis for talking about sanctuary in the Church. It is the means for safeguarding the integrity of the Church as an anticipatory public.

In our own time, not only in North America but elsewhere as well, the sanctuary has become identified as a refuge for the conscientious resistor and the persecuted refugee. It is the haven for those who stand confirmed by God's covenant even when disconfirmed by the straitjackets of nationalism's lesser covenants. Here the Church's integrity as people in covenant to God's Federal Republic is tested in contest with the lesser republics of our time. This is as it should be for sanctuary to be the theater of God's publicity.

At the center of the image of sanctuary today stands the refugee. The refugee creates an image which not only vivifies our grasp of sanctuary's meaning but also forces us to move beyond our little republics to a vision of a global federal republic where everyone would have a public place.

Our present republics co-exist by assigning citizenship and thereby the possibility of publicity on the basis of nationality. The person deprived of nationality became the focus of the United Nations after the enormous dislocations of World War II. However the question of public life for millions of refugees, aliens, and "guest workers" is still not answered, nor has displacement proven to be a temporary problem. It is a permanent feature of our life. Publishing the life of the refugee and the alien becomes a central act in the drama of the Church's witness to the Federal Republic in which we all are called to participate. The refugee is Abraham among us, calling us to that promised land.

II. Claiming the Vision

In this essay I have tried to retrieve and reform the symbol of federal republic. We have turned up numerous implications for Christian faith and public life. A theory of this governing symbol touches on every aspect of life. It grounds a political ethic without overlooking personality dynamics. It offers a theory of personality with profound political ramifications. It welds both of these to a theological partner.

The lines delineating this complex symbol give us a way for ordering our deepest affections. This theory is a kind of "analytical ethic," in Max Stackhouse's terms, which finds in the trustworthy disposition of things an orientation toward sustainable initiatives.[9] The struggle for an ethical ideal is also rooted in the nature of our action itself. In religious terms it is found in the biblical belief in a divine governance already at work but not brought to completion.

The viewpoint developed here helps us ferret out the essential strivings for covenanted publicity which underlie all human action. It leads us from the critique of sexism to the construction of redeeming publics. It tries to lead us from the contractual individualism of contemporary neo-conservatism to the covenantal bonds of public life upon the land. It moves us from the acts of liberation to the publication of our lives in federal publicity. This is the vision that helps us criticize narrowly biological, psychological or economic interpretations of life. It is also a vision that shapes our understanding of God's purposes. It refurbishes our knowledge of God in the light of biblical faith and our experience in the Christian public.

In a governing symbol like federal republic we are dealing not only with theories but with a highly charged symbol, whose flag has been splashed with blood, whose proclamation has been punctuated with tears. It evokes the loyalty of millions of people, even if in diverse ways. An ethical and religious theory tied to it touches on deep motivations. In this symbol we bring together energy and thought, giving us guidance for action. In the complex symbol, God's Federal Republic, we find judgment as well as hope. We find an intimate connection with our present lives and yet awareness of the gulf that separates us from our final destination.

By putting on these glasses we see the religious landscape differently. We are able to pull together a religious conception of life oriented around a transcendent vision and congruent with our psychology and sociology. We also can see our cultural landscape differently. Kingship symbolism traps our faith within the little households of a vanishing patriarchy. We are left hiding in a closet grasping the hair of memory without the living body of faith.

God's Federal Republic has two eyes for seeing our way ahead. Both are necessary. Federalism points to a way of bringing together the many publics which arise as people seek publicity. It creates covenantal relationships among many diverse publics. They are not to be placed in a hierarchical ladder but in a web of covenants grounding people in their relationships to each other, the land and the divine source of their life.

Republic indicates the character of these covenanted groups. They are arenas for evoking and shaping our need for profession and confirmation. The goals of publicity must always critique the narrowness of covenants as well as the distortions of public life. Republic always holds out the content of the life to be sustained in covenant.

Some critics might argue that such a symbol is too full, others that it is too empty. It may seem too full, in the sense that the symbol has been worshiped by too many different sects. It has too many meanings in a world of Republics and Federations. What could possibly be the connection between the German Federal Republic, The Republic of China, and the Republic of South Africa? This might lead others to say that the symbol is too empty. It is meaningless in the midst of such contention over the proper public structures to accompany it.

This symbolic diffusion testifies to the depth at which people claim a trans-rational vision. Not to work with such symbols is to escape from life. Secondly, a convergent symbol like Federal Republic narrows its range of possible interpretations. It demands a theory that takes up the implications of both partners to this wedding. The theory developed here has been designed to focus the arguments over the meaning of this governing symbol. Lastly, it is symbols like these that provide a cultural basis for helping the warring peoples of the world to talk to each other and which enable religious communities to engage this public debate in a critical fashion.

The argument, as I have shown, has long been underway. I have tried to reformulate it for our present situation and urge a particular line of development which can take up the concerns we have to overcome the dualisms of race and sex as well as to ground a public order of justice and peace. When we speak of *God's* Federal Republic we not only call into judgment all our pretensions at federal publicity, but also establish a hope for the ultimate perfection of our struggle for expression and confirmation—the republic where God presides among us all.

An earlier publicist could say: "I take leave of a partial public with the truest gratitude for its long endurance."[10] The Letter to the Hebrews goes further and calls us to have the faith of a wandering Abraham and Sarah who "looked forward to the city which has foundations, whose builder and maker is God."

NOTES

Introduction

[1] Robert Bellah, *et al.*, *Habits of the Heart: Individualism and Commitment in American Life* (Berkeley: University of California Press, 1985). For a related perspective see William Sullivan, *Reconstructing Public Philosophy* (Berkeley: University of California Press, 1982).

[2] For a rather polemical overview of this movement see Peter Steinfels, *The Neoconservatives: The Men Who Are Changing America's Politics* (New York: Simon and Schuster, 1979). For Novak's views see *Toward a Theology of the Corporation* (Washington: American Enterprise Institute, 1981). Neuhaus' argument for a religious presence in the public sphere is in *The Naked Public Square* (Grand Rapids: William B. Eerdmans, 1984).

[3] Jerry Falwell, with his associates, Ed Dobson and Ed Hindson, provides an historical overview and agenda in *The Fundamentalist Phenomenon: The Resurgence of Conservative Christianity* (Garden City, NY: Doubleday-Galilee, 1981). For a set of scholarly reflections see Robert Liebman and Robert Wuthnow, eds., *The New Christian Right: Mobilization and Legitimation* (New York: Aldine Publishing Company, 1983). Nancy Ammerman examines its local manifestation in *Bible Believers: Fundamentalists in the Modern World* (New Brunswick: Rutgers University Press, 1987).

1. Claiming a Governing Symbol

[1] My theory of symbol is influenced by Paul Tillich, "The Religious Symbol," *Myth and Symbol*, F. W. Dillistone, ed. (London: SPCK Press, 1966), 15–34, as well as sociologists like Hugh Duncan, *Symbols and Social Theory* (New York: Oxford University Press, 1969).

From Tillich I get the emphasis on the deep emotional grounding of symbols and the way they mediate more transcendent purposes, though I obviously believe they are more susceptible of rational discourse and intentional change over time. From Duncan I derive the understanding of the way symbols legitimate social structures. For a fuller explication of my approach see my earlier essay, "Cybernetics and the Symbolic Body Model," *Zygon*, 7:2 (June 1972), 98–109.

² *The Nerves of Government* (New York: Free Press, 1966).

³ Sallie McFague, *Metaphorical Theology: Models of God in Religious Language* (Philadelphia: Fortress Press, 1982), and Norman Perrin, *Jesus and the Language of the Kingdom: Symbol and Metaphor in New Testament Interpretation* (Philadelphia: Fortress Press, 1976). The language of "tensive" and "steno" symbols comes from Philip Wheelwright, *Metaphor and Reality* (Bloomington: Indiana University Press, 1962), esp. ch. 5.

⁴ McFague, 109–11, and David Tracy, "Metaphor and Religion: The Test Case of Christian Texts," *On Metaphor*, ed. Sheldon Sacks (Chicago: University of Chicago Press, 1978), 106, tend in this direction.

⁵ The present book brings to a conclusion an argument begun with my doctoral dissertation, "Body Thinking in Ecclesiology and Cybernetics," Harvard University, 1970. See also Mary Douglas, *Natural Symbols: Explorations in Cosmology* (New York: Pantheon, 1970).

⁶ For a critical survey of the literature from a pluralist perspective see Joseph R. Gusfield, *Community: A Critical Response* (New York: Harper & Row, 1975). Rosabeth Moss Kanter examines the deep commitments involved in communal utopias in *Commitment and Community: Communes and Utopias in Sociological Perspective* (Cambridge: Harvard University Press, 1972). Frank G. Kirkpatrick seeks to integrate atomistic/contractarian, organic/functional and mutual/personal models of community in *Community: A Trinity of Models* (Washington: Georgetown University Press, 1986). He presses in a covenantal and public direction without using the language I am advancing here.

⁷ For a history of this term see George Boas, *Vox Populi: Essays in the History of an Idea* (Baltimore: Johns Hopkins University Press, 1969).

⁸ Rauschenbusch spoke of "that Kingdom which is the only true Democracy" in *A Theology for the Social Gospel* (New York: Abingdon, 1945), 180. George A. Coe, the noted religious educator, persistently spoke of "the Democracy of God" in *A Social Theory of Religious Education* (New York: Charles Scribner's Sons, 1917), 54 *et pass.*

2. Kingship and Kingdom: The Heritage and the Harvest

[1] Still a fruitful source is Henri Frankfort, *Kingship and the Gods: A Study of Ancient Near Eastern Religion as the Integration of Society and Nature* (Chicago: University of Chicago Press, 1948). See also "Basileus," *Bible Key Words*, ed. G. W. Kittel, tr. A. A. Harvey (New York: Harper and Brothers, 1960), I.564–93; and Keith W. Whitelam, *The Just King: Monarchical Judicial Authority in Ancient Israel* (Sheffield: JSOT Press, 1979).

[2] In addition to Whitelam see Baruch Halpern, *The Constitution of the Monarchy in Ancient Israel* (Chico, CA: Scholars Press, 1982) and Martin Buber, *Kingship of God*, tr. R. Scheimann (New York: Harper & Row, 1967).

Because both later kings and early images of YHWH used warrior imagery, Buber claims that Israel thought of YHWH as king from its earliest days. This seems to be unsupported by any evidence, however. Buber sought a governmental order based on dialogue, persuasion, and interaction. He therefore read this back into his view of God's relation with Israel and Israel's relation to its human kings. Why he was willing to stick with the symbolism of kingship in the face of his dialogical model, however, is not clear. In fact, as I shall show, it is much more suitable for the symbolism of a federal republic.

[3] In addition to Kittel see Numa Denis Fustel de Coulanges, *The Ancient City: A Study on the Religion, Laws, and Institutions of Greece and Rome* (Garden City: Doubleday-Anchor, n.d. [1857]).

[4] Ellen and Neal Wood, *Class Ideology and Ancient Political Theory: Socrates, Plato and Aristotle in Social Context* (New York: Oxford University Press, 1978), 25, 233.

[5] For a classic critique of the platonic approach to government see Karl H. Popper, *The Open Society and Its Enemies* (5th ed. rev.; Princeton: Princeton University Press, 1966), Vol. I, ch. 10.

[6] On the meaning of Wisdom at the beginning of the Christian era see W. D. Davies, *Paul and Rabbinic Judaism* (2d ed.; London: SPCK Press, 1955), ch. 7, and with lesser political awareness, the articles in Robert Wilken, ed., *Aspects of Wisdom in Judaism and Early Christianity* (Notre Dame: University of Notre Dame Press, 1975). Schüssler Fiorenza (n. 7 below), 130–140, provides a feminist interpretation but without making its wider political meaning explicit.

[7] Elisabeth Schüssler Fiorenza, *In Memory of Her: A Feminist Theological Reconstruction of Christian Origins* (New York: Crossroad Publishing Company, 1984). Unfortunately, she sidesteps the problem of kingship symbolism by referring simply to "basileia," thus covering political symbolism in archaic language (110).

[8] Henry Myers, *Medieval Kingship* (Chicago: Nelson-Hall, 1982), 9. Myers' work underlies this treatment of kingship in the medieval period.

[9] From his "Oration on the Tricennalia of Constantine," quoted in Myers, 25.

[10] Richard Krautheimer, "The Constantinian Basilica," *Dumbarton Oaks Papers*, 21 (1967), 117–140; and Susan Lang, "A Few Suggestions Towards a New Solution of the Origin of the Early Christian Basilica," *Rivista di Archaeologia Cristiana*, 30:3–4 (1954), 189–208. I am indebted to Rev. Thomas Fait for this information.

[11] Quoted in Myers, 139.

[12] William Chaney, *The Cult of Kingship in Anglo-Saxon England* (Berkeley: University of California Press, 1970).

[13] No one summed up the theory of patriarchy and monarchical rights and duties better than James I.

> By the Law of Nature the King becomes a naturall Father to all his Lieges at his coronation: And as the Father of his fatherly duty is bound to care for the nourishing, education and vertuous government of his children, even so is the King bound to care for all his subjects.

(*The Political Works of James I*, intro. Charles H. McIlwain [Cambridge: Harvard University Press, 1918], 55.)

A seminal treatment of this development is John N. Figgis, *The Divine Right of Kings* (New York: Harper and Row, 1965). See also James Bryce's classic history, *The Holy Roman Empire* (New York: Schocken Books, 1961).

[14] Ann Douglas explores some of these dynamics from a feminist slant in *The Feminization of American Culture* (New York: Alfred A. Knopf, 1977). More research would be needed to develop the particular perspective I am advancing here. For a start see Janet F. Fishburn, *The Fatherhood of God and the Victorian Family: The Social Gospel in America* (Philadelphia: Fortress Press, 1982). Dennis McCann and Charles Strain also touch on this issue in *Polity and Praxis: A Program for American Practical Theology* (Minneapolis: Winston Press, 1985), 85–90.

[15] For a detailed history of this development see Ernst Kantorowicz, *The King's Two Bodies* (Princeton: Princeton University Press, 1957).

3. The Republican Heritage

[1] For this account of the classical period I am particularly indebted to Ernest Barker, *From Alexander to Constantine: Passages and Documents Illustrating the History of Social and Political Ideas, 336 BC–AD 337* (Ox-

ford: Clarendon Press, 1959); Victor Ehrenberg, *The Greek State* (New York: Barnes & Noble, 1960); and Hannah Arendt, *The Human Condition* (Garden City, NY: Doubleday-Anchor, 1959).

[2] Cicero, *De Legibus*, tr. C. W. Keyes ("The Loeb Classical Library"; Cambridge, MA: Harvard University Press, 1961), Bk. I., xiii, 337.

[3] Polybius, *The Histories*, Vol. III, tr. W. R. Paton (6 vols; London: W. Heinemann, and New York: G. P. Putnam's Sons, 1922–27), Bk. 6.

[4] Aristotle, *Politics*, 1295b.

[5] Aristotle, *Politics*, 1252a, 1276b; cf. *Nichomachean Ethics*, 1134a–b.

[6] A. P. d'Entreves provides a historical survey of natural law in *Natural Law: A Historical Survey* (New York: Harper & Row, 1965). For a typology of approaches see Francis H. Eterovich, *Approaches to Natural Law from Plato to Kant* (New York: Exposition Press, 1972). For an approach to its use in political theory, see Paul Sigmund, *Natural Law in Political Thought* (Washington: University Press of America, 1982) and for a recent struggle at reformulating the living tradition see Anthony Battaglia, *Toward a Reformulation of Natural Law* (Somers, CT: Seabury, 1981).

[7] For an example of the recovery of rhetoric for public debate see David Mall, *In Good Conscience: Abortion and Moral Necessity* (Libertyville, IL: Kairos Books, 1982).

[8] Vigen Guroian, working from the Armenian Orthodox tradition, provides some challenging approaches to a public theory of the ecclesia in *Incarnate Love: Essays in Orthodox Ethics* (Notre Dame, IN: University of Notre Dame Press, 1987), esp. chaps. 3, 6.

[9] Augustine, *The City of God*, tr. M. Dods (New York: Random House/Modern Library, 1950), II.21, for the following quotations.

[10] The psychological dynamics behind Augustine's search for authority and his rejection of emotional bonds between equal persons has been the subject of much analysis. See James Dittes, "Continuities between the Life and Thought of Augustine," *Journal for the Scientific Study of Religion*, 5:1 (October 1965), 130–140; and related articles in the same volume.

[11] *Confessions*, IX.23.

[12] Letter to Queen Theodelinda. I am indebted to Rev. William Wallaik for this reference from his thesis, "Christianity: The Ideal of Medieval Society" (Milwaukee: Salzmann Library, 1959).

[13] For the following perspective I am drawing on the work of Hans Baron, especially *The Crisis of the Early Italian Renaissance: Civic Humanism and Republican Liberty in an Age of Classicism and Tyranny* (rev. ed.;

Princeton: Princeton University Press, 1966). For Savonarola see Donald Weinstein, *Savonarola and Florence: Prophecy and Patriotism in the Renaissance* (Princeton: Princeton University Press, 1970).

[14] See especially *The Discourses*, Bk. I; *The Prince*, Ch. 1. See also J. G. A. Pocock, *The Machiavellian Moment: Florentine Political Thought and the Atlantic Republican Tradition* (Princeton: Princeton University Press, 1975), Ch. 6.

[15] For this shift see especially Baron, 418. Glen C. Dealy probes the survival of this cultural legacy of public action as distinguished from the private asceticism of Weber's Protestant personality in *The Public Man* (Amherst: University of Massachusetts Press, 1977).

[16] Baron, 395.

[17] Anthony Black, *Council and Commune: The Conciliar Movement and the Fifteenth Century Heritage* (London: Burns & Oates, 1979).

[18] Black, 88.

[19] Black, 155.

[20] Technically, we are dealing here with more than "Puritans." Other reform and revolutionary groups peppered the English landscape. For convenience I simply use the term Puritan as a generic category for various groups seeking changes in the ecclesiastical and governmental establishment at that time. See William Haller (note 22) and Don M. Wolfe, *Milton and His England* (Princeton: Princeton University Press, 1971).

[21] Harrington, *Oceana*, in J. G. Pocock, ed., *The Political Works of James Harrington* (New York: Cambridge University Press, 1977). For further interpretation of Harrington and his impact see Charles Blitzer, *An Immortal Commonwealth: The Political Thought of James Harrington* (New Haven: Yale University Press, 1960) and H. F. Russell Smith, *Harrington and His Oceana: A Study of a 17th Century Utopia and Its Influence in America* (Cambridge: Cambridge University Press, 1914).

John Milton, "The Readie and Easie Way to Establish a Free Commonwealth and the Excellence Thereof Compared with the Inconveniences and Dangers of Re-admitting Kingship in This Nation," *Complete Prose Works of John Milton*, Vol. 7, 1659–60 (rev. ed.; New Haven: Yale University Press, 1980), 407–63.

For Goodwin and others, including the "Putney Debates," see A. S. P. Woodhouse, ed., *Puritanism and Liberty* (Chicago: University of Chicago Press, 1951), 186, 212–20, 293–98.

[22] For an analysis of the concept of property in both Harrington and the Levellers of the English revolution see C. B. Macpherson, *The Political Theory of Possessive Individualism: Hobbes to Locke* (London: Oxford University Press, 1964), 140–54, 174–82. Macpherson brings out the

origins of those property concepts that have tended to cut people off from the public realm, while I am emphasizing those features of their thought they hold in common with classical perspectives on property—an aspect recognized by Macpherson as well. See Anthony Parel and Thomas Flanagan, eds., *Theories of Property: Aristotle to the Present* (Waterloo, Ontario: Wilfrid Laurier Press, 1979) for the wider background of this concept.

William Haller, *Liberty and Reformation in the Puritan Revolution* (New York: Columbia University Press, 1955), provides numerous insights into the tension between individualistic and communal thrusts in Puritan thought.

[23] John Milton, "The Doctrine and Discipline of Divorce" [1643]. See also my *Blessed Be the Bond: Christian Perspectives on Marriage and Family* (Philadelphia: Fortress Press, 1985), Ch. 2.

[24] Harrington, *Oceana* in Pocock, 216.

[25] Harrington, *Oceana*, 262: "Pian Piano," 384–86; and "A Political Discourse Concerning Ordination," in Pocock, 502–56.

[26] John Locke, *Two Treatises of Government*, ed. Peter Laslett (Cambridge: Cambridge University Press, 1960). J. W. Gough traces Locke's republican constitutionalism in *John Locke's Political Philosophy* (2d ed.; Oxford: Oxford University Press, 1973).

[27] Gerald Stourzh, *Alexander Hamilton and the Idea of Republican Government* (Stanford: Stanford University Press, 1970). I am also relying on Gordon Wood, *The Creation of the American Republic* (New York: W. W. Norton, 1969), and Leslie Wharton, *Polity and the Public Good: Conflicting Theories of Republican Government in the New Nation* (Ann Arbor, MI: Research Press, 1980).

[28] Montesquieu, *The Spirit of the Laws*, tr. Thomas Nugent (New York: Hafner Publishing Co., 1949), 129.

[29] See Pocock, *Machiavellian Moment*, Chaps. 9–14, for a detailed investigation of this change.

[30] Alexis de Tocqueville, *Democracy in America*, tr. G. Lawrence, ed. J. P. Mayer (New York: Doubleday Anchor Books, 1969), Bk. I:18.

[31] Stourzh, 70.

[32] Harold D. Lasswell developed this market model of politics with great sophistication in his little classic, *Politics: Who Gets What, When, How* (New York: McGraw-Hill, 1936).

[33] Most political theory has focused on the relationship between participants in the decision-making council and the general citizenry. I am emphasizing here the problem of the relation between the council and the professed sense of unity and destiny of a people. This is the issue to be highlighted by the religious notion of covenant. For the quandaries

of representation in political theory see Gordon S. Wood, *Representation in the American Revolution* ("Jamestown Essays on Representation"; Charlottesville: University Press of Virginia, 1969); Hannah F. Pitkin, *The Concept of Representation* (Berkeley: University of California, 1967); and, for the problem of majority rule versus proportional representation, see Ferdinand Hermens, *The Representative Republic* (Notre Dame, IN: University of Notre Dame Press, 1958).

³⁴ The biblical roots of governance according to law have often been overlooked, because Christianity became excessively involved in legitimating monarchical prerogative. See Max Lerner, *America as a Civilization*, Vol. I (New York: Simon & Schuster, 1957), "Keepers of the Covenant," 441–52. Edward S. Corwin provided the seminal article on this transposition from a natural law perspective in *The "Higher Law" Background of American Constitutional Law* (Ithaca, NY: Cornell University Press, [1928] 1955). See also Ernest Barker, "Natural Law and the American Revolution," *Traditions of Civility* (Cambridge: Cambridge University Press, 1948).

³⁵ Harrington, *Oceana*, 178.

³⁶ On the side of economic determinism see Karl Marx, "The German Ideology," *The Marx-Engels Reader*, ed. Robert C. Tucker (New York: W. W. Norton Co., 1972), 110–64; and for an American version with a political resolution see the famous "Federalist Paper No. 10" (Madison). The transformative impact of social interaction has been a staple of sociological reflection since Durkheim. See Peter Bachrach, "Interest, Participation and Democratic Theory," in J. R. Pennock and J. W. Chapman, eds., *Participation in Politics* ("Nomos," Vol. XVI; New York: Lieber-Atherton, 1975), 39–55.

³⁷ See Franklin Littel, *The Origins of Sectarian Protestantism: A Study of the Anabaptist View of the Church* (New York: Macmillan, 1964) and Donald F. Durnbaugh, *The Believer's Church: The History and Character of Biblical Protestantism* (New York: Macmillan, 1968) for some systematic inquiries into these roots.

³⁸ On the isolating and privatizing impact of separationist doctrines in Eastern Europe see *Church Within Socialism: Church and State in East European Socialist Republics*, ed. Erich Weingärtner, based on the work of Giovanni Barberini (Rome: IDOC International, 1976).

³⁹Stourzh, 99; Wharton, 46. This is also a central preoccupation of Arthur O. Lovejoy's essays in *Reflections on Human Nature* (Baltimore: Johns Hopkins University Press, 1961).

⁴⁰ Stourzh, 64.

⁴¹ Pocock, *Machiavellian Moment*, 439–53.

[42] In the deluge of writing on virtue today, see Stanley Hauerwas, *Vision and Virtue: Essays in Christian Ethical Reflection* (Notre Dame: Fides, 1974), ch. 12; Alasdair MacIntyre, *After Virtue* (Notre Dame: University of Notre Dame Press, 1981), and Robert Bellah et al., *Habits of the Heart: Individualism and Commitment in American Life* (Berkeley: University of California Press, 1985) esp. ch. 2. John P. Diggins, in *The Lost Soul of American Politics: Virtue, Self-Interest and the Foundations of Liberalism* (New York: Basic Books, 1984), struggles toward a more religious, communal and ecological view of virtue to offset classical liberalism's secular individualism. Most of the literature focuses on the need for a mythic, narrative context for virtue. I am focusing on the social structures that need to be linked to specific notions of virtue in order to pursue justice.

[43] See E. M. W. Tillyard's pithy classic, *The Elizabethan World Picture* (London: Chatto & Windus, 1973), esp. ch. 2.

[44] Harrington, *Oceana*, 171.

[45] Arthur Mitzman, *The Iron Cage: An Historical Interpretation of Max Weber* (New York: Alfred Knopf, 1970).

[46] Locke, *Two Treatises*, Bk I.86; Bk II.2–15.

[47] See Macpherson, *Possessive Individualism*, 9–46.

[48] Douglas Sturm and John B. Cobb, Jr. have made signal contributions engaging process thought, political theory and social ethics. See Sturm's "Process Thought and Political Theory: Implications of a Principle of Internal Relations," *Review of Politics*, 41:3 (July 1979), 375–401; and "The 'Path of the Law' and the Via Salutis: A Naturalistic Perspective," *Catholic University Law Review*, 26:1 (Fall 1976), 35–56. Among Cobb's numerous writings see *Process Theology as Political Theology* (Philadelphia: Westminster Press, 1982). See also the articles by Sturm and others in *Process Philosophy and Social Thought*, eds. John B. Cobb, Jr. and W. Widick Schroeder (Chicago: Center for the Scientific Study of Religion, 1981). For a very helpful reconceptualization of Dewey's political theory in the light of process thought see Franklin I. Gamwell, *Beyond Preference: Liberal Theories of Independent Association* (Chicago: University of Chicago Press, 1984).

[49] The biologist Ludwig von Bertalanffy ushered forth the general systems approach with "General Systems Theory," *General Systems*, I (1956), 1–10. Since then the perspective has been taken up by numerous authors in the social sciences, including Kenneth Boulding, Karl Deutsch, David Easton and Talcott Parsons.

[50] J. G. A. Pocock, *Politics, Language and Time* (New York: Atheneum, 1971).

[51] See Nathan Orr Hatch, *The Sacred Cause of Liberty: Republican Thought and the Millennium in Revolutionary New England* (New Haven: Yale University Press, 1977).

[52] Orestes Brownson, *The American Republic: Its Constitution, Tendencies and Destiny* (New York: P. O'Shea, 1865), 38.

[53] Karl Deutsch, *Nationalism and Social Communication: An Inquiry into the Foundations of Nationality* (2d. ed.; Cambridge, MA: MIT Press, 1966).

[54] Michael Harrington presents the argument for an American democratic socialism in *Socialism* (New York: Saturday Review Press, 1972).

[55] Montesquieu, *Spirit of the Laws*, Bk. IX. Sec. 1.

[56] Inaugural Address, Mar 4, 1801. Quoted in Wharton, 1.

4. Federalism: The Covenantal Heritage

[1] For an extended discussion of these motifs see Max L. Stackhouse, *Public Theology and Political Economy: Christian Stewardship in Modern Society* (Grand Rapids: William B. Eerdmans, 1987). M. Douglas Meeks develops a theology rooted in an understanding of the *oikos* in *God the Economist: The Doctrine of God and Political Economy* (Philadelphia: Fortress Press, 1987).

[2] See the essays in Daniel Elazar, ed., *Kinship and Consent: The Jewish Political Tradition and Its Contemporary Uses* (Philadelphia: Center for the Study of Federalism, 1983). George Mendenhall provided the starting point for recent study of covenant in the Bible with "Law and Covenant in Israel and the Ancient Near East," *The Biblical Archaeologist*, 18:2 (May 1954), 26–46 and 18:3 (September 1954), 49–76. Dennis McCarthy exposes additional motifs and uses in *Old Testament Covenant: A Survey of Current Opinions* (Richmond: John Knox, 1972).

[3] The theological perspective on land in Israel's covenant presented by Walter Brueggeman in *The Land* (Philadelphia: Fortress, 1977) contrasts with the break between heaven and earth that appears with Christianity as portrayed in W. D. Davies, *The Gospel and the Land* (Berkeley: University of California Press, 1974).

[4] Elisabeth Schüssler Fiorenza exposes this development in *In Memory of Her*, esp. 285–314.

[5] This becomes especially clear in *City of God*, Books 11–18.

[6] I am drawing here on Ernst Troeltsch's concepts in *The Social Teaching of the Christian Churches*, tr. Olive Wyon (New York: Harper & Brothers, 1960), 150–64.

[7] Students of alliteration could claim that medieval society was held together by *fides, foedus* and *feudum*. For the origins of *feudum* see F. L.

Ganshof, *Feudalism*, tr. P. Grierson (New York: Longmans, Green, 1952), 97.

[8] Henry Myers, *Medieval Kingship*, 124, 134–39.

[9] For an example of the medieval cult of kingship see Ernst Kantorowicz, *Laudes Regiae: A Study in Liturgical Acclamations and Medieval Ruler Worship* (Berkeley: University of California Press, 1958).

[10] I am following Frederick Carney's introduction and translation of Althusius' "Politica Methodice Digesta . . . " in *The Politics of Johannes Althusius* (Boston: Beacon Press, 1964). See also Carl J. Friedrich, *The Philosophy of Law in Historical Perspective* (2d ed.; Chicago: University of Chicago Press, 1963), ch. 8.

[11] Troeltsch sees this development in the context of what for him was the essence of the Gospel—personality (*The Social Teaching*, Vol II, 694–724). This development reaches full flower in the American colonies with Roger Williams and Isaac Backus. For Backus, the lesser known but very influential American Revolutionary divine, see William McLoughlin, *Isaac Backus and the American Pietist Tradition* (Boston: Little, Brown, and Co., 1967).

[12] See Champlin Burrage, *The Church Covenant Idea: Its Origin and Its Development* (Philadelphia: American Baptist Publication Society, 1904); and Christopher Hill, "Covenant Theology and the Concept of a 'Public Person,' " in Alkis Kontos, ed., *Powers, Possessions and Freedom: Essays in Honor of C. B. Macpherson* (Toronto: University of Toronto Press, 1979), 3–22.

[13] A. S. P. Woodhouse, ed., *Puritanism and Liberty*, provides the Agreements, 342–666, 443–44. See also defenses of Church covenants, 299–301. For the Solemn League and Covenant of 1643 see Samuel R. Gardiner, ed., *The Constitutional Documents of the Puritan Revolution, 1625–60* (3rd ed.; Oxford: Clarendon Press, 1979 [1906]), 267–71.

[14] Immanuel Kant, "Eternal Peace," in *The Philosophy of Kant: Immanuel Kant's Moral and Political Writings*, ed. Carl J. Friedrich (New York: Modern Library, 1949), 340–476, esp. 437–46.

[15] See Perry Miller's classic study in *The New England Mind: The Seventeenth Century* (Boston: Beacon Press, 1961), chaps. 13–16, and a typical expression of this covenantal theology in Thomas Shepard, "The Covenant of Grace," in Perry Miller, ed., *The American Puritans: Their Prose and Poetry* (Garden City, NY: Doubleday-Anchor, 1956), 133–48.

[16] For the political significance of Puritan and Jeffersonian approaches to land use see Daniel Elazar, "Land Space and Civil Society in America," *Western Historical Quarterly*, 5:3 (July 1974), 261–84.

[17] Max L. Stackhouse, *Creeds, Societies and Human Rights* (Grand Rapids: William B. Eerdmans, 1984). Milner S. Ball argues that cove-

nant underlies the whole American constitutional enterprise in *The Promise of American Law: A Theological, Humanistic View of Legal Process* (Athens: University of Georgia Press, 1981).

[18] See my "Land Ethics: Toward a Covenantal Model," *The American Society of Christian Ethics: Selected Papers From the Annual Meeting*, ed. Max Stackhouse (Waterloo, Ontario: Council for the Study of Religion, 1979), 45–73, for an extended discussion of the components of covenant.

[19] *Two Treatises of Government*, Bk. II, Ch. 7.

[20] Robert Bellah, *The Broken Covenant: American Civil Religion in Time of Trial* (New York: Seabury Press, 1975), 37.

[21] For an exploration of these religious dynamics in election life see Michael Novak, *Choosing Our King: Powerful Symbols in Presidential Politics* (New York: Macmillan, 1974).

[22] Michael Walzer, "Liberalism and the Art of Separation," *Political Theory*, 12:3 (August 1984), 315–30. Milner S. Ball advances a conception of law as social medium rather than as bulwark in "Law Natural: Its Family of Metaphors and its Theology," *Journal of Law and Religion*, 3:1 (1985), 141–65.

[23] Hannah Arendt, *On Revolution* (New York: Viking Press, 1965), 241–44. Charles L. Mee, Jr. claims that the idea of expanding publics was central to James Madison's approach to the formation of the United States Constitution in 1787 (*The Genius of the People* [New York: Harper and Row, 1987], ch. 9).

[24] "Of all the features of American constitutionalism, federalism has had the most decided impact abroad," wrote Carl J. Friedrich in *The Impact of American Constitutionalism Abroad* (Boston: Boston University Press, 1967), 43. Friedrich's own work in the construction of the modern German constitution was certainly a major element in this impact.

Sobei Mogi's compendious survey of the history of American, British, and German federalism reduced the Hebraic-biblical contribution to a footnote, but is otherwise very useful. *The Problem of Federalism: A Study in the History of Political Theory* (London: George Allen & Unwin, 1931). S. Rufus Davis has updated the inquiry with more theoretical form in *The Federal Principle: A Journey Through Time in Quest of a Meaning* (Berkeley: University of California Press, 1978).

[25] See the introduction by John Anderson to *Calhoun: Basic Documents* (State College, PA: Bald Eagle Press, 1952) and note Calhoun's own emphasis on countervailing power as necessary to a viable federalism (76).

[26] Joseph Allen, *Love and Conflict: A Covenantal Model of Christian Ethics* (Nashville: Abingdon Press, 1984), 69–72, 154–67.

²⁷ This is of course to turn Karl Marx on his head. In *The Communist Manifesto* Marx and Engels claimed that the rise of republicanism was to be supplanted by socialism and communism. In fact, however, Marx was dealing with pre-conditions of republican life, which may be one reason Marxist-led movements have taken root in pre-republican societies but fared poorly in nations with a more fully developed public life. Communist visions can be seen in fact as another form of nostalgia for village life in the face of modern technology.

²⁸ The effort to reunite civil constitution with religious culture is central to the understanding of Iran's revolutionary constitution as presented by Hamid Algar, *Constitution of the Islamic Republic of Iran*, tr. H. Algar (Berkeley: Mizan Press, 1980). In the United States an analogous development occurs in the efforts to subordinate civil pluralism to cultural covenant as set forth most famously by Jerry Falwell and "the Moral Majority."

²⁹ Daniel Elazar, *American Federalism: A View from the States* (3rd ed. rev.; New York: Harper & Row, 1984). See also his more recent book, *Exploring Federalism* (University, AL: University of Alabama Press, 1986).

³⁰ The movement from clan loyalty to civic consciousness can be seen as a central theme of social development. Donald Hanson traces its lineaments in English history in *From Kingdom to Commonwealth: The Development of Civic Consciousness in English Political Thought* (Cambridge: Harvard University Press, 1970).

³¹ For a history of the development of participation, right of dissent, access to information and the like, see Milton Derber, *The American Idea of Industrial Democracy, 1865–1965* (Urbana: University of Illinois Press, 1970). See Michael Harrington, *Socialism*, for a full position statement. For an effort taking up issues of federalism and the wall between private and public see Ronald Mason, *Participatory and Workplace Democracy: A Theoretical Development in Critique of Liberalism* (Carbondale: Southern Illinois University Press, 1982). For a current political analysis see also Martin Carnoy and Derek Shearer, *Economic Democracy* (White Plains: M. E. Sharpe, 1980). For participative management see Joseph Cangemi, *et al.*, *Participative Management: Employee-Management Cooperation* (New York: Philosophical Library, 1983).

³² "The New Abolitionist Covenant" to abolish nuclear weapons was produced in the late 1970's by a number of groups, including the Fellowship of Reconciliation, Nyack, New York. For over forty years the World Federalist movement has sought to advance a global political structure patterned on the American model, but without real self-con-

sciousness of its religious roots. Additional material on covenants is available from the Center for the Study of Federalism, Temple University, Philadelphia, PA 19122.

[33] Peter Berger and Richard Neuhaus, *To Empower People: The Role of Mediating Structures in Public Policy* (Washington: American Enterprise Institute, 1977). The theme in modern sociology emanates from Emile Durkheim's discussion in *The Division of Labor in Society*, tr. G. Simpson (New York: Free Press, 1964), as well as from Alexis de Tocqueville.

[34] For attention to this public context of professionalism see Paul Camenisch, *Grounding Professional Ethics in A Pluralistic Society* (New York: Haven Publications, 1983), ch. 5; and William F. May, *The Physician's Covenant: Images of the Healer in Medical Ethics* (Philadelphia: Westminster Press, 1983), ch. 4. Unfortunately, I am not aware of an equal level of attention by ethicists to the covenantal responsibilities of labor unions.

For the interaction of covenantal ideas with corporate and constitutional forms see Douglas Sturm's penetrating essay, "Corporations, Constitutions, and Covenants: On Forms of Human Relation and the Problem of Legitimacy," *Journal of the American Academy of Religion*, 41:3 (September 1973), 331–54.

[35] The idea of the covenant of being seems to go back at least to Jonathan Edwards. Karl Barth sees creation as the external covenant of God's grace, revealed redemptively in Jesus Christ. See *Church Dogmatics*, tr. G. Bromiley and T. F. Torrance (Edinburgh: T. & T. Clark, 1960), Vol. III, Pt. 1. As Herbert Hartwell puts it, "creation is the external basis of God's covenant of grace with man and . . . this covenant is the internal basis of creation." *The Theology of Karl Barth* (Philadelphia: Westminster Press, 1964), 115.

Thomas Oden uses the covenant idea to ground his psychologically influenced theology in *The Structure of Awareness* (Nashville: Abingdon, 1969), 83–99.

H. R. Niebuhr's covenantalism lies behind his relational theory of the self in *The Responsible Self* (New York: Harper & Row, 1963).

William James' pragmatic psychology led him to speak of the universe as ordered like a federal republic. See Henry S. Levinson, "William James and the Federal Republican Principle," *Publius*, 9:4 (Fall 1979), 65–86.

Whitehead's highly influential philosophy is more rightly called "organic" than covenantal. The philosophy of relation important to the covenantal view I am advancing here can be found in *Process and Reality: An Essay in Cosmology* (New York: Harper & Brothers, 1960), Part III, "The Theory of Prehension"; and *Adventures of Ideas* (New York: New

American Library, 1955), 90, where Whitehead places the development of persuasion in terms of the history of commerce rather than publicity, thus revealing the historical context shaping his own perceptions.

James Luther Adams explores the power and limits of Whitehead's root metaphor in "The Lure of Persuasion: Some Themes from Whitehead," *The Prophethood of All Believers*, ed. George K. Beach (Boston: Beacon Press, 1986), 186–205.

For the original theological appropriation of Whitehead's ideas see Charles Hartshorne, *The Divine Relativity* (New Haven: Yale University Press, 1948), esp. 147–58. John Cobb, a successor in this tradition, gives explicit attention to ecological issues in *Is It Too Late?* (Beverly Hills: Bruce, 1972).

5. The Covenanted Public: A Contemporary Theory

[1] John Dewey, *The Public and Its Problems* (New York: Henry Holt & Co., 1927); Walter Lippmann, *The Public Philosophy* (Boston: Little, Brown & Co., 1955); Hannah Arendt, *The Human Condition;* John Courtney Murray, *We Hold These Truths;* and Jürgen Habermas, "The Public Sphere," *New German Critique*, 3 (Fall, 1974), 360–75.

[2] Jürgen Habermas, *Legitimation Crisis*, tr. T. McCarthy (Boston: Beacon, 1975); Michael Harrington, *Socialism;* Milton Friedman, *Capitalism and Freedom* (Chicago: University of Chicago Press, 1962).

[3] The modern concept of rights, usually seen as a defense of our natural privacy, can also be seen as a response to a divine command, as with the statement of the World Alliance of Reformed Churches (Arnold O. Miller, ed., *Christian Declaration on Human Rights* [Grand Rapids: William B. Eerdmans, 1977], 129–43).

[4] John Dewey, *The Public and Its Problems*, 15.

[5] Carl Friedrich, *The New Image of the Common Man* (Boston: Beacon Press, 1950).

[6] This is a typical theme in Arendt's work. See *The Human Condition*, ch. 1.

[7] Arendt, *The Human Condition*, 156ff; and Walter Lippmann, *Public Opinion* (New York: Macmillan, [1922] 1961), 25–31.

[8] Ivy L. Lee, "Publicity and Propaganda," in W. Brooke Graves, ed., *Readings in Public Opinion: Its Formation and Control* (New York: D. Appleton & Co., 1928), 577. For the chief founder of publicity as a science and practice see Edward L. Bernays, *Crystallizing Public Opinion* (New York: Boni & Liveright, 1923).

[9] Dewey, *The Public and Its Problems*, 167–73; and Friedrich, *The New Image of the Common Man*, ch. 3.; as well as numerous articles in Graves, *Readings in Public Opinion*.

[10] Jürgen Habermas, "Towards a Theory of Communicative Competence," *Inquiry*, 13 (Winter 1970), 360–75; Dewey, *The Public and Its Problems*, 174; and Lippmann, *Public Opinion*, ch. 36. For a use of Habermas' ideas with more sensitivity to cult and culture see Charles Davis, *Theology and Political Society* (London: Cambridge University Press, 1980).

[11] See Hugh D. Duncan, *Communication and Social Order* (New York: Oxford University Press, 1968). Karen Hermassi provides helpful perspectives on the interpenetration of drama and politics in *Polity and Theater in Historical Perspective* (Berkeley: University of California Press, 1977).

[12] In *Blessed Be the Bond* (61–62) I used the concepts of "expression" and "confirmation." In using the concept of profession instead of expression I draw attention to the public side of expression, though the essential content of the two ideas is the same.

[13] Arendt, *The Human Condition*, 219. Cf. Habermas, "Hannah Arendt's Communications Concept of Power," *Social Research*, 44:1 (Spring 1977), 3–24.

[14] These theses from Habermas' earlier article "Wahrheitstheorien" are discussed by Thomas McCarthy in *The Critical Theory of Jürgen Habermas* (Cambridge, MA: MIT Press, 1978), 305–10.

[15] See Richard Sennett's earlier work with Jonathan Cobb, *The Hidden Injuries of Class* (New York: Random House, 1972), 171.

[16] For similar views see Carl Friedrich, *The Philosophy of Law in Historical Perspective*, ch. 21; and Habermas, *Legitimation Crisis*, 68–74.

[17] See Barbara Laslett, "The Family as Public and Private Institution: An Historical Perspective," *Journal of Marriage and the Family*, 35:3 (August 1973), 480–92.

[18] Habermas, *Legitimation Crisis*, 111–17; and McCarthy, *The Critical Theory of Jürgen Habermas*, 299–307.

Philip Rossi argues that Immanuel Kant's theory of reason and freedom, which is the ancestor of this intellectual heritage, assumes a public life of mutuality in which hope, imagination, and story construct our real and moral world. *Together Toward Hope: A Journey to Moral Theology* (Notre Dame: University of Notre Dame Press, 1983).

Michael Walzer explores the significance of this pluralism for a more differentiated theory of justice in *Spheres of Justice: A Defense of Pluralism and Equality* (New York: Basic Books, 1983).

[19] The phrase is C. B. Macpherson's in *The Political Theory of Possessive Individualism*. See also his *Democratic Theory: Essays in Retrieval* (Oxford: Clarendon Press, 1973), ch. 6, for a similar effort to recover a political theory of property.

[20] For some sharp critiques of political pluralism see William E. Connolly, ed., *The Bias of Pluralism* (New York: Atherton Press, 1969).

[21] Gerd Theissen, *A Critical Faith: A Case for Religion*, tr. J. Bowder (Philadelphia: Fortress Press, 1979), 33; Leon Festinger, *A Theory of Cognitive Dissonance* (Evanston: Row, Peterson, 1957); Robert B. Zajonc, "Thinking: Cognitive Organization and Processes," *International Encyclopedia of the Social Sciences* 15 (1968), 615–22; and Ronald Laing, *The Divided Self* (London: Tavistock, 1969), ch. 3; and *The Politics of Experience* (New York: Ballantine, 1972), ch. 3, 5.

[22] Carl Rogers, *Client Centered Therapy* (Boston: Houghton Mifflin, 1951), ch. 11.

[23] James Fowler, *Becoming Adult, Becoming Christian: Adult Development and Christian Faith* (San Francisco: Harper & Row, 1984), ch. 5. See also Walter Brueggemann, "Covenanting as Human Vocation: A Discussion of the Relation of Bible and Pastoral Care," *Interpretation*, 33:2 (April 1979), 115–29.

[24] Christopher Lasch, *The Culture of Narcissism: American Life in an Age of Diminishing Expectations* (New York: W. W. Norton, 1978) and *Haven in a Heartless World: The Family Besieged* (New York: Basic Books, 1977); Richard Sennett, *The Fall of Public Man* (New York: Random House, 1978); Parker Palmer, *The Company of Strangers*.

[25] Paul Zweig, *The Heresy of Self Love* (Princeton: Princeton University Press, 1979); Peter Homans, "Introducing the Psychology of the Self and Narcissism into the Study of Religion," *Religious Studies Review*, 7:3 (July 1981), 193–99.

[26] Kenneth Burke, *The Rhetoric of Religion* (Boston: Beacon Press, 1969); Hugh D. Duncan, *Communication and Social Theory*; Erving Goffman, *Interaction Ritual* (Garden City, NY: Doubleday, 1967); Jacob L. Moreno, *Who Shall Survive? Foundations of Sociometry, Group Psychotherapy and Sociodrama* (Beacon, NY: Beacon House, 1953), xvi–xxviii.

6. Theological Reverberations of God's Federal Republic

[1] Others working along these lines are Helmut Peukert, *Science, Action, and Fundamental Theology: Toward a Theology of Communicative Action*, tr. James Bohman (Cambridge, MA: MIT Press, 1984), and Dennis McCann and Charles Strain, *Polity and Praxis: A Program for American Practical Theology* (Minneapolis: Winston Press, 1985). See also J. Leon Hooper's sensitive development of John Courtney Murray's thought in this direction in *The Ethics of Discourse: The Social Philosophy of John Courtney Murray* (Washington: Georgetown University Press, 1986).

[2] See my earlier articles, "Liturgy and American Society: An In-

vocation for Ethical Analysis," *Anglican Theological Review*, 56:1 (January 1974), 16–34; and "Liturgy and Ethics: A Response to Saliers and Ramsey," *Journal of Religious Ethics*, 7:2 (Fall 1979), 203–14, for a fuller discussion of these themes.

³ Robert Bellah, "Christianity and Symbolic Realism," *Journal for the Scientific Study of Religion*, 9:2 (Summer 1970), 89–97; John Shea, *Stories of God: An Unauthorized Biography* (Chicago: Thomas More Press, 1978); Stanley Hauerwas, *A Community of Character: Toward A Constructive Christian Social Ethic* (Notre Dame: University of Notre Dame Press, 1981); Sallie McFague TeSelle, *Speaking in Parables: A Study in Metaphor and Theology* (Philadelphia: Fortress Press, 1975); and Victor Turner, *Dramas, Fields and Metaphors: Symbolic Action in Human Society* (Ithaca: Cornell University Press, 1974).

⁴ The assumption that the source or object of theology is a pre- or trans-public reality can still be seen even in the work of David Tracy, *The Analogical Imagination*, 355–64, and Parker Palmer, *A Company of Strangers*, 22–26, both of whom have given major attention to the idea of the public. Their main concern has been for the Church and the Gospel to enter the public sphere, mine is for its very theology to appropriate symbols of covenant and publicity at the core of its message and life. This also differs from Martin Marty's concept of the public church in *The Public Church* (New York: Seabury-Crossroad, 1981), while sharing his interest in emerging patterns of public engagement in the churches.

⁵ See again Jürgen Habermas, "On Systematically Distorted Communication," *Inquiry*, 13 (Autumn 1970), 205–18, and "Towards a Theory of Communicative Competence," *Inquiry*, 13 (Winter 1970), 360–75; and Charles Davis, *Theology and Political Society*.

⁶ Parker Palmer, *To Know as We Are Known: A Spirituality of Education* (San Francisco: Harper and Row, 1983), 31.

⁷ John Burnaby provides the classic study of this thrust in Augustine in *Amor Dei* (London: Hodder, 1938). While I share Augustine's formal notion of our lives as a search for their ultimate good, I differ in my view of the content of that desire, i.e., publicity rather than peace.

⁸ This recasts Whitehead's concepts of God's primordial and consequent natures set forth in *Process and Reality*, 134–35, 521–24 and develops further his notion of the "presiding occasion" of a "society" (166–67). See also Hartshorne, *The Divine Relativity*, 50, 142.

⁹ Max Stackhouse, *Ethics and the Urban Ethos*, 63, 111.

¹⁰ Quoted from Thomas Pennant, *Of London* (1790), Preface, by Ernest Barker in his Preface to *From Alexander to Constantine*, xii.